D1244631

ANATOMY
of an
ASSASSINATION

By the same author:

Assassination—The World Stood Still

ANATOMY
of an
ASSASSINATION

JOHN COTTRELL

FUNK & WAGNALLS / NEW YORK

Copyright © 1966 by John Cottrell
All Rights Reserved.
Library of Congress Catalog Card Number: 68-18160

Published by Funk & Wagnalls, *A Division of* Reader's
Digest Books, Inc., by arrangement with Frederick
Muller.

Manufactured in the United States of America.

To Mary

CONTENTS

ILLUSTRATIONS

ACKNOWLEDGMENTS

IN PRESENTING the new evidence contained in Chapter Nine, I am immeasurably indebted to Ray A. Neff, Head of the Department of Health in Cape May County, New Jersey, through whose diligent research these facts were uncovered, and to Robert H. Fowler, editor, who first published this evidence in *Civil War Times Illustrated* (August, 1961). All the material for Chapter Nine was provided by Neff and Fowler; documentary illustrations of Neff's findings are also reproduced by courtesy of *Civil War Times Illustrated*, published in Gettysburg, Pa.

A special word of gratitude is due to Colin Rickards, author and political commentator, who gave invaluable assistance in tracking down some of the sources for this work which are fully listed at the end of the book. My thanks also to Mrs. Meena Stentitford, who so patiently worked on the typing of the MS in the face of constant additions and amendments.

JOHN COTTRELL.

Lincoln Drive, Woking.

INTRODUCTION

HISTORY MAY never repeat itself precisely in every detail, but it came remarkably close with the assassination in Dallas on November 22, 1963. The similarities between the murder of President Lincoln and that of President Kennedy nearly a century later are astonishing. Both were shot on a Friday, in the back of the head, and with his wife seated at his side. Both never regained consciousness. Both were killed at a time when they were fighting on the civil rights issue more outspokenly than any other Presidents have done. Both were succeeded by a Southerner named Johnson.

On the day he was killed, Lincoln remarked to a bodyguard, William Crook: 'Do you know, I believe there are men who want to take my life. And I have no doubt they will do it.' On the morning before his assassination, Kennedy remarked: 'If anybody really wanted to shoot the President of the United States it would not be a very difficult job—all one has to do is get on a high building some day with a telescopic sight and there's nothing anybody can do to defend such an attempt.'

Twenty-eight soldiers trapped the crippled John Wilkes Booth and yet failed to take Lincoln's assassin alive. The vast resources of the Dallas police failed to preserve the life of Lee Harvey Oswald while he was in custody.

More obscure similarities have been noted—that Lincoln was elected in 1860 and Kennedy in 1960; that the names of both

Presidents contain seven letters; that the wife of each President lost a son while she was First Lady; that the names of the assassins, John Wilkes Booth and Lee Harvey Oswald, each contain fifteen letters; that Andrew Johnson was born in 1808 and Lyndon Johnson in 1908; that Boston Corbett, who claimed he had shot Booth, was later found insane, while Jack Ruby, who shot Oswald, pleaded insanity at his trial.

All these are curious, though wholly insignificant, coincidences. But the two senseless crimes have two highly significant features in common. Firstly, both crimes could have been prevented if security officials had acted upon information they possessed concerning the respective assassins. Secondly, in both cases the assassin was shot before he could fully explain his actions, so that history was denied a complete and satisfactory account and the way was left open to fantastic speculation. Six other Presidents or Presidents-elect have been the targets of gunmen; two others, Garfield and McKinley, have been assassinated. But in each case the assassin faced a legal trial at which all the evidence could be openly debated and weighed.

Thus, a hundred years from now, historical investigators will almost certainly be still probing the circumstances behind President Kennedy's death, just as they are still searching now for clues concerning the killing of Lincoln a century ago. Since Oswald, alone among assassins of Presidents, did not explain his motives or even confess to his crime, the Kennedy assassination is perhaps even more exposed to the whims of theorists.

After a detailed study of their report, and having seen and heard some of the key witnesses, I unreservedly accept the conclusion of the Warren Commission that Lee Harvey Oswald killed President Kennedy and Police Patrolman J. D. Tippit. The commission report, based on testimony taken from 552 witnesses, provides overwhelming evidence to this effect. But as a leader in the London *Daily Mail* expressed it—'People will rarely believe a simple explanation for a dire event. They search for the intrigue and the hidden motive. John F. Kennedy is among the immortals whose end will be subjected to ceaseless wordy warfare. His shade will be the victim of the endless curiosity, or eternal credulity, of the mind.'

This story concerns the search for the intrigue and hidden motive behind the first assassination of an American President and the reasons why so many mysteries have arisen out of a crime witnessed by hundreds of people. In both the killings of Lincoln and Kennedy it has been suggested that there was a gigantic political plot behind the deed, that both Booth and Oswald were the instruments of some prominent person or powerful organisation, and that both were silenced to prevent them revealing the men behind them. There is more justification for this belief in the case of Lincoln since the assassination took place in time of war, when conspiracies were frequently being discovered and when the powerful radicals in Washington were bitterly opposed to the President's plans for a 'soft peace'.

Over the years, researchers have assembled a vast array of facts to strengthen suspicions of a high-level conspiracy. Especially, a formidable case has been built up to suggest that Lincoln's murder may have been engineered by his own Secretary of War, Edwin McMasters Stanton—the man who solemnly stated over the President's body, 'Now he belongs to the ages.' In his fascinating study of mystery and intrigue, *Why Was Lincoln Murdered?*, Otto Eisenschiml[1] provided the foremost indictment of Stanton. But in one respect he erred. Eisenschiml wrote that Stanton's detective chief, General Lafayette Baker, 'left no papers, so far as is known, and whatever additional data he had, or whatever suspicions he harboured, were buried with him'. In fact, Baker's suspicions were not buried with him. They have since come to light—more than ninety years after his death —and provide sensational new evidence to support the belief that Stanton may have headed a power group in Washington that sought to eliminate the President of the United States.

This latest evidence is presented in Chapter Nine. At the same

1. Grosset and Dunlap, New York, 1937.

time I should stress that it is not my primary purpose to fan the flames of suspicion which have flickered and flared for over a century. American writers like Eisenschiml have done their work well to create serious doubts about the official verdict of history.

Extensive research, however, has led me to believe that, one hundred years after Lincoln's death, there remains room for a work which endeavours to present the facts as objectively as possible, without aiming to prove any particular theory. This, then, is a newspaperman's report of the strange events before and after the assassination. For the most part, events are dramatic enough in themselves without embellishment. Dialogue is not invented, but based on records, and I have noted where sources conflict hopelessly over statements of fact. Was Lincoln betrayed? I offer my conclusions, but this is strictly a question which the reader must resolve for himself.

1

PROLOGUE TO MURDER

AT SIX O'CLOCK on the morning of February 23, 1861, the sprawling, pretentious city of Washington, bedecked in red, white and blue, lay still and silent. The day before had seen birthday celebrations in honour of the first American President from whom the Federal capital took its name; close at hand were more momentous occasions, the official welcome for the strange Westerner chosen to be 16th President of the United States, and his inauguration with the traditional grand procession, speeches, fireworks and dancing. But, for the moment, the city slept, unconscious of any historic event in these last hours of darkness.

At Washington depot, the silence was shattered with the arrival of the first morning train from Philadelphia. For the railway workers another day had begun, a day which would bring more festive sightseers flooding into an already hopelessly overcrowded city. From the train's last sleeping car, which had been reserved by a woman for her 'invalid brother', there stepped a tall, angular figure in a slouched hat, muffler and short, bob-tailed overcoat. He was closely attended by two companions— a short, bearded Scottish gentleman who called himself Mr. E. J. Allen, and a burly fellow, Ward Hill Lamon, whose overcoat bulged where he carried two pistols, two derringers and two large knives.

As the groups of sleepy-eyed passengers moved along the

platform, only one person at the depot paid attention to these three arrivals. He glanced anxiously about him, then sidled up to the tall, lanky stranger, grabbed his hand, and cried, 'Abe, you can't play that on me.'

Immediately, Ward Hill Lamon drew back his massive fist, ready to smash it into the intruder's face. The tall stranger instinctively held back his escort's strong arm. 'Don't strike him,' he said hastily. 'It's Washburne.'

Thus, without bands, without banners, Abraham Lincoln, President-elect of the United States, arrived in the capital; unrecognised and welcomed only by one man, Congressman Elihu Washburne. In the cause of security, Lincoln had ruined plans for a formal welcome to Washington by arriving secretly, many hours ahead of schedule.

Joseph Howard, an irresponsible newspaperman, with a flair for invention rather than factual reporting, sent in a story to the *New York Times*. The President-elect, he reported, 'wore a Scotch plaid cap and a very long military coat, so that he was entirely unrecognisable'. With various embellishments, this story was taken up by innumerable journals. It was a gift to cartoonists and to Lincoln's many political enemies who branded him a spineless coward. Ridiculed in words and in pictures, the President-elect became a laughing stock for the whole country and he would regret his surreptitious entrance into the capital for the rest of his days.

The one-time rail-splitter, now on the last stage of his fifty-two-year journey from log cabin to the White House, had many times proved his exceptional courage, but he remained no less sensitive to suggestions that he feared for his safety. This was the first time he had heeded the advice of his security officers. Never again would he be persuaded to submit himself to such extreme measures to safeguard his own, often threatened, life.

In March, 1837, when Abraham Lincoln rode into Springfield, Illinois, on a borrowed horse to set himself up as a lawyer, he carried all his personal possessions in his saddlebags, was eleven hundred dollars in debt, and had a background which scarcely suggested the brilliant professional career that was to follow. Twenty-eight years had passed since he was born on a Sunday morning in Kentucky, the son of an illiterate farmer. He had grown tall, lean and wiry (two inches over six feet by the age of sixteen); had developed enormous strength in his long arms and huge hands; had acquired a sound education even though the aggregate of all his schooling amounted to less than one year. In a decade of remarkably varied experience he had worked as a ferryman, rail-splitter, lumberman, surveyor, postmaster and blacksmith, run a mill and a grocery store, refereed cockfights and horse races, served as a captain in the Black Hawk War, and represented New Salem in the Illinois State Legislature. He had little knowledge of the world at large, though six years before he had sailed as far south as New Orleans, where he witnessed the full misery of human slavery, with Negroes in chains, whipped, and auctioned like cattle. It is recorded that he saw the revolting sight of a pretty mulatto girl being pawed by prospective buyers and then made to trot up and down like a prize horse so that bidders might see how well she moved. According to Billy Herndon, his law partner and biographer, Lincoln told his companions: 'By God, boys, let's get away from this. If ever I get a chance to hit that thing' (meaning slavery), 'I'll hit it hard.' Doubtless the young Lincoln was deeply moved, but there is no first-hand evidence that he expressed great concern over slavery until many years later.

In November, 1860, when Lincoln prepared to leave Springfield, he was almost fifty-two years old, a prominent lawyer and politician, out of debt, married to a lady of high social standing, and elected to the highest office in the land. But neither a wife nor political success had brought him happiness. On the afternoon before his departure he would call at his dingy law office for the last time and confide to his partner Herndon that he had a feeling he would never see Springfield again. 'I am sick of office-holding already, and I shudder when I think of the tasks that are still ahead.'

On November 7, 1860, the day after his election as President, Lincoln went to his Springfield home in the afternoon and sprawled on a haircloth sofa. In front of him was a bureau with a swinging mirror, and as he looked into the mirror he was startled at seeing two images of himself, one bright, the other deathly pale. Perplexed, he got up to examine his reflection, but the illusion vanished. When he told Mrs. Lincoln about the phenomenon, she interpreted it as meaning that he would enjoy good health in his first term of office and would die in the second. The future President possessed a most logical mind and would argue: 'There are no accidents in my philosophy. Every effect must have its cause.' Nevertheless, his upbringing among super-stitious people had left him with a certain belief in the significance of dreams. He became convinced that he was destined to die violently, that he would never return to Springfield from Washington alive.

Lincoln's fears were well-founded. From the moment of his election his life was in dire peril. He was destined to be Chief Magistrate of a 'Divided House', feared and hated by the South, threatened with assassination even before he took office. Despite his many denials, the slave states feared that he was an aboli-tionist and, if he were not, that he would be unable to hold back the powerful radicals of his newly formed Republican Party. On November 10, U.S. Senator Jefferson Davis wrote, 'If South Carolina has determined to secede, I advise her to do so before the Government passes into hostile hands.' On December 20, South Carolina seceded, to be swiftly followed by Mississippi, Florida, Alabama, Georgia and Louisiana. Texas's renunciation of the Union came on February 1, 1861. The secessionists seized Federal forts and arsenals, hauled down the Stars and Stripes from custom houses. On February 10, Jefferson Davis of Mississippi was trimming roses with his young wife Varina when he was handed a telegram informing him that he had been elected

Provisional President by the delegates to the Montgomery convention of the Confederate States of America. He was destined to lead rebel states with some nine million people (including nearly four million slaves) as opposed to some twenty-two million Northerners.

When Lincoln was elected by a minority of the votes of the nation, and without a single vote in ten Southern states, there was no real doubt about his attitude towards the great slavery question. As early as March, 1837, he had stated in writing that he believed 'that the institution of slavery is founded on both injustice and bad policy, but that the promulgation of abolition doctrines tends rather to increase than abate the evils . . . that the Congress of the United States has no power under the Constitution to interfere with the institution of slavery in the different States'. He had reiterated that view countless times in his speeches over the years, so that it was nonsense to suggest that he was a radical abolitionist. On the other hand, he was firmly opposed to the extension of slavery in the territories.

Lincoln was a moderate. What was uncertain in the suspenseful weeks immediately after his election was how this prairie lawyer would deal with the growing rebellion. In those crucial weeks, President Buchanan, a staunch Democrat, had failed to take firm action or even to threaten force when the states of the Lower South appeared on the brink of secession. In his annual December message to Congress he asserted that 'while a State could not lawfully secede, neither could the Federal government coerce it'. He proposed a Constitutional Convention to frame amendments guaranteeing slaves in the states and the territories and assuring the recovery of fugitive slaves. During January and February, as one state after another seceded, as one Federal fort after another was taken over by state forces in the Lower South, Buchanan did nothing. And by his lack of firmness he missed the one real chance of preventing civil war.

In January, 1861, panic prevailed in Washington as the Federal capital abounded with rumours that the city, surrounded by slave territory, was to be seized. In February, this fear subsided, but now there were rumours of Southern plans to prevent the counting of the electoral vote, scheduled for February 13. Meanwhile, as Buchanan fiddled with his policy of non-committal, as the Union dissolved, as the republic tottered on the brink of civil war, the reluctant leader who would eventually have to deal with the greatest crisis in the country's history was obliged to wait helplessly in Springfield for three months. There he could do nothing but worry, losing forty pounds in weight in the process, and face a never-ending bombardment by office-seekers, who had filled every hotel and boarding house in his home town and who would harass him for the rest of his days.

How, if at all, would Mr. Lincoln resist the rebels who regarded slavery as the cornerstone of their civilization? He was expected to reveal his intentions in his Inaugural Address on March 4. But many people wondered whether he would ever reach the inauguration platform. Charles Francis Adams, whose father would soon be appointed American Minister in London, reported, 'It is beyond a doubt that the revolutionists have determined to take forcible possession of the Government at Washington before the fourth of March.'

In the first week of February the careworn President-elect managed to slip away from the hordes of office-seekers, journeying seventy miles to visit the grave of his father, Thomas Lincoln, and to bid farewell to his stepmother in a little country village in Coles County. The old lady wept and told him: 'I didn't want you to run for President, Abe, and I didn't want to see you elected. My heart tells me that something will happen to you and that I'll never see you again till we meet in heaven.'

In his final week in Springfield, Lincoln received some seven hundred friends at his modest home on Eighth Street, and among the callers was Hannah Armstrong, whose son he had successfully defended on a murder charge three years before. In that trial, Lincoln had scored a most notable triumph, dramatically nonplussing the principal witness for the prosecution, who claimed positively to have seen the fatal blow struck in the moonlight, by showing with an almanac that the moon had set at that time. Now Mrs. Armstrong grieved because she believed she would never see Abe Lincoln alive again. 'Hannah,' he joked, 'if they do kill me I shall never die again.'

Lincoln's strange and tortuous journey to Washington began early on the cold, drizzling morning of February 11, when a crowd, variously estimated at a thousand to fifteen hundred, gathered at the small Great Western station to see him off. The President-elect travelled with his wife, three sons, State politicians, personal friends, secretaries and newspaper correspondents. A military escort of four army officers had been provided by the War Department, but Lincoln's chief, self-appointed bodyguard was powerfully built, 6 ft. 2 in. tall Ward Hill Lamon, a devoted old friend who had once worked in law partnership with Lincoln and who was now obsessed by the fear that the President-elect might be attacked at any moment. Lamon carried with him a veritable arsenal of pistols, derringers, knives and brass knuckles; also a banjo on which he played Negro ballads, including Lincoln's favourite, 'The Blue-Tailed Fly', to amuse the passengers.

At the Springfield depot that morning, Lincoln climbed aboard a passenger car and, with his head bowed and his face written with sadness, stood for a moment in silence. Then he looked up from the rail of the rear platform and addressed the crowd gathered patiently beneath a vast canopy of umbrellas. For once in his life he struggled in vain to hold back the tears.

'My friends,' he began, 'no one, not in my situation, can appreciate my feeling of sadness at this parting. To this place, and the kindness of these people, I owe everything. Here I have lived a quarter of a century, and have passed from a young to an old man. Here my children have been born, and one is buried. I now leave, not knowing when, or whether ever, I may return, with a task before me greater than that which rested upon

Washington. Without the assistance of that Divine Being who ever attended him, I cannot succeed. With that assistance I cannot fail. Trusting in Him who can go with me, and remain with you and be everywhere for good, let us confidently hope that all will yet be well. To His care commending you, as I hope in your prayers you will commend me, I bid you an affectionate farewell.'

With those words Abraham Lincoln took his last view of Springfield before embarking on the twelve-day rail-ride to Washington and supreme office as 16th President of the United States. It was just two days since Jefferson Davis had been elected first President of the Confederate States of America.

En route for Washington, Lincoln was to make more than twenty speeches in the major cities of five states, meet governors and legislators, shake the hands of tens of thousands of citizens and be greeted by crowds at every whistle-stop. On February 12, exactly fifty-two years after his birth in a log cabin, he rode in a great procession through Cincinnati. The following day, with Washington in a state of extreme tension, Congress formally declared him President-elect after the canvassing of electoral votes. Without the expected disturbances, Vice-President John C. Breckinridge of Kentucky announced, 'Abraham Lincoln, of Illinois, having received a majority of the whole number of electoral votes, is elected President of the United States for four years, commencing the fourth of March, 1861.'

On February 14, Lincoln arrived in Pittsburg. At a town called Freedom he accepted the challenge of a coal-worker who called out from the crowd that he was at least as tall as the President-elect, so famed for his great height. Lincoln invited the man on to the platform, stood with his back to the dust-covered labourer, who proved to be of exactly the same stature, six feet four inches tall. The crowd cheered, but professional men shook their heads and said it was no way for a future President to behave.

When his train stopped at Westfield, New York, Lincoln endeared himself to the people by asking for Grace Bedell, an eleven-year-old child who, four months before, had written to him to suggest that he would be more distinguished looking if he grew whiskers. At the time he had replied, 'Do you not think people would call it a piece of silly affectation were I to begin wearing them now?' But now, as the little girl was brought to the platform, he was able to tell her, 'You see I have let these whiskers grow for you, Grace.' Then he kissed her and shook her hand. It prompted the *St. Louis Republican* to sneer, 'If kissing pretty girls is a Presidential privilege, Mrs. Lincoln, who knows her rights and knowing dares maintain them, ought to insist on a veto power for herself.'

On February 18, as Lincoln crossed the Empire State of New York towards Albany, there came news that, amid scenes of great rejoicing in Montgomery, Alabama, Jefferson Davis, like Lincoln a son of Kentucky, had taken the oath as President of the Confederate States of America. In a speech, Lincoln humbly declared: 'While I hold myself without mock modesty, the humblest of all individuals that have ever been elevated to the Presidency, I have a more difficult task to perform than any one of them. When the time comes I shall speak as well as I am able for the good of the present and this country—for the good both of the North and the South. . . .'

In New York, Lincoln rode in a thirty-carriage procession through the nation's business capital where the majority of citizens had not supported his election. The crowds were no less in size but showed markedly less enthusiasm. Curiosity brought the big-city Easterners out in their thousands to see the awkward-looking backwoods lawyer who was to be their next President. When Lincoln attended the opera at the fabulous new Academy of Music, sophisticated New Yorkers snickered because he covered his huge hands with black kid gloves while everyone else correctly wore white. He was in strange territory now and, though his reception was the most extravagant that he had en-countered on his journey to Washington, it also appeared the most heartless.

Hostile newspapers called him a 'gorilla' and a 'baboon'. News reporter Henry Villard described how, as he travelled eastwards, Lincoln disappointed many who were seeing him for the first time, with his 'most unprepossessing features, the gawkiest figure, and the most awkward manners'. But Walt Whitman, who saw him in New York, remarked on the nobility of the man with 'his dress of complete black, stovepipe hat pushed on the head, dark-brown complexion, seam'd and wrinkled yet canny-looking face, black bushy head of hair, disproportionately long neck'.

In Philadelphia, where he raised a flag over Independence Hall at six o'clock on the morning of Washington's Birthday, Lincoln assured the people that there would be 'no bloodshed unless it be forced upon the Government and then it would be compelled to act in self-defence'. He said that the ideals of the Declaration of Independence were still alive, still offered hope 'that in due time the weights would be lifted from the shoulders of all men, and that all should have an equal chance. If the country could not be saved without giving up that principle,' he said, 'I would rather be assassinated on this spot than surrender it.'

The day before the flag-raising ceremony in Philadelphia, Lincoln was met by 'Mr. E. J. Allen', the man who was to guard him on the last, secret stage of the journey to the capital. The true identity of this short, bearded gentleman was Allan Pinkerton, founder of the famous detective agency, and he had been hired by the Philadelphia, Wilmington and Baltimore railroad to investigate rumours that secessionist military groups, centred in Baltimore, planned acts of sabotage to disrupt traffic and prevent the movement of troops to the south. Through his spies placed in Baltimore secret societies, Pinkerton received confirmation of such plots. He also became firmly convinced that there was a well-organised plan to assassinate Lincoln as he crossed Baltimore to change trains. As a result, the railroad company armed some two hundred guards who were disguised as workmen along the line, and Pinkerton sped to Philadelphia to warn the President-elect.

Lincoln, already accustomed to threats on his life, refused to be alarmed and would not listen to the detective's suggestion that he should change his schedule. Soon after, however, he was met by Frederick Seward, son of the famous New York Senator who had been Lincoln's chief rival for the Republican nomination. The younger Seward brought a warning from his father and from General Winfield Scott, the veteran Commander-in-Chief of the Army; they had received independent reports of a plot to kill the President-elect when he passed through hostile Baltimore. Lincoln, finally impressed of the extreme danger, reluctantly agreed to the secret night journey to Washington, once he had fulfilled his engagements in Philadelphia and Harrisburg. But he had grave doubts about the wisdom of the plan, asking, 'What would the nation think of its President stalking into its capital like a thief in the night?'

Lincoln moved on to Harrisburg where he visited both branches of the legislature then in session, and at six o'clock in the evening he retired to his room. But, instead of staying overnight as planned, he slipped out the back door of the hotel, disguised in a threadbare old overcoat and an uncharacteristic soft wool hat. With Lamon, he shared the single carriage of a special train which ran without lights, and, as a final precaution, the telegraph wires from Harrisburg were grounded to prevent news of Lincoln's departure being sent ahead.

Soon after ten o'clock the train drew into the Pennsylvania railroad station, where they were met by Pinkerton, and for the next hour the detective drove them about the city in a darkened cab to pass the time in changing trains and stations. Then, with a shawl drawn high on his face, the President-elect boarded the New York-Washington train, taking the rear berths of the last sleeping car which had been reserved by a woman detective for her 'invalid brother'. Only Pinkerton and Lamon travelled with Lincoln, but, unknown to them, another armed detective had taken a berth on the last car. This conscientious New York police officer was hurrying to Washington to warn the authorities that the President-elect was in danger of assassination on his journey through Baltimore the next day. The officer's name was John Kennedy.

Meanwhile, Mrs. Lincoln, hysterical over the separation from her husband, travelled on the President-elect's special train from Harrisburg, as originally scheduled. On the afternoon after Lincoln's secret arrival in Washington, his official train drew into Baltimore's Calvert station where some ten thousand people gathered in vain to welcome him. Many came to demonstrate and there was a great chorus when someone called for three cheers for the Confederacy, three for Jeff Davis—'and three groans for the rail-splitter'. The hostility of the crowd suggested that Abraham Lincoln was well advised to stay out of Baltimore that day.

Distinguished-looking General Winfield Scott, Commander-in-Chief of the Army of the United States, hero of two wars, was in the evening of his glorious career. For nearly half a century he had been famed as a mighty warrior. He had been victorious over the British in 1814, had defeated the Mexicans in 1848. Now he was old and feeble, infirm with dropsy and vertigo, still carrying bullets within his six feet five-inch frame. Yet, at nearly seventy-five, he soldiered on, no less conscientious in his preparations for one more inauguration day.

Washington was so overcrowded that hundreds of homeless visitors spilled over from the hotels and boarding houses, sleeping in doorways of public buildings, on market stalls and pavements, or strolling the streets all night. But the control of huge crowds on March 4 was one of the General's lesser worries. For weeks the city had been buzzing with rumours of plots against Lincoln. Scott received a report that Southern sympathisers planned to blow up the inauguration platform; there was a widely spread rumour that a company of Virginia horsemen would make a lightning raid in the evening to capture the new President at the Union Ball.

On his inauguration day, Thomas Jefferson had walked to the Capitol without a single guard. In contrast, General Scott planned Lincoln's inauguration drive from Willard's Hotel to the Capitol like a full-scale military operation, involving every soldier in the city. The entire route was guarded, with riflemen hidden on the rooftops of buildings in Pennsylvania Avenue and stationed at windows of the Capitol, with troops lining the sidewalks, with two batteries of artillery stationed near the Capitol and another near the Treasury building, with cavalry guarding every intersection.

The weather fitted the nation's mood—bright and clear becoming cloudy with a chill wind. It was a bleak day at noon when bachelor President James Buchanan of Pennsylvania, his face pale and withered, called at Willard's Hotel to escort his successor to the Capitol in an open carriage. As they drove together along the Avenue, jammed each side with onlookers, Mr. Lincoln looked ill at ease. For once he was most elegantly dressed, in new black suit, black boots and shining tall hat, and he carried a magnificent ebony cane topped with a golden head the size of a chicken's egg. But few people crowding the sidewalks could see him through the forest of prancing cavalry, and he reached the Capitol without incident.

Delivering his address from the temporary inauguration platform on the east front of the Capitol, the new President stressed: 'I have no purpose, directly or indirectly, to interfere with the institution of slavery in the states where it exists. I believe I have no lawful right to do so, and I have no inclination to do so.' In this he was merely reiterating a statement he had made many, many times before, and supporting a bill which had just been passed in the last hours of the 36th Congress. That bill forbade the Federal Government from ever interfering with slavery in slave states, and thus Congress had assured the South that, whatever action might be taken against slavery extension, it would never interfere with the domestic institutions of the States.

Lincoln further declared: 'Apprehension seems to exist among the people of the Southern States, that by the accession of a Republican Administration, their property, and their peace, and personal security, are to be endangered. There has never been any reasonable cause for such apprehension.' But he also stated firmly, 'No State, upon its own mere notion, can lawfully get out of the Union,' and, unlike his predecessor, he did not sidestep the main issue of how the government would endeavour to prevent the Union from being broken up. The Union would constitutionally defend and maintain itself, though, he explained: 'In doing this there needs to be no bloodshed or violence and there shall be none, unless it be forced upon the national authority. The power confided to me will be used to hold, occupy, and possess the property and places belonging to the government, and to collect the duties and imposts; but beyond what may be necessary for these objects, there will be no invasion—no using of force against, or among the people anywhere. . . . Plainly the central idea of secession is the essence of anarchy. . . . One section of our country believes slavery is right, and ought to be extended, while the other believes it is wrong, and ought not to be extended. This is the only substantial dispute. . . .'

The key phrase was Lincoln's declaration that his power would be used 'to hold, occupy, and possess' the government's property. He was calling a halt to the Southern rebellion and seizure of Federal property. On the other hand, he had omitted from his final draft a pledge that his power would be 'used to reclaim the public property and places' already seized by the Confederates. Thus he had not openly declared war, but had given the proud South one last opportunity to avoid a great conflict.

In reality, however, any real hope of both preventing civil war and preserving the Union had already faded away. Lincoln's speech was hailed by the Union as a 'peace offering', but such was the temper of the South at this stage that, despite the well-reasoned and conciliatory tone of the President's eloquent address, his speech was denounced by secessionists as being virtually a declaration of war.

Inauguration night brought the spectacular Union Ball, and, at eleven o'clock, after shaking more than three thousand hands in two and a quarter hours, a President, tired and troubled after only a few hours of office, led off the grand march. This time he wore white kid gloves. The ladies in their enormous crinolines, with their heads topped by elaborate creations of flowers and feathers, made a scene of great colour and splendour as they moved gaily through waltz, polka, schottische and mazurka. And not least conspicuous was Mrs. Mary Todd Lincoln, blue-gowned, her hair crowned by a large blue feather, and wearing a necklace and bracelets of gold and pearls. This was her night, the realisation of her lifelong dream. Even as a teenage society girl she had contended to her Kentucky friends that one day she would be the First Lady of America. Now her ambition was fulfilled.

Washington society was gay and carefree that night, but the mood was soon to change. Little more than a month of grave anxiety and suspense would pass before the President's declared intention to 'hold, occupy, and possess' was put to its sternest test. At four-thirty in the morning of April 12—despite the warning that such action would 'inaugurate a civil war greater than any the world has yet seen'—the first shots were fired on Fort Sumter, the island fortress in Charleston harbour, the most vital fort in Confederate territory which remained under Federal control. With traditional Southern courtesy, the South Carolinians allowed a visitor, Edmund Ruffin, a hard-bitten, sixty-seven-year-old farmer from Virginia, to pull the first gun of the war. Then General P. G. T. Beauregard's encircling batteries pounded the rock all day and through the rain-swept night.

On Sunday, April 14, the hated symbol of Federal authority fell after thirty-three hours of bombardment with more than three thousand shot and shell. The moment of truth had arrived; the bloodiest war was on.

Abraham Lincoln never expressed himself more clearly on the great slavery question than when, in the summer of 1862, he sent

\ his famous letter to Horace Greeley, founder of the *New York Tribune*, foremost editor of his day. The President wrote: 'My paramount object in this struggle is to save the Union, and is not either to save or destroy slavery. If I could save the Union without freeing any slave, I would do it; and if I could save it by freeing all the slaves, I would do it; and if I could save it by freeing some and leaving others alone, I would also do that. What I do about slavery and the coloured race I do because it helps to save the Union. . . .'

— Though he had stressed over and over again that it was not his purpose 'directly or indirectly to interfere with the institution of slavery in the states where it exists', more and more the circumstances of war were forcing him to reconsider. In March, 1862, Congress had legislated against the use of the armed forces by any officer for the purpose of capturing and returning fugitive slaves; in July it had ruled that slaves who escaped across Union lines from owners hostile to the United States were free, and that slaves owned by persons convicted of treason or rebellion should be made free. The President was now authorised 'to employ as many persons of African descent as he may deem necessary and proper for the suppression of this rebellion'. Moreover, Congress passed a bill providing for gradual, compensated emancipation in the District of Columbia, with not more than 200 dollars to be paid for a slave's freedom; also an act recognising the Negro republics of Haiti and Liberia. Steamship tickets to these countries were to be provided to any freed slaves who wished to settle there. Outright emancipation was the logical next step.

Yet Lincoln still hesitated, still advocated a policy of gradual compensated emancipation, with colonisation as the final solution. He was reluctant to issue an edict of emancipation, as the radicals demanded, fearing it would turn the Border States against the Union and prompt half his army officers to quit the battle. Indeed, some army men forecast that entire regiments would throw down their arms if it were so suggested that they were not fighting for the Union, but merely 'to free the niggers'.

The President's own view was that the slaves should be freed by purchase in the Border States. He argued that this expenditure on buying the slaves would shorten a war now costing the North something like two million dollars a day and prove a considerable saving in the end. He also clung tenaciously to his dream of founding a great Negro colony, at first in the Republic of New Grenada in Central America, and then on Isle 'a Vache, a possession of Haiti.

In August, 1862, for the first time, a committee of free Negroes was invited to the White House by the President, who told them that it was better for both white and black that they be separated. He explained his plan for 'colonising people of African descent', but they showed no enthusiasm for it. Some months later, Frederick Douglass, the fine orator and most distinguished of fugitive slaves, would explain to Lincoln in opposing his colonisation policy, 'The coloured race can never be respected anywhere till they are respected in America.'

In reply to the Abolitionists who constantly urged him to issue a proclamation giving freedom to the slaves, Lincoln would say: 'It would do no good to go ahead any faster than the country would follow. We didn't go into war to put down slavery, but to put the flag back.' By the late summer of 1862, however, he could stall no longer in the face of powerful arguments at home and abroad. His plans for Negro colonisation had met with abject failure, and the radicals of his party were screaming for more positive action. His overseas ministers were also advising him that a definite policy of emancipation would deter European recognition of the Confederacy, and with each day it became clearer to him that such a step was now in the best interests of the Union. On September 22 he issued his preliminary Proclamation of Emancipation which declared that if the states in rebellion did not return to their allegiance by the first day of 1863, he would issue a second proclamation by which the slaves in those states would become 'forever free'. But his uncertainty remained. When news of his action brought serenaders to the White House with a brass band, he addressed the crowd from a balcony, saying, 'I can only trust in God I have made no mistake.'

The President's December message to Congress proposed that the Constitution of the United States be amended to provide that every state abolishing slavery before January 1, 1900, should be paid for its freed slaves in U.S. bonds. 'Without slavery the rebellion could never have existed; without slavery it could not continue.' Of his thirty-seven-year plan of gradual emancipation, he said, 'The proposed emancipation would shorten the war, perpetuate peace, ensure this increase of population, and proportionately the wealth of the country.' He was confident that it 'would secure peace more speedily, and maintain it more permanently, than can be done by force alone'. And he added, 'I cannot make it better known than it already is, that I strongly favour colonisation.'

The radicals still said he would not dare to issue his threatened Emancipation Proclamation on January 1, 1863, though, at Christmas, the President declared: 'My mind is made up. It must be done. I am driven to it. There is no other way out of our troubles. But although my duty is plain, it is in some respects painful, and I trust the people will understand that I act not in anger but in expectation of greater good.'

The radicals were wrong. On New Year's Day, after three hours of hand-shaking at the annual White House reception, Lincoln took up a pen in aching hand and shakily signed the proclamation that would officially transform the civil war into a moral crusade. 'I never, in my life, felt more certain that I was doing right, than I do in signing this paper.'

That paper, drawn up 'upon military necessity', declared that all persons held as slaves by the rebels should be 'thenceforth and forever free' and it offered Negroes the chance to fight in the Union Army. In reality, applying only to states outside the Union, it did not free a single slave. But henceforth no European country could seriously contemplate giving open support to a Confederacy which was fighting for human slavery against a government fighting for human rights. And while thousands of soldiers deserted because they had enlisted to fight for the Union, not to free slaves, thousands of Negroes would join up in the first six months after the proclamation. By the end of the war some 188,000 coloured men would have been enrolled in the Union Army.

Morally and militarily, it was a great step forward. But, in the North, anti-war campaigners sneered at the way Lincoln had changed his way of styling the 'niggers'—'Negroes' in 1859, 'coloured men' in 1860, 'intelligent contrabands' in 1861, and now 'free Americans of African descent'. And no single act by Abraham Lincoln was better designed to make him the most violently hated enemy of the South. The Confederate States screamed their disgust, called the proclamation an invitation for Negroes to kill, burn and rape. It was, said the *Richmond Examiner*, 'the most startling political crime, the most stupid political blunder yet known in American history. Southern people have now only to choose between victory and death'.

Of Lincoln, the *Examiner* asked: 'What shall we call him? Coward, assassin, savage, murderer of women and babies? Or shall we consider them all as embodied in the word of fiend, and call him Lincoln the Fiend?' And so Lincoln, the loving father of the North, would remain, in the eyes of Southern fanatics, the greatest monster in American history.

During the civil war years no man received more threats on his life than President Lincoln. Yet, for eighteen months after his arrival in Washington, there were no armed men in or near the Executive Mansion. A fatalist by nature, the President displayed complete indifference to his own safety. Ordinary citizens would hesitate to walk through Washington streets alone after dark, but Lincoln, accustomed to strolling out late at night in his Springfield days, continued the habit in the capital. He regularly ventured out alone at night, taking a short cut through trees and shrubbery in the White House grounds to make his last daily visit to the War Office. He also went riding alone at night, and sometimes, without escort, made informal visits to the theatre. With his elongated figure, crowned with stovepipe hat, he provided an unmistakable target, and at least twice he had that tall hat removed by bullets in the night.

War Secretary Edwin Stanton frequently complained of the unnecessary risks taken by the President and eventually military protection was forced upon him. Stanton appointed a cavalry escort to accompany him whenever he drove through the city, but Lincoln considered this too ostentatious and disliked giving an impression to the public that he feared for his life. On afternoon carriage drives he playfully tried to shake off the outriders, and he continued to ride alone at night.

According to a newspaper report in October, 1862, the President argued that the only way to eliminate all risk to his person was to shut himself up in an iron box where he could not perform his duties as President. He was quoted as saying: 'Why put up the bars when the fence is down all around? If they kill me, the next man will be just as bad for them; and in a country like this, where our habits are simple, and must be, assassination is always possible, and will come if they are determined upon it.'

No one feared for the President's life more than Ward Hill Lamon, now U.S. Marshal for the District of Columbia. Early in 1863, Lamon warned Lincoln that there was a plot to depose him and put a military dictator in his place. The President replied: 'I think, for a man of accredited courage, you are the most panicky person I ever knew; you see more dangers to me than all the other friends I have . . . now you have discovered a new danger; now you think the people of this great government are likely to turn me out of office. I do not fear this from the people any more than I fear assassination from an individual.'

That year Lincoln continued to ride sometimes without escort on his daily three-mile trips between the White House and the Soldiers' Home, where his family stayed in the hot summer months. One night, at about eleven o'clock, he was approaching the grounds of the Soldiers' Home when he heard the crack of a single rifleshot. His 'eight dollar plug-hat' went flying, and his horse, 'Old Abe', galloped off with him. The President told Lamon, 'I was left in doubt whether death was more desirable from being thrown from a runaway federal horse, or as the tragic result of a fire-ball fired by a disloyal bushwacker in the middle of the night.'

But he still played down the dangers when talking to Lamon. 'In the face of this testimony in favour of your theory of danger to me, personally, I can't bring myself to believe that anyone has shot or will deliberately shoot at me with the purpose of killing me . . . I have about concluded that the shot was the result of accident. It may be that someone on his return from a day's hunt, regardless of the course of his discharge, fired off his gun as a precautionary measure of safety to his family after reaching his house.' Lincoln considered it a minor incident compared with the great escapes of his soldiers in battle. 'This whole thing seems trivial. No good can result at this time from giving it publicity. . . . I do not want it understood that I share your apprehensions. I never have.' Lamon concluded that the time 'may not be far distant when this republic will be minus a pretty respectable President'.

According to the Marshal, Lincoln only once ever referred to an individual as being a possible threat to himself—one Adam Gurowski, an elderly, hot-headed political writer who had been sacked as a State Department translator. This malcontent bitterly attacked the President and Secretary of State Seward and frequently brought his grievances to the White House. Said Lincoln: 'I have sometimes thought he might try to take my life. It would be just like him to do such a thing.'

But Gurowski was just one among thousands who possibly hated the President enough to kill him. In March, 1864, the *New York Tribune* printed a letter, believed to have come from a Southern source, which emphasised the need for more caution in guarding Lincoln. It stated that one hundred and fifty picked men were to go secretly north and take quarters in Washington, Georgetown, Baltimore and Alexandria for the purpose of kidnapping him. To prevent pursuit, every bridge between Washington and Indian Point was to be mined. It also stated that last summer a club or society of wealthy citizens of Richmond had begun to raise funds for the kidnap plot.

According to *Tribune* stories published in March and April, a certain Colonel Margrave had proposed to the Confederate War Department a plan for kidnapping Lincoln and taking him to Richmond, or, if that failed, to assassinate him. But the *New York World* remarked that this 'ridiculous canard' had been repeated in nearly every journal in the land, and commented wryly: 'It is absurd on its face. Mr. Lincoln is of much more service to the rebels where he is than if they had him in Richmond.'

At this time, Francis Bicknell Carpenter, the thirty-seven-year-old artist, was engaged for many months at the White House on an official portrait of the President. He recalled that several times he had walked about Washington with Lincoln, late at night and without escort. When he told him about the *New York Tribune* report, Lincoln smiled. 'Well, even if true, I do not see what the rebels would gain by killing or getting possession of me. I am but a single individual, and it would not help their cause or make the least difference in the progress of the war. Everything would go right on just the same.'

Lincoln was not merely casual about his own safety; he was downright reckless. On July 12, when Washington was seriously threatened by Confederate forces under Jubal A. Early, he witnessed the engagement from such an exposed position that an officer at his side was killed and a surgeon, only five feet away, was hit in the ankle by a bullet. Only when ordered to do so by Major-General Horatio Wright did the President move to a safer position.

In August, a guard on duty at the main gate to the grounds of the Soldiers' Home heard a gun-shot at about eleven o'clock in the evening. A few minutes later, Lincoln, bareheaded, rode furiously towards him. The guard, John W. Nichols, made a search with a corporal and, at a nearby driveway intersection, they found the President's silk hat—with 'a bullet through the crown'.

By now Stanton was becoming more and more anxious about Lincoln's safety; he ordered that, while the President might venture to the War Department alone after dark, he was always to be escorted home by four soldiers and a non-commissioned officer. In the autumn of that year the cavalry guard at the Soldiers' Home was regularly reminded to be especially alert. Yet the President was still in the habit of slipping out without warning for a late-night walk in the extensive grounds.

That autumn, Lamon was so convinced that Lincoln was in grave danger that he sometimes spent nights sleeping in the hall outside the President's bedroom. He considered theatres to be especially dangerous places, and in December he wrote to Lincoln complaining bitterly about his casual approach in visiting the theatre in the company of one or two elderly officials who would be incapable of protecting him. Lamon offered to resign his marshalship if the President doubted his sincerity in making the warning.

Lincoln did not doubt it; nor did he heed his old friend's advice. In 1864, it was estimated that the President had visited Grover's Theatre as many as a hundred times since his arrival in Washington, and often he had been to the theatre without escort. Such informality would be ended late in 1864 with the appointment of four Presidential bodyguards, recruited from the Washington metropolitan police force. The precise purpose of this police detail was not generally appreciated by the public since they were assigned to the White House at a time when much publicity was being given to the vandalism of souvenir-hunters visiting the Executive Mansion. But their specific duty was, in turn, to remain within a few yards of the President at all times and to look out for suspicious characters.

The four bodyguards were Alfonso Dunn, John F. Parker,

Thomas Pendel and Alexander Smith, and when Pendel was soon appointed doorkeeper he was replaced by William H. Crook. Each man was plainclothed and carried a .38 Colt revolver. Two served on an 8 a.m. to 4 p.m. shift, a third guarded the President from 4 p.m. until midnight, the fourth took the remaining hours of early morning with his post in the hall directly outside the President's bedroom door. Crook later recorded, 'The night guards were expected to protect the President on his expeditions to and from the War Department, or while he was at any place of amusement, and to patrol the corridor outside his room while he slept.'

Abraham Lincoln was sick of the Presidency even before he formally took office. He disliked the heavy social programme and all the formalities his duties entailed; above all, he had no taste for the task of distributing appointments. Many thousands of men were unemployed at the time of his inauguration and it was known that the Republicans, in power for the first time, would replace all Democratic government workers down to the lowest of clerks. By far the greatest part of the President's daily routine was taken up by the thousands of applicants for these posts. Night and day they pestered him, in Springfield and at Willard's Hotel when he was President-elect, at the White House within two hours of his arrival. Even while he faced the critical problem of Fort Sumter, he was besieged by office-seekers. A Michigan Congressman wrote, 'The city is overwhelmed with a crowd of rabid, persistent office-seekers—the like never was experienced before in the history of government.' One applicant even stopped Lincoln as he drove through the city and waved a recommendation paper towards him. 'No. No,' said the President. 'I won't open shop in the street.' Once he was so persistently pestered by a politician seeking new office or suggesting changes that he remarked to a friend that last thing at night 'I look under the bed to see if So-and-so is there, and if not, I thank Heaven and bounce in.' Another time he was handed so many recommendations on behalf of two rival candidates for a lucrative Ohio postmaster-ship, and so harassed by delegations pleading each man's case, that he had all the recommendations piled on a pair of scales and ruled that the man with the heavier papers should have the appointment. A week after his famous Gettysburg speech of November, 1863, the President went down with a mild form of smallpox. He joked: 'There is one good thing about this. I now have something I can give everybody.'

The war years swelled the White House invasion into a great tidal wave of favour-seekers, as added to the job applicants came thousands of tragic citizens—mothers, wives and sweethearts—pleading for pardons on behalf of their condemned menfolk, or begging for their young men to be spared from the draft. They came weeping and praying, mothers in widows' weeds, young wives with babes in their arms, bringing the full tragedy of war to the White House. Thirty thousand cases were brought before army courts martial in one year; never was one man approached so often to spare so many. Lincoln, the great pardoner, rarely refused mercy where there were the slightest grounds for mercy to be granted. He used to joke: 'If I have one vice, and I can call it nothing else, it is not to be able to say "No." Thank God for not making me a woman, but if He had, I suppose He would have made me just as ugly as He did, and no one would ever have tempted me.'

Some cases could not arouse even his ready sympathy, such as that of the Missouri guerilla leader Nichols, who had a reputation for pushing gunpowder into the ears of Unionist prisoners and setting it alight to blow off their heads. It was said that he carried human ears in his clothing when captured. But Lincoln, who had the highest regard for human life, was reluctant to dispatch any man to the grave. Something inside him died with every report of great losses in battle, and by the summer of 1864 the giant Westerner, once famed for his phenomenal strength, was physically withered and mentally worn out by three years of excessive work and worry. Carpenter, engaged on his portrait, remarked of his subject: 'In repose, it was the saddest face I ever knew. There were days when I could scarcely look into it without crying.'

Cruelly, the President had also been struck by personal tragedy in February, 1862, when eleven-year-old Willie, a delicate, studious boy, idolised by his parents, became feverish after riding his pony in the chilly rain. Lincoln reluctantly allowed the White House ball to be held as scheduled but ruled that there should be no dancing. Still, music and laughter incongruously filled the rooms of the Executive Mansion while the poor, blue-eyed boy steadily weakened above. The President had no heart for playing the host and crept upstairs to be with his son. Two weeks later Willie was dead. Lincoln uncovered the child's face, stared a long while, and murmured, 'It is hard, hard, hard to have him die.' The loss left Mrs. Lincoln with a broken heart. She was too ill to attend the funeral on a day which brought near-hurricane-force gales that ripped off the rooftops of houses, and she never again entered the guest room where her Willie died or the Green Room in which he was embalmed. The sight of his picture, the very mention of his name, was long after enough to make her disintegrate in tears and wailing; not until New Year's Day, 1865, would she lay aside her heavy mourning and resume her social duties.

Nor was the President spared cruel attacks on his family. His grief-stricken wife had so many relatives on the Confederate side that it became widely rumoured in 1863 that she was a Southern spy and the malicious suggestion was brought to the attention of Senate members of the Committee on the Conduct of War, who called a secret morning session to discuss it. To the members' astonishment and embarrassment, Lincoln, uninvited, walked in on the 'secret' meeting. Solemnly, he stood before the members and stated, 'I, Abraham Lincoln, President of the United States, appear of my own volition before this Committee of the Senate to say that I, of my own knowledge, know it is untrue that any of my family hold treasonable communication with the enemy.'

He turned and left without further word. The members sat speechless for a while; then, deeply moved, they dropped the subject completely and adjourned for the day.

Walt Whitman wrote of Lincoln in a letter, 'I do not dwell on the supposed failure of his government; he has shown I sometimes think an almost supernatural tact in keeping the ship afloat at all.' The President had indeed carried a terrible burden, meeting his generals' constant demands for more men, seeking to unify the various shades of opinion within his own party, facing grave difficulties abroad, and becoming deeply involved in the controversial military tactics of his armies. He worked at a pace no ordinary mortal could have maintained, never spared himself in the struggle to restore the Union he so greatly cherished. But, for all this, the President received precious little appreciation from the politicians; in 1864 he was being attacked almost as bitterly in the North as in the South.

Early that year it was reported that not one Senator could be named as favourable to Lincoln's renomination for the Presidency, that in the House only one Congressman positively supported him. Lincoln was the 'man in-between', who had either gone too far or not far enough for the politicians. Some felt he was too weak to put down the rebellion, others that he was too strong to allow a peaceful solution. Moreover, since no President for thirty years had served a second term, some felt that a one-term tradition had been established. Yet his hold over the common people was as strong as ever. The great majority of the Army was solidly behind 'Old Abe'; the masses trusted him and were not prepared to risk trying another in his place.

Despite the strong opposition of members of his own party, Lincoln won unanimous renomination at the Baltimore convention in June, but, as military blunders brought more heavy casualties, many Republicans regretted the choice and demanded that Lincoln withdraw. Opposition newspapers were now describing the President as an 'ape, gorilla, filthy storyteller, liar, thief, braggart, buffoon, monster, tortoise, tyrant, fiend, butcher

and perjurer'. One satirist, composing a mock biography, wrote:
'Mr. Lincoln stands six feet twelve in his socks which he changes
once every ten days. His anatomy is composed mostly of bones,
and when walking he resembles the offspring of a happy marriage
between a derrick and a windmill. . . . His head is shaped something like a rutabago, and his complexion is that of a Saratoga
trunk. . . . He swears fluently. . . . He can hardly be called handsome, though he is certainly much better looking since he had
the smallpox.'

His enemies heaped abuse upon him, ambitious politicians
schemed behind the scenes. But Lincoln, greatly boosted by
timely military successes, would win the day. On the rain-swept
election day of November 8 he received 55·09 per cent of the
popular vote as opposed to the 44·91 per cent of the Democratic
candidate, General George B. McClellan. In the Electoral College,
Lincoln had a formidable 212 votes to McClellan's 21, but then
he only narrowly won three states with the largest electoral
votes, New York, Pennsylvania and Ohio. On the other hand,
the soldiers gave him a vote of confidence with 116,877 votes
against McClellan's 33,748, and hundreds of thousands of more
soldiers, who would certainly have backed him, had no chance to
vote, either because they were busy fighting or because their
home-state legislatures would not accept their votes in the field.

Thus, Lincoln, who desired a second term to complete the task
of restoring the Union and beginning the reconstruction of the
South, was returned to the White House. Many Confederate
newspapers judged his election as being to the advantage of their
cause. But General Grant wired from the front, 'The victory is
worth more to the country than a battle won.'

From the White House, Lincoln told the celebrating crowd,
'So long as I have been here I have not willingly planted a thorn
in any man's bosom.' But Ward Hill Lamon was more alarmed
than jubilant at his hero's success. On election night he rolled
himself up in his cloak and spent the night on the floor outside
the President's door, with, as Lincoln's secretary, John Hay,

recorded in his diary, 'A small arsenal of pistols and bowie knives around him.'

Senators squirmed uncomfortably in their chairs. Members of the Cabinet looked away in shame or else buried their faces in their hands. There was no way of escaping the fact—red-faced Andrew Johnson, the one-time illiterate tailor's boy from Tennessee, now about to be sworn in as Vice-President of the United States, was drunk. The previous night he had over-indulged himself at a stag party given by Colonel John W. Forney, clerk to the U.S. Senate, and the after-effects were plain to see as, flushed and fortified with three large whiskies, he shuffled into the stuffy Senate Chamber shortly before noon. They became even more painfully evident as he stumbled through a confused, egotistical speech about the poverty of his youth and his lack of education.

Hannibal Hamlin, the outgoing Vice-President, tugged at his successor's coat-tails; Forney whispered to him. But there was no stopping Andy Johnson who, hoarse-voiced, rambled on through his embarrassing address. Inaudibly, he repeated the oath of office, and then, most ludicrous of all, he took the Bible in his hand and bellowed, 'I kiss this Book in the face of my nation of the United States.' The bumbling, repetitious speaker was an embarrassment to all, and after his pathetic performance President Lincoln gave instructions that Johnson should not be permitted to speak outside from the inauguration platform. He also took such pains to avoid his deputy that more than a month would pass before he invited his new Vice-President to the White House for the first time. It was also the last time. The day Lincoln chose to see him was Good Friday, April 14.

As long as he lived, Andrew Johnson would be haunted by the memory of that day of indignity and shame. His political enemies were to exploit the incident to the full, and in his term as President millions of citizens would hear stories of Johnson's habitual drunkenness. But Johnson was no drunkard; rather he was the most maligned political figure of his time. In 1868 he would be the first American President to be put on trial for 'high crimes and misdemeanors' and his impeachment, based on a purely political case, would fail by only one vote.

For all his weaknesses, Johnson was not a man without virtues. A coarse-mannered Southerner, who had grown up to detest the cotton-owning aristocracy, he was a fearless patriot and had never given the faintest hint of fear in the face of assassination threats. He had fought secession as hard as any man. Several times, in a slave state, he had drawn the revolver he always carried in his right hip pocket to hold off crowds ready to lynch him. Johnson's alcoholic condition on inauguration day was understandable, if not excusable. During the previous winter he had been laid down for weeks with typhoid fever; with the addition of his heavy political duties and the excitement of his election, he was suffering from both physical and nervous exhaustion. He had written to Lincoln asking whether he might take the oath of office without leaving Nashville. The President replied: 'It is our unanimous conclusion that it is unsafe for you not to be here on the fourth of March. Be sure to reach here by that time.'

Following the Vice-President's sad display in the Senate Chamber, a more noteworthy event passed almost unnoticed. It happened after the newly-elected senators had been sworn in and the dignitaries moved in procession through the hallways to the east front of the Capitol. Suddenly a man broke through the police guard and headed towards the inauguration platform. He was promptly seized by police officers, but he was not seriously regarded as a menacing intruder and, after the ceremonies, was released.

Some weeks later police would identify the intruder as John Wilkes Booth, the nationally famous actor, son of Junius Brutus Booth, the greatest tragedian of his day, and the brother of actors Edwin and Junius Booth, both famed as Shakespearian players. But this belated identification would seem unreliable. In fact, John Wilkes Booth had no need to rush through the police lines.

He took a seat on the inauguration platform, a place provided for him by his fiancée Miss Bessie Hale, whose father, having just failed to win re-election as Senator for New Hampshire, was about to be appointed Minister to Spain. Later John Wilkes would tell a friend that he had been close enough to the President to have shot him on his inauguration.

As the huge crowds dispersed, John Wilkes Booth walked along the Avenue with Mr. Walter Burton, the National Hotel night clerk, who was an ardent admirer of Mr. Lincoln. Burton never suspected for a moment that his companion, frustrated by the dismal failure of plots to kidnap the Chief Executive, was now contemplating the greatest crime of all—the assassination of the President.

While Washington buzzed with the scandal of Johnson's shocking lapse, the subject of more serious discussion on that inauguration day of a century ago was the controversial 'malice towards none' speech of the reinstated President. Despite lashing rain and violent gales, vast crowds had gathered on Saturday morning beneath the inauguration platform at the east front of the Capitol. Marshal Lamon, ever concerned for the President's safety, had arranged for thirteen U.S. marshals and thirteen citizen aides to escort Lincoln from the White House to the Capitol. But the security measures did not compare with those at the 1861 inaugural. During the morning the President had driven to the Capitol by himself to deal with paper work hours before the procession began.

Sudden sunshine pierced the dark clouds as Lincoln made his short address before Chief Justice Chase administered the oath of office. The solemn, five-minute address ended with the godly words, 'with malice towards none; with charity for all; with firmness in the right, as God gives us to see the right, let us strive on to finish the work we are in; to bind up the nation's wounds; to care for him who shall have borne the battle, and for his widow, and his orphan—to do all which may achieve and cherish

a just and lasting peace, among ourselves, and with all nations.'
It brought a tumult of applause; many people were moved to
tears. But it was also a speech which would be roundly criticised
as being too conciliatory towards the South.

The hoi polloi of the North loved Abe Lincoln; how deeply
tens of thousands would not fully appreciate until his death. His
second inaugural provided the occasion for the most extravagant
celebrations, and the 'Coronation Day' brought more chaos to
Washington than the crowning of a royal head in a European
capital. The city was crammed to bursting point as, by train,
coach and foot, the revellers came. Once again thousands of
visitors had to sleep on floors and in chairs, on porches and on
pavements; public appeals had to be made for people to stay out
of the city if possible.

But, for all the mass demonstrations of loyal affection, President
Lincoln was an isolated, bitterly abused figure in those last days
of the war. Politically, he was a minority leader. All the South
stood against him, plus the Democrats of the North. The radicals
of the Republican party opposed him, and most of the nation's
leading newspapers. The leader's party was severely split with
many members in the Senate and the House speaking out strongly
against his reconstruction plans, and seeking to rub the proud,
defeated South in the dust. On the evening after Lincoln had
spoken of 'malice towards none', the Vice-President was to roar
out his hatred of Jefferson Davis to a crowd celebrating beneath
illuminated public buildings. In answer to their lynch-mob cries
Johnson shouted, 'Yes, hang him twenty times because treason is
the greatest of the crimes.' And Johnson was a Southerner and a
Democrat. Republican radicals were even more bitterly opposed
to Lincoln's 'soft peace'.

In seeking a lenient peace, the President stood virtually alone.
Even among his close friends he could count on few who wished
to support him in this view, and his most loyal supporters could
not agree with his intention to push ahead with the post-war
reconstruction of the South without consulting Congress. From

Lincoln with his favourite son, Tad

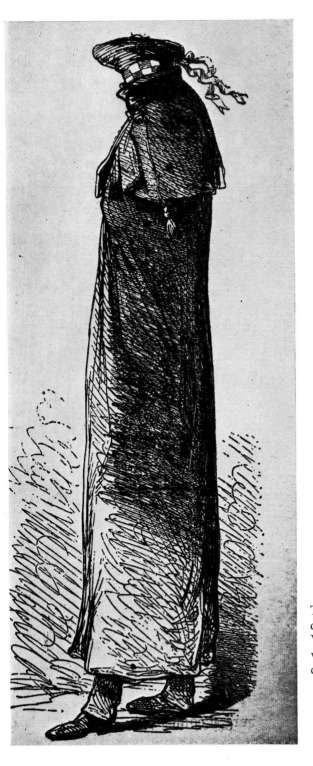

The President-Elect was caricatured arriving in Washington in disguise, wearing a Scotch plaid cap and a long military coat

all sides he was cruelly attacked, both politically and personally. His enemies sank to the lowest depths in mocking his physical appearance and abusing him as being a man of low intelligence, education and manners, and a teller of smutty stories. Horace Greeley, the grotesque-looking newspaper baron, once Lincoln's friend, had turned against him the year before after he had unsuccessfully campaigned in the *New York Tribune* for peace at any price. On April 14 he would hand in an editorial to his managing editor, Sidney Howard Gray, which was so 'brutal, bitter, sarcastic and personal' in attacking the President that Gray, after having his boss's vitriol set up in type, hid the galley in shame.

In the defence of Fort Sumter, Major Robert Anderson had lost only one man and he the victim of an accidental explosion. In the holocaust that followed six hundred thousand men were to perish and not until the dawn of 1865 would the end of the killing come in sight. Despite their far greater losses, the North now had more men than when the conflict began, and in his December message to Congress, Lincoln was able to report, 'We are gaining strength, and may, if need be, maintain the contest indefinitely.' The tide was turning inexorably against the South. In mid-December, the Southern invasion of Tennessee was repulsed. Sherman's ruthless military machine ploughed across Georgia as far as the sea, and on December 22 the general wired to Lincoln, 'I beg to present you as a Christmas gift the city of Savannah, with 150 heavy guns and plenty of ammunition; also about 25,000 bales of cotton.'

On the night of January 15, the Union forces took Fort Fisher, the fortress that defended Wilmington, the last port of the South into which blockade-runners could bring supplies. In February, Sherman's hordes of sixty thousand swept over the state where the bloody business of secession had begun. South Carolina would be ravaged without mercy. Sherman's aim: 'to whip the rebels, to humble their pride, to follow them to their inmost recesses, and make them fear and dread us'.

Meanwhile, life in Washington was far from being peaceful and serene. At eight in the evening of inauguration day, to a background of music by a Marine band, two thousand people stampeded into the White House grounds for a public reception. Women and men alike were severely bruised in the free-for-all rush to enter the Executive Mansion and shake the President's hand in the stuffy Blue Room, and when the wild stampede had passed it left a trail of havoc behind. The savage souvenir-hunters had torn curtains, cut chair coverings, peeled off wallpaper, ripped out bell cords. It was not an unfamiliar scene, but this was one of the worst acts of vandalism seen there. Bodyguard Crook wrote that 'the White House looked as if a regiment of rebel troops had been quartered there, with permission to forage'. He recalled the President saying: 'Why should they do it? How can they?'

Chaos returned to the White House on Monday night with the holding of the Inauguration Ball for more than four thousand guests. Mrs. Lincoln, who had returned to her extravagant ways, wore a dress costing two thousand dollars. There were lancers, waltzes, schottisches and polkas, but soon the floor was so jammed that serious dancing became impossible. Then followed an un-civilised scramble to attend the midnight supper of beef, veal, poultry, game, smoked meats, terrapin, oysters, salads, jellies, ices, tarts, cakes, fruits, nuts, coffee and chocolate. It was intended to feed the guests in shifts of three hundred at a time, but many more pushed through for places. In minutes the magnificent table, with a monster sugar model of the Capitol in the centre, was reduced to ruins. Couples piled their plates and picnicked in corners and on the floor; men snatched whole chickens; ladies grabbed huge ornamental confectionaries; glasses and plates were smashed as the hopelessly overworked waiters were jostled in the crowd.

The start of Lincoln's second term also released a fresh avalanche of office-seekers who descended in hordes on the White House each day. These vultures would help to exhaust the President so much that one newspaper recommended driving them out of the city to save the President from a breakdown. That breakdown nearly came on March 14. Lincoln spent this Tuesday in bed, though he insisted on holding a Cabinet meeting in his room. Influenza was the officially announced diagnosis. In fact, his doctor's verdict was 'complete exhaustion'. The President did not have the strength to rise. But next day he was back at his desk working quietly, and, at his wife's request, he accompanied her to an opera at Grover's Theatre.

Throughout that first month of his second term, one Union victory followed swiftly upon another as the South fought on gallantly, stubbornly, and hopelessly for their lost cause. By sheer weight of numbers the army of General Ulysses S. Grant was moving towards certain victory, and so sure was the conclusion that, late in March, Grant invited the President to join him at City Point, Virginia, and witness the final act. The invitation offered Lincoln an opportunity of welcome relief from his tiresome duties in Washington and he readily accepted. On March 23 he sailed on the *River Queen* with his wife, son Tad, and bodyguard Crook.

Unfortunately the President could not escape all the torments of Washington life; the emotionally unstable Mary Todd Lincoln took along the absurd jealousy and explosive temperament that her husband had endured with monumental patience for almost a quarter of a century. En route for City Point, Mrs. Lincoln told the President that she understood Grant had arranged for all generals' ladies to stay at the rear and she supposed she would be the only lady at the front. Her husband knew nothing about it, but when they had joined the Army of the Potomac, Mrs. Lincoln learned that Grant had indeed made such an order, with one exception, his wife, Julia.

A few days later the subject arose again as Mrs. Lincoln and Mrs. Grant rode in an army ambulance to attend a troop review at the battle lines. They were escorted by an army driver and General Adam Badeau, Grant's military secretary, who chanced to mention that only one other lady had been allowed to remain in the front area—the wife of General Charles Griffin, who had obtained a special permit from the President. Immediately, Mrs. Lincoln flew into one of her wild fits of jealousy.

'Do you mean that she saw the President alone?' she screamed. 'Do you know that I never allow the President to see any woman alone?'

Badeau recalled: 'She was absolutely jealous of poor, ugly Abraham Lincoln. I tried to pacify her and to palliate my remark, but she was fairly boiling over with rage. "That's a very equivocal smile, sir," she exclaimed. "Let me out of this carriage at once. I will ask the President if he saw that woman alone." '

When the carriage rolled on, Mrs. Lincoln tried to grab the reins from the driver. Mrs. Grant, a plain, cross-eyed woman, always unsure of herself in the First Lady's presence, was near to tears as she begged Mrs. Lincoln not to alarm herself so. The rest of the journey was made in almost unbearable silence.

Next day Mrs. Lincoln had another mad bout of jealousy on the visit to the Army of the James, commanded by General Ord, on the north side of the river. Once again the various distinguished visitors from Washington rode on horseback, while the two women travelled in a carriage. This time Mrs. Ord accompanied her husband, and since the ambulance was full she rode ahead of the other ladies, for a while by the side of the President. Again Mary Lincoln flew into a frenzy. 'What does the woman mean by riding by the side of the President, and ahead of me? Does she suppose that he wants her by the side of him?' When poor Mrs. Grant tried to pacify her, she turned like a wild cat on the wife of the Commander of the U.S. Army. Brutally she shouted, 'I suppose you think you'll get to the White House yourself, don't you?' Mrs. Grant replied quietly that she was quite satisfied with her present position which was far greater than she had expected to attain. But Mrs. Lincoln went on: 'Oh, you had better take it if you can get it. 'Tis very nice.'

At the front, Mrs. Lincoln turned on Mrs. Ord, called her vile names in the presence of a crowd of officers, and reduced the bewildered woman to tears. Throughout the visit to the armies the First Lady bitched crazily about the conduct of Mrs. Griffin and Mrs. Ord. She stated loudly to Grant that General Ord should be removed from his position, and she repeatedly abused well-meaning Mrs. Grant. Once she rebuked the general's lady for sitting in her presence. 'How dare you be seated,' she said, 'until I invite you.'

Badeau wrote in his book, *Grant in Peace*: 'I never suffered greater humiliation and pain on account of one not a near personal friend than when I saw the Head of the State, the man who carried all the cares of the nation at such a crisis—subjected to this inexpressible public mortification. He bore it as Christ might have done; with an expression of pain and sadness that cut one to the heart, but with extreme calmness and dignity. He called her "mother" with his old-time plainness; he pleaded with eyes and tones, and endeavoured to explain or palliate the offences of others, till she turned on him like a tigress; and then he walked away, hiding that noble, ugly face that we might not catch the full expression of its misery.'

The great military progress provided much to console President Lincoln during his stormy visit to the front. On Wednesday, March 29, he watched the launching of Grant's great assault on the Petersburg lines. The following week-end Robert E. Lee's lines were broken as Grant pushed forward from the east and Sheridan swept down from the west, and on Monday a telegram from Lincoln to the War Department told War Secretary Stanton that Petersburg was evacuated and that Grant believed Richmond had fallen too. Soon after, Lincoln's next message came from Richmond itself. On that eventful April 3, the blue-coats had surged into the Confederate capital.

During his stay at City Point, Lincoln had been cautioned by Stanton against visiting the front. But now the President casually walked into the burning chaos of Richmond, where the risk to

his own life could scarcely have been greater. As he approached
the fallen capital, Negroes crowded around him and knelt before
him, while one old-timer of sixty called, 'Bless de Lawd, dere
is de great Messiah.' The President told them: 'Don't kneel
to me. You must kneel to God only and thank Him for your
freedom.'

Meanwhile, Washington went wild with joy. Workers in the
now undisputed capital quit their offices, children skipped school
and shops closed down, as the citizens poured out in their tens of
thousands to celebrate in the streets. Bands played, cavalry
paraded, saloons were packed. There was a deafening salute of
three hundred guns for Petersburg and five hundred for Richmond. The evening of April 4 brought grand illuminations of
the city, music, dancing and fireworks. The great orgy of
jubilation had begun.

All the news was good for the North, except for one notable
casualty on the domestic front. It was learned that Secretary of
State William Seward had met with a near-fatal accident when
his horses bolted during an afternoon drive in Washington. The
veteran statesman was left unconscious in the street, with a broken
right arm and severely shattered jaw. When Lincoln heard of his
friend's misfortune he resolved to hurry back to the capital.
Arriving home from the front on Palm Sunday, April 9, he
hastened directly to Mr. Seward's residence and found the statesman lying in pain, swathed in bandages, with a steel frame supporting his mutilated jaw. The President sprawled his huge frame
on the bed, and, resting on one elbow, told his crippled Minister
of the Army's great progress. He spoke softly to him for half an
hour, then tiptoed out of the darkened room. Seward had fallen
into a feverish sleep.

Soon after this visit the President received a telegram from
Grant: 'General Lee surrendered the Army of Northern Virginia
this morning on terms proposed by myself.' The war was virtually over. On the rainy Monday morning, Washington woke
to the news of Lee's surrender, proclaimed by more gun salutes

that thundered so loudly that they cracked window-panes on Massachusetts Avenue. It was the second successive Monday devoted to celebrations, a holiday for most workers, with bands, bells and speeches sustaining the sound of victory throughout the day. But this time the President was at home and great crowds flocked like happy children to see 'Father Abraham'.

The soft, misty evening of Tuesday, April 11, brought the formal celebrations of Lee's surrender. Government buildings were illuminated again; huge crowds filled Pennsylvania Avenue and pressed around the White House, chanting 'Lincoln, Lincoln . . .' After four years of bloodshed and tears, the masses waited for a stirring victory speech, eloquently praising the victors and condemning the vanquished rebels. They were disappointed. Instead of words resounding with triumph, the humble President gave them a sober, heavy speech about the grave problems of reconstruction that lay ahead, about his wish for the elective franchise to be conferred on some coloured men—'the very intelligent and on those who served our soldiers'.

This view of Negro suffrage was far too moderate to satisfy the Republican radicals. But, as Lincoln spoke from a balcony, one man among the thousands on the White House lawns found the proposal far too extreme. For actor John Wilkes Booth, talk of giving the ballot to Negroes was the final indignity thrust upon his beloved South.

As the brass band struck up *Dixie*, he turned to his companion, a boyish-looking man called Davy Herold,[1] and hissed: 'Nigger citizenship. Now, by God, I'll put him through. That's the last speech he will ever make.'

Mr. Lincoln was in a melancholy mood. That same evening the war-weary President entertained a few friends informally at

---

1. Sources are equally divided in naming Herold or Lewis Paine as Booth's companion that night. But Herndon gives Frederick Stone, Herold's defence counsel, as his authority for stating that Booth made this remark to Herold.

the White House. He talked about dreams and how often they were mentioned in the Bible. 'If we believe the Bible, we must accept the fact that, in the old days, God and His angels came to men in their sleep and made themselves known in dreams.' Encouraged by Mrs. Lincoln who had so long suffered with nightmares, he went on to recall a recent dream which, he said, had haunted him ever since.

'There seemed to be a death-like stillness about me,' he began. 'Then I heard subdued sobs, as if a number of people were weeping.' He explained in detail how he had wandered in his dream from room to room until he arrived in the East Room, where he saw a corpse lying on a catafalque guarded by soldiers and surrounded by weeping mourners.

' "Who is dead in the White House?" I demanded of one of the soldiers.

' "The President," was his answer. "He was killed by an assassin."

'Then came a loud burst of grief from the crowd, which awoke me from my dreams. I slept no more that night, and, although it was only a dream, I have been strangely annoyed by it ever since.'

Ward Hill Lamon believed that Mr. Lincoln probably had this dream on March 19, the night after he had attended a performance of *Faust*. But he did not dismiss the story as a meaningless nightmare, for he remained as firmly convinced as ever that the President's life was in great danger. After listening to the account, both Lamon and Secretary of the Interior John P. Usher urged Lincoln not to risk going out any more after dark.

The President teased Lamon about his obsessive anxiety. 'What does anybody want to assassinate me for? If anyone wants to do so, he can do it any day or night, if he is ready to give his life for mine. It is nonsense.'

2

'I MUST HAVE FAME'

WHEN ONE CONSIDERS the totally inadequate security measures in operation at that time, it may not be readily appreciated how far government officials were preoccupied in April, 1865, with the possibility of an assassination attempt against the President. In fact, no other topic except the progress of the war was more frequently discussed. For more than six months, somewhat coloured reports of threats on Lincoln's life had appeared regularly in the Northern press. The vast network of secret agents under Colonel Lafayette C. Baker, chief of the Detective Bureau, was for ever uncovering new Confederate conspiracies and intrigues; without warrant or reasonable evidence, his detectives would seize suspects for third-degree-type questioning, and hold them for weeks without registering any formal charge. At no time, however, did the police or secret servicemen question so respected and popular a figure as John Wilkes Booth. It was generally assumed that an assassination plot would be the work of skilled professionals employed by the Confederate States of America, never of a small group of amateurs.

Despite his well-known sympathy for the Confederate cause, Booth was not a person to be readily suspected of plotting against the government. The North abounded with Southern sympathisers who made more likely suspects than such a prominent and successful actor. Booth was a dashing young man who enjoyed good looks, good health and good fortune (he had earned as much as twenty thousand dollars a year on the stage). In days when so many suffered the privations of war, he seemed a man to be envied by all. True, he had not achieved the fame of his father, Junius Brutus, a star of the first magnitude who had been hailed as the foremost tragedian on the London and American stage; nor the fame of his elder brother, Edwin, sometimes rated America's greatest Shakespearian player. But, at twenty-six, he had at least risen to the stature of a matinée idol. Strangers would nod to him as he passed by in the street; theatre managements eagerly sought his services; he was popular among fellow actors who knew him as a gay young dandy, generous in buying drinks, and with a fondness for practical jokes. John Deery, the national billiards champion, once said: 'No man have I ever known who possessed a more winning personality. In his way with his intimates he was as simple and affectionate as a child. John Wilkes Booth cast a spell over most men with whom he came in contact and, I believe, all women without exception.'

Handsome, lean, and of medium height (5 ft. 8 in.), John Wilkes dressed elegantly, had silky jet-black hair and moustache, shining white teeth, ivory skin, and an easy charm. He was a fine athlete, horseman, swordsman and marksman. Above all, he was a great lover, who could boast unrivalled success with the ladies. Women, of high and low station, found him irresistible. Hotel maidservants attended to his needs with rare devotion to their duty; waitresses rushed to serve him in restaurants; adoring female fans packed the theatres when he was on tour. His mail brought showers of scented love letters, and in his diary he carried photographs of four beautiful actresses of his day, Fay Brown, Effie Germon, Alice Gray and Helen Western.

Booth prided himself on his reputation as a great lover. He took women as he pleased and it pleased him often, though it was said of him that he never seduced a girl he knew to be pure. There is no evidence to suggest that he ever lost his heart completely to one woman; rather he treated love-making as a game.

A man of considerable charm and culture, he fully understood the refined art of making a lady companion feel appreciated and desirable. He gave his lady friends much satisfaction; he also broke many hearts.

There was actress Henrietta Irving, who, during a tour in April, 1861, rushed into Booth's room, lunged at him with a knife, and grazed his face. She then ran to her own room and stabbed herself in the breast, though not fatally. Then there was Booth's most regular mistress, attractive little Ella Turner Starr, whom he installed in her own sister's whore-house, not far from the White House. She used to join him when he stayed at Washington's National Hotel. When Ella learned that her lover had assassinated the President, she would place his picture below her pillow and bury her face in chloroform in an unsuccessful suicide attempt.

Booth was secretly engaged to Bessie Hale, the daughter of John Parker Hale, former Senator for New Hampshire, a staunch Lincoln man who, in April, 1865, was to become Minister to Spain. But he was not deeply in love with her; rather the vain actor was responding to the ex-Senator's opposition to the match. He easily won over the infatuated Bessie, but, while he was engaged to her, he happily had affairs with other women. Early in March he secretly met the mysterious Eva, believed to be the daughter of another Senator. She left him a note scribbled on an envelope:

> 'For all sad words from tongue or pen,
> The saddest are these—it might have been.
> March 5th, 1865—In John's room.'

On April 3, the day Grant's blue-coats surged into Richmond, Booth booked into New York City's Aquidneck Hotel, and, as was his practice, he was accompanied by a girl friend. Without attempt at pretence, he signed the register, 'J. W. Booth and Lady.'

In his undoubted success with the ladies, John Wilkes took very much after his father. Junius Brutus Booth, the head of this remarkably talented family, was born in London in 1796, the son of a lawyer, the grandson of a Jewish silversmith, and from his early teens he had a reputation for being something of a lady-killer. At thirteen he was accused by a servant girl of being responsible for her pregnancy; at seventeen he was unsuccessfully defended by his father on an identical charge, this time in a court of law. Bored with the life of a clerk in his father's law office, Junius joined a group of strolling players, acting throughout the country and later in the Low Countries. He gained unrivalled training for a stage career, and in Brussels he also gained a bride. A Miss Adelaide Delannoy, twenty-two, eloped with him, and they married in May, 1815. Their first child, a girl, died in infancy; then came a son, Richard Junius. Now Booth's reputation as an actor was rising rapidly until by 1820 he was virtually second only to the great Edmund Kean as a star of the London stage.

But Junius Booth was far too restless an individual to be rooted in London as an actor and family man. Moreover, his liking for the ladies was as compelling as ever. In Amsterdam he missed a command performance before the Prince of Orange because he was busy cuddling Dutch girls in a saloon. Then, back in London, he was attracted by a dark, eighteen-year-old flower-girl, Mary Ann Holmes from Reading in Berkshire. With remarkable success he began leading a double life—playing the devoted family man in London and taking the attractive, full-figured Mary Ann with him on engagements abroad.

This time it was no mild flirtation. Junius was madly in love and Mary Ann was expecting his child. So it happened that in the spring of 1821 he sailed with his mistress to the United States where he quickly won even greater fame as a Shakespearian actor. Booth made his American début as Richard III in Richmond, Virginia, conquered New York, enjoyed a triumphant tour of the South. Yet he found theatre life strangely unsatisfying and in 1823 sought temporary escape by taking a lonely log cabin in Maryland, three miles from Belair, and, one year later, leasing farmland nearby.

Junius frequently returned to the stage, but only so that he might afford the luxury of supporting two families—his wife and child in England and his mistress and two children, Junius and Rosalie, in Maryland. In America, Mary Ann was accepted as his wife, a role she more than adequately fulfilled by bearing him eight more children (Henry, Mary Ann, Frederick, Elizabeth, Edwin, Asia, John Wilkes and Joseph). Booth's father crossed the Atlantic to manage the farm while his son was on tour and twice Junius revisited England. Incredibly, he took Mary Ann with him in 1825 and still managed to maintain two households in England without his lawful wife discovering his double domestic life.

In America Junius became recognised as the greatest tragedian of his day. He could pack any theatre, often earned a hundred dollars a performance. Yet he was still restless, still dissatisfied. He had done everything in his profession and lacked any sense of purpose. A deeply spiritual man, he studied numerous philosophies, but failed to discover any clear pattern for living. More and more he sought escape in drink until it became not unusual for him to appear intoxicated on the stage. His drinking, mixed with personal sorrows, finally brought signs of mental disturbance.

In 1824 it was reported in the New York *Commercial Advocate* that Booth, in a 'violent fit of insanity', waved his dagger at actor James Wallack and said, 'I must cut somebody's throat today, and whom shall I take?'

As a devoted family man Mr. Booth suffered a series of heartbreaking experiences. Firstly, his four-year-old son Frederick died; then, with the loss of his baby daughter Elizabeth, he became alarmingly deranged. Junius had only just recovered when another daughter, Mary Ann, died. This time the pain was too great to bear. On stage in Boston he shrieked, 'Take me to the lunatic asylum,' and that night he walked miles out of town in his stocking feet and underwear. He had a guilt complex and believed he was being punished by God for having recently broken his vegetarian habits.

Despite his many lapses, Booth maintained his star status on the American stage, and in 1836 he again visited England with Mary Ann and their children. But misfortune still shadowed him. In London, another child, eleven-year-old Henry Byron, died of smallpox. He was his father's favourite son. Booth had other troubles, too. A brother-in-law, James Mitchell, was blackmailing the secret head of two families and eventually he had the effrontery to move in on the Booths in Maryland, bringing his wife and eight children with him. Junius suffered another blow when his pony Peacock died. This was no minor tragedy in the distorted mind of the actor; he arranged a formal funeral, invited the neighbours, and made his wife attend, dressing her up in a white sheet and persuading her to sit on the carcass. Then, while his children looked on in frightened wonder, he stalked about the dead animal, with a gun in one hand and a Bible in the other. Tears streamed down his face.

Mad Mr. Booth was devoted to all animals, firmly believing they were reincarnated humans. He banned the killing of wild life on the farm and the privileged included poisonous snakes. Once when a copperhead was injured by a plough, Booth made a bed for the reptile in his wife's only hat-box and nursed it until it could crawl away. Another time he wept over the bodies of some dead pigeons, bought them a plot in a cemetery, and summoned a clergyman to preach a funeral sermon. His most dramatic act of madness came in 1838 when, from a ship off South Carolina, he jumped overboard to search for fellow actor William Conway who had drowned himself in that region. People called him 'the mad tragedian', and yet, for all his mental wanderings, he could still inject more life into a Shakespearian role than any other man of his time.

Junius Brutus Booth found no peace in the last years of his strange, tragic life, for he was finally confronted with the sins of his youth. The generous old man had made the grave indiscretion of sending for his only legitimate son, Richard, who was scraping a modest living by teaching Latin and Greek. When Richard discovered on his arrival that there was a second, widely recognised, 'Mrs. Booth', with six children, he wrote to his mother that she was being cruelly wronged. Late in 1846 the outraged Adelaide sailed from Liverpool and took rooms with her son in Baltimore, twenty-five miles from the Booths' 200-acre farm. Fearful domestic rows followed as, aided by a lawyer, the deceived woman fought for her marital rights; once she called at the farmhouse and railed at poor Mary Ann. Years would pass before the stubborn Adelaide gave up all hope of winning back her famous husband. Finally, in March, 1851, she had no difficulty in obtaining a divorce and two months later Mr. Booth, now fifty-five, at last married the gentle, warm-hearted woman who had borne ten of his children. Eighteen months later, the eccentric, sometimes insane, actor developed a high fever and died, leaving only a few hundred dollars for his widow. Adelaide, broken-hearted, had meanwhile taken to drink, and she died six years after him.

Mr. Booth had never encouraged his sons to follow in his footsteps as an actor; it was always his expressed wish that they should work with their hands. Yet three of his sons, Junius, Edwin and John Wilkes, inherited some of his artistic genius and sought fame and fortune on the stage. Of these, the most gifted was Edwin, sometimes rated America's greatest Shakespearian actor. Edwin, born in 1833, was the seventh child, followed by Asia, John Wilkes and Joseph Adrian, all handsome children with the dark looks and bright eyes of their mother. Johnny, gay and full of life, was the great charmer of this proud Maryland family. He would ride as a boy through the forests waving an old Mexican War sabre as he charged imaginary foes, and, lying in the grass on a hot summer day, he would tell his school friends how one day his name would shine bright and permanent as the stars, how he intended his name to go down in history for some impossible feat equivalent to overthrowing the Colossus of Rhodes. 'I must have fame, fame!' he once cried.

In the eyes of his loving mother this swashbuckling boy could do no wrong; he was her favourite child and she called him 'Pet'. But as darling Johnny approached manhood, he began to reveal the darker side of his nature—an intolerant, sometimes malicious, streak. He despised his father as the weak sentimentalist he was, and, though he would be casual in his own relations with women, he could never forgive the old man for delaying so long in making an 'honest woman' of his mother. John had not the slightest sympathy for his father's sacred attitude towards animals; it is said that he killed dogs and cats to make his father cry like a child and add to his mental instability. But this seems doubtful, since, according to his sister Asia, he shared her great love of wild life. Certainly, John Wilkes could be both loyal and loving in the extreme. For all his father's weaknesses, he was proud of his family name, adored Asia, and displayed great affection for the mother who had always spoiled him.

When John Wilkes was fifteen years old a gypsy read his palm and said: 'A bad hand, full of sorrow and trouble. You'll break hearts; they'll be nothing to you. You'll die young and leave many to mourn for you. You'll make a bad end and have plenty to love you. You'll have a fast life—short, but a grand one. Young sir, I've never seen a worse hand, and I wish I hadn't seen it. But if I were a girl I'd follow you through the world for your handsome face.'

Booth was seventeen when he made his stage début in Baltimore in 1855. He overplayed the role of Richmond, recited his lines inaccurately, and was roundly booed. But he had resolved to become a great star since learning that his brother Edwin had earned as much as five thousand dollars for one month's work in Boston. He worked hard and within five years Southern audiences, not the most discerning of theatregoers, came to idolise him. Though he could not yet be described as a truly great actor, his star quality was undeniable.

Mary Lincoln, dressed for one of her extravagant White House balls

Vice-President Andrew
Johnson, alleged to be drunk
at the Inauguration

John Wilkes Booth, actor
and assassin

Some critics generously rated him as highly as his brother Edwin. For while Edwin might interpret roles with more subtlety, John Wilkes gained a reputation for playing them with greater intensity. He was the most passionate of Romeos, the most acrobatic of Macbeths, the most insane of Hamlets. The *Baltimore Sun* first dubbed him 'the gymnastic actor'. One fellow player, E. L. Tilton, was toppled into the orchestra pit while fencing with him in a play; others were cut by his sword in stage duels. Actor W. J. Ferguson recorded, 'I saw him, after a rehearsal, take on two men at once with the foils and disarm them both within seconds.'

In April, 1863, Booth made his first professional appearance in Washington, playing Richard III at Grover's Theatre, and by that year he had won fame at least to equal that of his eldest brother, Junius, and was seriously rivalling Edwin. Sometimes he stayed with his most distinguished brother in New York, but politically, they stood in opposite camps. The Booths, like so many families, were left a house divided when war came. Edwin and Junius favoured the North, Asia wavered a long time before siding with the Union. Little Joseph, the only one to see action, was a doctor with the Confederates in the attack on Fort Sumter. John spoke passionately for the South, but he never fought for the cause he so eloquently supported. In common with so many mothers, the widowed Mrs. Booth cared nothing for the issues, only for the preservation of her children. Indeed, John's excuse for non-enlistment was that he had promised his mother he would never join the fight. In fact, John Wilkes did temporary military service before the war. He served briefly with the Richmond Grays who, under Colonel Robert E. Lee, were on duty at the execution of abolitionist fanatic John Brown at Charles Town, Virginia. Conceivably, the grim experience of witnessing that hanging deterred him from further service.

Because of his determination to outshine his famous brothers, he spent much of his time in the North after the war had begun. There he could win greater prestige, and at the same time he could give some small service to the Confederate cause. As an actor, Booth was allowed to pass freely between North and South, and he took advantage of this freedom even though his outspokenness sometimes landed him in trouble. Early in 1863 he was arrested in St. Louis for expressing the wish that 'the whole damn government would go to hell'. He had to swear allegiance to the Union besides paying a fine before he was released. Yet he went on smuggling quinine, so desperately needed by Southern hospitals, and in private he continued to pour his eloquent scorn on the crude, treacherous North who, he argued, could only conquer by sheer weight of numbers, never by courage or patriotism. Above all, he abused President Lincoln whom he despised for 'his pedigree, his coarse low jokes, his vulgar smiles and his frivolity'.

In 1860, the year after old John Brown and a small band of followers seized the Federal Arsenal at Harper's Ferry, Lincoln said the affair corresponded 'with the many attempts related in history at the assassination of Kings and Emperors. An enthusiast broods over the oppression of a people till he fancies himself commissioned by Heaven to liberate them. He ventures the attempt, which ends in little else than his own execution.' So it was with the sensitive actor who had been named after John Wilkes, the English M.P., Lord Mayor of London, convict, exile and agitator for civil liberty.

History endowed Lincoln with many of the attributes of a saint, but in Booth's narrow-seeing eyes he was a devil incarnate, bent on destroying all the noble and courtly traditions of the South which he loved so passionately. In contrast, he saw the North as an uncultured land of crude commercialism, the big bully among two brothers. To help us appreciate the strange ramblings of his mind, we have the letter which he left, together with some bonds and oil stock certificates, with his sister Asia a few days before he planned to make his first attempt to capture Lincoln and take him as a hostage to the South. Booth wanted to assure his proper place in history and this letter was to be handed over to the authorities in the advent of his capture or death. This letter asked that, right or wrong, he should be judged by God, not man. 'For be my motive good or bad, of one thing I am sure, the lasting condemnation of the North.' He went on:

'The country was formed for the white, not the black man. And looking upon African slavery from the same standpoint held by the noble farmers of our constitution, I, for one, have ever considered it one of the greatest blessings (both for themselves and us) that God ever bestowed upon a favoured nation. Witness heretofore our wealth and our power; witness their elevation and enlightenment above their race elsewhere. I have lived among it most of my life, and have seen less harsh treatment from master to man than I have beheld in the North from father to son. Yet, Heaven knows, no one would be willing to do more for the Negro race than I, could I but see the way to still better their condition. But Lincoln's policy is only preparing a way for their total annihilation. The South are not, nor have they been, fighting for the continuation of slavery. The first battle of Bull Run did away with that idea. Their causes since the war have been as noble and greater far than those that urged their fathers on. Even should we allow that they were wrong at the beginning of this contest, cruelty and injustice have made the wrong become a right, and they stand now (before the wonder and admiration of the world) as a noble band of patriotic heroes. . . . The South can make no choice. It is either extermination or slavery for themselves (worse than death). . . . I know my choice.

'But there is not time for words. I write in haste. I know how foolish I shall be deemed for undertaking such a step as this, where, on one side, I have many friends and everything to make me happy, where my profession alone has gained me an income of more than twenty thousand dollars a year, and where my great personal ambition in my profession has such a great field for labour. . . . I love justice more than I do a country that disowns it, more than fame or wealth, more (Heaven pardon me if wrong), more than a happy home. . . . My love (as things stand today) is for the South alone. . . .

'A Confederate doing duty upon his own responsibility.

'J. Wilkes Booth.'

In November, 1864, the three Booths appeared together on one stage for the first time. It was the theatrical event of the year in New York—with Edwin as Brutus, Junius as Cassius, and John Wilkes as Mark Antony. John, lusting for more fame, had his golden chance to prove himself greater than his brothers. He was sick of being described as 'the brother of the great Edwin Booth', and on this one gala night, given the role which offered the greatest opportunities, he played Antony with all the feeling he could command and certainly won the contest if success can be measured by volume of applause alone. But the following night Edwin opened in *Hamlet* and scored a monumental success. He was still the king of the Eastern stage while, as the popular saying had it, Junius Brutus was king in the West and John Wilkes king in the South.

Early in 1865 Edwin Booth figured in a little, but most noteworthy drama off-stage. It happened late at night when he was waiting on a congested New Jersey railway platform for a train to take him to Philadelphia. People were pressing all around when a young man, trapped against the side of a sleeping-car, began to slip between the wheels and platform as the train moved off. Just in time Booth grabbed the man by the collar and hauled him to safety. He had saved the life of Robert Lincoln—the President's son. Less than two months later his brother John would take the life of the father.

It would seem that John Wilkes Booth first resolved to kidnap Lincoln at the time of his re-election. But his fanatical hatred of the President had smouldered and flamed for years before, at least since Lincoln's first election in 1860 and his proclaimed intent to maintain the Union. Now, possibly with a deep sense of guilt, since he had never risked his life for the Southern cause, he was set upon some positive action.

Booth's first scheme was to capture the President, smuggle him to Richmond and hold him to ransom in exchange for Confederate prisoners so desperately needed to boost the dwindling Southern Army. When he began making plans, in November, 1864, he decided that the best route out of Washington with his prisoner would be across the Navy Yard Bridge to southern Maryland—the recognised corridor for spies and smugglers moving between North and South. From Port Tobacco he would take a boat across the Potomac to Virginia.

Posing as a prospective farm buyer and horse trader, Booth reconnoitred the intended escape route. Then, during a winter visit to New York, he cautiously outlined his plan to an actor friend, Samuel Knapp Chester, hoping he would join him in the enterprise. Chester, a wary family man of no great ambition, was horrified at the complex operation. Booth argued passionately, stressed how desperately the South needed more men, while the North had an inexhaustible supply. But Chester could not be swayed by such an argument, nor by Booth's promise of fame and fortune for the kidnappers. He wanted no part of it, though he agreed not to betray his colleague. Booth pressed more firmly and explained that he would implicate him anyway if he breathed a word of the plot. He boasted that there were between fifty and a hundred in the conspiracy and that he merely wanted Chester, familiar with theatres, to open the back door of Ford's Theatre at a prearranged time. Still Chester remained obdurate. He felt sick just to contemplate the plan.

Undiscouraged, Booth went on with his plans for the President's capture (he never referred to it as kidnapping since that was a crime, whereas he considered capturing the Commander-in-Chief of the Yankee armies as a legitimate act of war). It is estimated that he invested some four thousand dollars of his own income in the enterprise during the first three months of 1865. Horses had to be bought, stabled and fed; the rabble that made up his team of conspirators had to be supported. Though Booth had boasted to Chester of fifty to a hundred men in the plot, he could muster at the very most no more than seven followers, mostly simple-minded men who were attracted by the actor's immense personal charm and by his money.

Still in need of an accomplice familiar with the theatre, he sought the service of John Matthews, a small-part player in Washington who had often worked at Ford's. But Matthews rejected the proposal at once and strongly advised Booth against it. The arrogant actor never forgave this minor player for his effrontery and later branded him 'a coward . . . not fit to live'.

Booth found his recruits more easily among the 'dead beats', men without prospects or strong will. The first to be recruited were two of his former school friends—Michael O'Laughlin, twenty-seven, and Sam Arnold, twenty-eight—whom the actor summoned to Washington from Baltimore. From boyhood they had grown up in awe of John Wilkes, admiring his success both on and off the stage. In contrast, they had humdrum lives— Arnold as a humble store clerk, O'Laughlin working for his brother in the produce and feed business. Neither was enthusiastic about the plot. They had become more cautious and cynical after war experiences as Confederate soldiers, and Arnold especially was frightened by the risks. For a time, however, Booth was able to reassure them by stressing that they were part of a huge secret group.

A more professional conspirator was John Harrison Surratt, a six-foot-tall, fair-haired man whose goatee beard belied his twenty years. This audacious youth, whose widowed mother ran a seven-bedroomed boarding house in Washington, had been recommended to Booth as a man expert in negotiating the underground route to Richmond. For two years Surratt had operated the run between Richmond and Montreal, acting as a spy and a dispatch messenger for the Confederacy; it was said that he hid documents in a hollow heel of his boot and beneath the floor boards of his carriage. Surratt doubted Booth's sanity when he was first approached, but he was persuaded that the abduction plot, by the very nature of its daring, would succeed.

David E. Herold, an out-of-work drug store clerk who had once delivered a bottle of castor oil to the White House for Mr. Lincoln, needed no persuading. Twenty-three years old, he had the looks of a teenager and the mind of a child. He had a passion for practical jokes, loved to shoot partridge and to march behind brass bands, and he would readily follow such a colourful leader as John Wilkes Booth on the wildest of schemes. But apart from an intimate knowledge of the Maryland countryside, this insignificant youth had no obvious contribution to make to the conspiracy.

George A. Atzerodt, twenty-nine, another original member of Booth's team, had one definite value: experience of secretly ferrying Southerners and Northerners alike across Pope's Creek at night. Otherwise this carriage-maker from Port Tobacco, some thirty-six miles south of Washington, was a worthless recruit. Prussian in origin, he was a small man with shifty eyes, a scraggly beard, and dirty appearance. He drank too much and he was easily frightened.

Excluding the Baltimore men, Arnold and O'Laughlin, the conspirators held occasional meetings at Mrs. Mary Surratt's small boarding house at 541 H Street,[1] where, in an upstairs room, they would practise wrestling with knives and handling pistols. There is no absolute proof that Mrs. Surratt was aware of the precise purpose of these meetings (her son John was said to have told her they were discussing oil speculation), but she must surely have gained a vague understanding of what was being planned. Certainly all her sympathies lay with the South. She had three children—Isaac, a Confederate soldier; John, a Confederate courier; Anna, a seventeen-year-old girl who was secretly smitten with the charming and famous actor who so often visited her home.

Mrs. Surratt, who had once owned a few slaves, was a small,

1. Now 604 H Street.

plain woman of forty-five; she had a reputation for being generous, kind-hearted, and a pious Roman Catholic. Life had not been easy for her in the three years since the death of her husband, who had had a farm and a tavern in southern Maryland. She had eventually leased the farm and tavern to Mr. John Lloyd, a drunkard, and had moved to Washington. But while she efficiently ran her little boarding house, she always had difficulty in paying her bills. In fact, the widow was in debt to the tune of several hundred dollars and her greatest concern at this time was the collection of four hundred and seventy-nine dollars owed to her by an elusive gentleman called John Nothey, who years before had bought seventy-five acres from her husband.

Booth's amateur group, never wholly enthusiastic, became less and less earnest as they played out their comedy of errors. The kidnap plot was doomed to be a pathetic failure. They lay in wait for a President who never arrived when and where they anticipated, and with each abortive attempt Booth's followers became more panicky and disheartened. Some lacked the nerve for a long-drawn-out conspiracy; they became convinced that their failure could only mean that the government was secretly aware of their activities.

The first attempt to seize Lincoln was planned for the night of Wednesday, January 18, 1865, when the President was expected to visit Ford's Theatre for a performance of *Jack Cade*, starring the veteran tragedian Edwin Forrest. The previous week-end, Herold was sent to southern Maryland to prepare a relay of horses for the flight from Washington, and Atzerodt home to Port Tobacco to lay on a large boat to take the kidnappers and prisoner downriver. The precise plan is not known, but apparently it was John Surratt's task to cut off the theatre lights while Booth entered the President's box, gagged and tied his prisoner, and then lowered him to Surratt on the stage. Then they would escape through the back door to a waiting carriage. Because they were so pessimistic about the prospects of such an involved and hazardous operation, Booth decided to leave Arnold and O'Laughlin out of this attempt.

As it happened, all their careful planning was wasted. The President did not attend the theatre that night, and, in fear that they had been discovered, the plotters quickly dispersed—Surratt to the South, Herold to his mother's house, and Atzerodt to Port Tobacco. Booth, after playing Romeo two nights later, went to New York and was out of Washington for nearly a month. Meanwhile, the President twice visited Ford's in February, once accompanied by General Grant.

During these weeks of inactivity the conspirators regained some confidence. None of them appeared to be under suspicion and a fresh attempt was planned. At this stage a sixth man joined Booth's unimpressive group, one Lewis Thornton Powell, alias Lewis Paine, the youngest, the simplest, and yet the most potentially dangerous conspirator of all. Paine, all brawn and no brain, was a twenty-year-old Alabama man of gladiatorial build and muscular power, and Booth's most valuable recruit in that he could be relied upon to follow orders blindly, however extreme his task might be. He was fearless. He did not have a loose tongue or a weakness for wine and women. Above all, he was the one conspirator besides Booth who would not hesitate to kill.

Like the actor he worshipped, Paine had jet black hair and a reasonably handsome face; otherwise the two men were entirely different. Paine had fought as a Confederate soldier and, as a seventeen-year-old, he had learned to kill without feeling. Among his war souvenirs was a skull which he used as an ash tray; without bombast he would casually explain to friends that it was the head of a Union soldier he had killed. He had made an admirable soldier, a veteran of Antietam, Chancellorsville and Gettysburg, and after being wounded and captured he had escaped from a Union hospital. Then, in January, 1865, he changed his name from Powell to Paine and stayed on in the North to rest from the dreary war. Paine only joined the conspirators by an unlikely chance. Late in February he was in Baltimore when Booth was seeing Arnold and O'Laughlin about a second attempt at Lincoln's capture. Booth recognised him on the street as being an enthusiastic young man who some five years before had come backstage to praise him after a performance. He reintroduced himself, bought the unemployed ex-soldier some clothes, gave him money, and then took him to the Surratt boarding house in Washington where, complete with clerical collar, he played the unlikely role of a Baptist preacher by the name of the Rev. Lewis Wood.

Booth now had a loyal servant who would willingly follow him as far as the grave. Yet Paine was not quite the 'perfect killer' for the actor's purposes. His one big weakness was an inability to move about Washington without losing himself. If he was to kill, this deadly robot would have to be directed on to his target. One other weakness was his violent temper. Though he was a quiet fellow, not easily excited, there were rare occasions when he lost control and became wildly violent. Paine scarcely knew his own strength; once when he grabbed the throat of a maid-servant who had insulted him he very nearly strangled her.

One day Booth took Paine for a stroll along Pennsylvania Avenue, pointed out the White House and remarked how easy it would be to conceal oneself in the grounds and lie in wait for the President when he ventured out for one of his late-night walks. Paine agreed to hide in the bushes in front of the building and to shoot the President as he returned from one of his regular visits to the War Office. He waited, but did nothing. Later he explained to his leader (he called Booth 'Cap') that he had been near enough to strangle the President, but he had hesitated and missed his chance. In fact, Lincoln had been accompanied that evening by a burly officer, famed for his physical strength and quite capable of resisting a lone assailant. His name was Major Thomas Eckert, chief of the War Department Telegraph Office.

The tension which Booth must have been suffering at this time was indicated one day early in March when he sat in his hotel room with a map spread out on the table and weighted down with a knife and a pistol. Suddenly a very old friend, actor John McCullough, entered the room. Booth, lost in his violent dreams, jumped instinctively from his chair, grabbed the knife, and sprang towards the intruder. Just as he was about to lunge forward he regained his senses, stopped, and apologised for his display of bad nerves.

The conspirators began to reassemble during March[1] and in the third week Booth gave John Surratt a pass to Ford's Theatre. The Confederate spy made up a party which included the deserter Lewis Paine and they actually occupied part of the President's double box at an evening performance. By now the actor was making his preparations with greater thoroughness and no less determination. That same night, or possibly the following evening, in a private dining-room at Gautier's Restaurant, he held the only meeting ever attended by all the members of his gang at the same time. Booth did things in style. There was champagne, plenty of whisky, oysters, cold meats and cheeses. The meeting lasted all night.

Booth presided most formally, introducing each conspirator in turn. Herold, Atzerodt, Surratt and Paine already knew one another well, but Arnold and O'Laughlin had not met the others before. Booth then held the stage with a detailed account of the manner in which Lincoln would be successfully abducted from Ford's Theatre. Paine would have the honour of helping him to rope up the President, and they would lower the Chief Magistrate to Sam Arnold who would appear with a gun on the stage. O'Laughlin would cut off the gas lights. Herold would have charge of a carriage waiting in the alley outside Ford's. Surratt

1. In their book *Twenty Days* (Harper and Row) Dorothy Meserve Kunhardt and Philip B. Kunhardt Jr. have published photographs which they claim prove that Paine, Atzerodt, Herold, John Surratt and Ned Spangler (stage hand at Ford's Theatre) attended Lincoln's second inauguration on March 4, 1865. They are identified among the crowd standing only a few feet below the President's stand, while a high-hatted gentleman above the platform is marked out as being Booth.

and Atzerodt would join them after they had crossed the Navy Yard Bridge and guide them to the waiting boat.

If, after his carefully thought out speech, Booth expected some sign of enthusiasm, he certainly received none. The majority were now reluctant conspirators whose nerves had been severely frayed by the long delay. They believed that the government was already aware of their intentions and waiting to spring on them. Sam Arnold boldly came out and said what several were thinking when he suggested that they abandon the plan as being too hazardous. Perhaps Lincoln could be seized in a less public place, possibly on the outskirts of Washington. Wasn't the President soon to visit the Soldiers' Home[1] in the suburbs? When Arnold added impatiently that he was going to give up the enterprise altogether if they didn't succeed within another week, Booth coldly replied that anyone who thought of quitting should be shot. But Arnold stood his ground and the actor shrewdly apologised, explaining he had drunk too much champagne. There was no sense in losing another member of his already inadequate band.

The conspirators talked on until dawn, by which time it was clear that the majority supported Arnold's plan. Booth relented, and the following evening, when he was playing the part of the evil Pescara in *The Apostate* at Ford's, he learned the vital news that Lincoln was due in two days' time to attend a matinée of *Still Waters Run Deep* at the Soldiers' Home, three miles out of the city. Elaborate preparations were made to hold up Lincoln's carriage en route. Again the plan ended in comic farce. When the conspirators rode up to a carriage that appeared at the scheduled time (around 2 p.m.) they found that it had only one passenger and the man was not Lincoln. At this first sign of difficulty the conspirators began to fall out. Surratt and Arnold argued that the coach was a decoy and that the cavalry would

1. This was a convalescent camp situated beyond the city limits and approached by a lonely road. Lincoln, who had a modest stone cottage in the grounds, frequently visited this isolated retreat despite the warnings of friends and officials.

pursue them at any moment. Booth, determined as ever, protested that this was simply the first coach; the President would appear soon after. But Mr. Lincoln did not pass by.

For fifteen minutes they waited nervously. Then the group of frightened men angrily broke up. Arnold and O'Laughlin, fearing their plot had been discovered, fled to their homes in Baltimore, swearing they had finished with Booth's mad schemes. John Surratt, disgusted at the amateurism of it all, also quit, returning to Richmond to resume work as a secret courier taking Confederate dispatches to Canada.

In fact, this kidnap plot had been thwarted only by a freak chance. Lincoln had fully intended to visit the Soldiers' Home, but at the last moment another engagement cropped up. Governor Oliver P. Norton had requested that the President attend a hastily arranged ceremony at which one of the Governor's regiments, the 140th Indiana, would present him with a captured Confederate banner. The little ceremony took place on the verandah of the National Hotel from where the President addressed the crowd in the street below. So, ironically, Lincoln was at Booth's hotel at the very time that the actor was waiting to seize him en route for the Soldiers' Home.

There was another noteworthy occurrence while the kidnappers had been waiting in vain for Lincoln's carriage. At the Surratt house, one of the boarders, Mr. Louis J. Weichmann, found his landlady weeping because her son John had gone off on horseback with six other men and she felt sure they were set on some mischief. Weichmann's curiosity must have been further aroused at 6.30 p.m. when John Surratt rushed into the house, carrying a gun and complaining that nothing seemed to go right. This conspirator was followed by the giant Paine, also armed, and later by Booth, who growled about his ill-luck as he stamped into the house clenching a riding whip in his hand.

Though he was a War Department clerk, working in the office of the Commissary-General of Prisoners, Louis Weichmann fitted remarkably well into the secessionist atmosphere of this boarding house. He was friendly with Atzerodt, the Confederate ferryman, and he sometimes lent clothes to both Atzerodt and Paine. He shared a bed with the Confederate courier, John Surratt, whom he had known since schooldays. But Weichmann, a big, flabby man, who had failed in his studies for the priesthood and had failed to make a success of schoolteaching, was a moral coward. In private, he was as full of secessionist talk as anyone; in public he curried favour with the authorities. He was a man of many opinions and few principles.

During March, probably the day after he saw Booth and his friends return from some fruitless escapade, Weichmann was in the office of the Commissary-General of Prisoners when clerks were discussing the President's ill-health and the prospects of the Union if he were to die. When the conversation turned to the many reports of assassination plots, Weichmann broke in with the astonishing statement that an attack on the President was actually being planned in the house where he was lodging. Possibly he wished no more than to impress his colleagues. If he had been certain of his facts he would surely have reported his suspicions to official quarters. Now he found his remark was viewed most seriously. Captain Gleason of this office questioned him further and Weichmann begged him to keep the matter secret lest his friends at the boarding house should learn of his grave allegations. Gleason refused and said he would have to report the matter to Lieutenant Sharp, an Assistant Provost Marshal on the staff of General Augur, commandant of all troops in the district. Now, suddenly eager to co-operate and safeguard his own position, the greasy Weichmann properly reported his suspicions to Captain McDavitt, U.S. Enrolling Officer. He gave this officer the names of all the boarders and regular visitors to the Surratt house.

Officers Sharp and McDavitt almost certainly filed reports and later detectives testified that they had the boarding house under surveillance for weeks. And yet no direct action was taken. The suspects were not even brought in for questioning.

In the circumstances, the conspirators were not entirely un-justified in their fears that the authorities had learned of the kidnap plot. But despite all the fears and failures, Booth's resolution never wavered. On Saturday, March 25, he returned to Washington from a visit to New York and took his usual room at the National Hotel. Lincoln was out of the city, having accepted General Grant's invitation to join him at the front. Two days later, how-ever, Booth saw a Press announcement that the President and his family would attend Ford's on the Wednesday to see the Italian opera *Ernani*. Immediately he sent a message to O'Laughlin asking him to come to Washington and to bring Arnold if possible. But Booth's Baltimore friends had had enough. Neither man went to the capital. The Irishman did not answer because he did not want to rejoin the plot nor, at the same time, to break off completely his profitable friendship with the wealthy actor. Arnold sent a letter, but only to complain that Booth had passed through Baltimore a week before without troubling to call on him. 'How inconsiderate you have been,' wrote Arnold bitterly. Again he warned the actor that the Government suspected a plot and advised him to see first 'how it will be taken at R——d'. So Booth's army of 'between fifty and a hundred' was now reduced to a mere quartette—himself, the adolescent Herold, the cowardly Atzerodt, and Paine, the brainless killer.

Only the most extreme fanatic could contemplate the direction of a conspiracy against the President after such a miserable record of failure and with such unreliable support. Booth was such a man. His abduction plot was again nullified on Wednesday, March 29, for Lincoln did not return in time to attend the opera as his wife had originally planned. That day the President was watching the launching of Grant's great assault on the Petersburg lines. But nothing could convince Booth of the senselessness of his plans, and the fall of the Confederacy served only to inflame his hatred of Lincoln. On April 3, the day Richmond fell, Booth was staying in New York with an unidentified girl friend. Later, his sister Asia was to offer the opinion, 'If Wilkes Booth was mad, his mind lost its balance between the fall of Richmond and the terrific end.'

Back in Washington, on April 11, as he stood among the great crowd on the White House lawn listening to Lincoln's words in favour of giving the ballot to some Negroes, Booth swore he would kill the President who seven days before had spoken about 'malice towards none, with charity for all'. That same week, a distinct change in Booth was observed by John Deery, the national billiards champion, who kept a large saloon situated over the front entrance of Grover's Theatre. The saloon-keeper noticed that his actor friend was drinking more and talking less than he had ever known him do before. 'He now sometimes drank at my bar as much as a quart of brandy in less than two hours. . . . It was more than a spree. . . . He seemed to be crazed by some stress of inward feeling, but only one who was very intimate with him could have told it.'

April 13 was a glorious spring day in Washington. Warm sunshine dispelled the wintry greyness of the city; flower-beds everywhere were a blaze of colour. It was a day designed to turn a young man's thoughts to the lightest pleasures, yet the sunshine failed to penetrate the dark corners of the mind of John Wilkes Booth. That day his resolution to strike one great and final blow for the Confederacy was strengthened when he learned that General Ulysses S. Grant, conqueror of the proud South, had arrived in the city. Surely, he reasoned, Lincoln would soon make a theatre outing to show the war hero to his adoring public. The actor's hopes were further raised when Mr. C. Dwight Hess, manager of Grover's Theatre, told him that he was inviting the President to attend a performance the following night of *Aladdin, or the Wonderful Lamp*. Booth immediately called on John Deery and asked him to reserve the front right-hand box at Grover's on his behalf. He explained that he did not wish to make the booking himself since Hess, as an old friend, would feel obliged to give him complimentary tickets. On this occasion he wanted to pay for himself.

That evening Booth rounded up his three followers and warned them to be prepared for action. He had abandoned the plan to capture the President. Instead, he intended to rid the country of him altogether. An attack might also be made on the Vice-President and as a preliminary move he instructed Atzerodt to take a room at Kirkwood House and spy on Andrew Johnson. Then, as his last act on the eve of the crime of the century, he sat in his hotel room writing a final short letter to his mother. With remarkable restraint he apologised because he had had nothing to write about recently.

'Everything is dull,' he concluded.

3

LINCOLN'S LAST DAY

THE DAY DAWNED misty and cold in Washington. Although spring had proclaimed her arrival with an abundance of flowers in bloom, overcoats and mufflers served as a reminder that the long, hard winter was not quite at an end. City life began around 7.30 a.m., as, over cobblestones, by foot and by carriage, workers headed for shops and offices. Many would crowd into the churches, for this was Good Friday, the day they crucified Our Lord. Many, too, would pack the saloons where, for ten rowdy days, men had over-indulged themselves in re-fighting the great battles, planning the peace and singing 'When This Cruel War Is Over'. The womenfolk still anxiously checked the latest newspaper lists of the dead, still complained of exorbitant wartime food prices. But for the first time people were confidently talking of the civil war as something of the past.

The war, with six hundred thousand men gone, was virtually ended; except for the battle-worn force of General Joseph Johnston, and a few small, scattered units, the Confederate Army was smashed. Ten days had passed since Washington was launched on a drunken victory spree with the news of the fall of Richmond; each succeeding day had brought fresh cause for jubilation. On Wednesday, April 12, a five-hundred gun salute in front of the City Hall had shattered more windows. Thursday had brought the arrival of the greatest hero of the hour, General Ulysses S.

Grant, who was mobbed as he foolishly ventured on to the Avenue for a quiet walk from Willard's Hotel to the War Department. That night there had been more grand illuminations; over three thousand five hundred candles had flickered in the windows of the Post Office building, nearly six thousand at the Patent Office. Now, on Friday the fourteenth, more ceremonies were planned. This day, the fourth anniversary of the historic surrender, the shell-torn Union flag would be raised again above Fort Sumter.

Washington in 1865 was a city of livery stables, wood yards and taverns, of gas-lights, hooped skirts and tall hats, of sin, turbulence and intrigue. It was dominated by the Capitol and Washington Monument, and though the White House attracted huge crowds, this was a neglected mansion, badly in need of renovation. Willard's was the most fashionable hotel, a popular meeting place for official Washington, where celebrities breakfasted on such dishes as fried oysters, steak and onions, and blancmange. The National was equally famous, though some years before its business had declined sharply after many guests had been struck down with severe stomach disorders. It was frequented by members of Congress because of its approximity to the Capitol, and at present the guests included former Senator, John P. Hale of New Hampshire and his family, Speaker of the House Schuyler Colfax of Indiana, and actor John Wilkes Booth. Vice-President Johnson stayed at the smaller Kirkwood House on the corner of Twelfth Street and Pennsylvania Avenue.

The city's population had swelled at an alarming rate in the war years with the arrival of tens of thousands of newcomers, freed slaves, blockade-runners, office-seekers, gamblers, traders, undertakers, embalmers, makers of artificial limbs, pickpockets, and, not least, the prostitutes. In 1863, a newspaper investigation had concluded that there were about five thousand prostitutes in the city as opposed to about five hundred in the entire District of Columbia before the war. There were dealers in sex to cater for all classes. Sophisticated beauties, operating in superbly furnished houses, were able to attract custom from the high ranks of the Army, Navy, and leading professions. Nor were the morals of society ladies, who still favoured the low-cut, fragile evening dresses popularised in the 1850s, all that they seemed on the surface. Politicians' wives led busy social lives, flirted outrageously, and, if a husband was engaged in business at the time, were accustomed to selecting another male escort for the day.

Gambling was no less a vice in Washington. There were gaming houses for top people on Pennsylvania Avenue and in one establishment a Congressman was reputed to have broken the bank by winning a hundred thousand dollars in one night. In mid-1863 Colonel Baker, chief of the Detective Bureau, had reported to War Secretary Stanton that 163 gaming houses needed his attention. President Lincoln's secretary, John Hay, wrote, 'This miserable sprawling village imagines itself a city because it is wicked, as a boy thinks he is a man when he smokes and swears.' In the circumstances, the day police force of fifty patrolmen supported by the municipality was hopelessly inadequate. As for the night force of fifty men, employed by the Federal Government, they were largely responsible for the protection of public buildings, not for citizens who ventured into the poorly lit streets at considerable personal risk.

On Good Friday, drunk and disorderly revellers were to be seen and heard all over the city, though around noon, the holy hour, when many thousands were at church or at home, Washington was unusually still and quiet. But one sound inevitably remained, the familiar roll of dust-covered army wagons returning from the war. By now grey uniforms had become more common than blue in the capital as the last days of war brought an unending tide of Confederate deserters. Day by day the ragged lines of hungry disheartened men had limped into the city. February had brought twelve hundred of them; in March had come twenty-eight hundred men, broken in spirit and ready to take the oath of allegiance to the Union.

President Lincoln looked a sick man. He was fifty-six years old, but with his tired, baggy eyes, yellow complexion, sunken cheeks, unkept black beard, stooped shoulders and shuffling walk, he could have passed for nearer seventy. He suffered from chronic indigestion, had difficulty in sleeping, was thirty pounds under-weight, and complained of perpetual cold in hands and feet. No sign remained to suggest that this was the physical giant who once reputedly had the strength of three men; who, aided with ropes and straps harnessed about him, had lifted a box of stones weighing nearly a thousand pounds; who could sink an axe deeper and throw a cannonball farther than any man in his neigh-bourhood; who, as Herndon wrote when describing Lincoln's fam-ous wrestling match with Jack Armstrong of New Salem, 'fairly lifted the great bully by the throat and shook him like a rag'.

In Herndon's judgment, 'No man in America—scarcely a man in the world—could have stood what Lincoln did in Washington and survived through more than one term of the Presidency.' But the war years had taken a such terrible toll on the old rail-splitter that Surgeon-General Dr. Barnes now feared that a complete nervous and physical breakdown was imminent. It was exceedingly doubtful whether Lincoln could survive a second term without relaxing the fearful pace he had set himself; more than ever it seemed that events would justify Mrs. Lincoln's gloomy interpretation of the 'double image' omen of four and a half years before.

Lincoln himself had confided in Harriet Beecher Stowe, author of *Uncle Tom's Cabin*, his belief that he would not live long after the war, whatever the outcome. In his desk he kept a file marked 'Assassination' which contained eighty threats on his life. But the President was not frightened of unnatural death; rather he was resigned to it. He once remarked that he did not consider he had ever accomplished anything without God. 'If it is His will that I must die by the hand of an assassin, I must be resigned.' He further explained his resignation to death by saying that to live in constant fear of being killed was to die over and over again. Though Lincoln dismissed their significance to friends, his unhappy dreams most surely prepared him for a violent end. Some influence still remained from his boyhood days in Gentryville, Indiana, where superstition thrived in the extreme. The country people of those parts believed in witches and wizards and a hundred and one unfavourable omens. Friday was the day they greatly feared. It was a day, they said, when to begin any task was to invite a long succession of disasters.

On Good Friday, as was his habit, Lincoln rose from his nine-foot-long bed shortly before seven o'clock. When he emerged from his bedroom he was immediately confronted by favour-seekers, some of whom had camped all night in the White House hall to snatch a word with him. After four years he was all too familiar with this scene and had learned the impracticability of giving way to all the demands on his time. They came to seek public appointments, special passes to the South, reversals of military sentences, financial assistance, or merely to lodge grievances. Very few had justified requests, otherwise they might have been granted by the department directly concerned. The *National Republican*, fearing for the health of the President, had recently argued that he should be spared this ordeal. But still the vultures came.

Slowly, but purposefully, Lincoln made his way down the White House hall, politely brushing off the citizens who eagerly rushed to his side, pleading, weeping, demanding. The daily gauntlet-run ended as always with the President passing a soldier on guard and disappearing into his huge second-floor office. There, at 7.30 a.m., he sat at his desk, reading through official correspondence. Meanwhile, at his home a few blocks away, the Secretary of War, Edwin McMasters Stanton, was having breakfast with his wife. He asked her to send regrets to Mrs. Lincoln who had invited them to join a theatre party planned for the evening. As he had explained so often, he had no taste for the theatre and disapproved of the President making such appearances. Stanton then left to visit the bedridden Seward, and as the elderly statesman was being shaved he told him the latest news from the Army.

At 8 a.m. the President joined his family for breakfast. As he spooned his egg—this and a cup of coffee usually sufficed for his first meal—he listened to his elder son Robert recalling the last days of the fighting and his impressions of General Grant with whom he had recently served. Mrs. Lincoln, in a remarkably gay mood that morning, broke into the conversation to say that it was much too cold outside for her other son, twelve-year-old Tad, to play in the White House grounds. The President nodded. But he was more interested in hearing about the victorious Army.

Robert, a handsome, twenty-one-year-old officer on Grant's personal staff, nicknamed 'The Prince of Rails' by the Press, had just arrived home eager to tell his father of the stirring events he had seen through the eyes of a young warrior untouched by the full horrors of war. Mrs. Lincoln, however, had no wish to hear of the tactical brilliance of Grant, the courage of Sheridan, the drama of the siege of Petersburg. She lived in her own little world, vitally concerned with social and domestic matters.

In fun, Robert handed his father a picture of General Robert E. Lee. Without smiling, the President studied the picture long and hard. Then he said solemnly: 'It's a good face. I am glad the war is over at last.'

Mrs. Lincoln turned to the most pressing matter of her day. Although she had tickets for a gala celebration night at Grover's Theatre, she would much prefer to see *Our American Cousin*, starring Laura Keene, at Ford's. The President, only half listening, instinctively agreed to go if she wished it. He had no inclination to visit any theatre that evening, but he had long since learned the futility of opposing his wife's wishes.

Robert Lincoln promptly excused himself from the theatre trip;

he had not had a night in a proper bed for weeks and desperately wanted to catch up on his sleep. But Tad[1] was very interested in the visit to Ford's and complained that no one had troubled to invite him. He was a mischievous, energetic boy, the President's favourite companion. Once, when a party of Boston ladies were viewing the stately East Room, he careered into the room, riding a wheeled chair drawn by two goats. Another time, late in the evening, he dismissed the regular White House guard and put cooks, doormen and messengers on sentry duty. Even the crusty Stanton was won over by the warm-hearted boy, whom he commissioned a lieutenant and provided with a suitable uniform. Tad had a cleft palate and lisped, misfortunes which only made Lincoln love him all the more. Only Tad was allowed to burst into the President's office at any time of day and interrupt the most important conferences. Often he would stay in the office until he fell asleep; then his father would gently lift him in his great arms and carry him off to bed.

Mrs. Lincoln passed over Tad's little joke at the breakfast table. Forever organising, she persisted with her plans for the evening. Would General Grant and his wife be joining them in their theatre box? The President thought it likely and suggested it would be most fitting to let the people have a rare glimpse of their conquering hero. Would 'Father' be able to find time for a carriage drive with her that afternoon? Mr. Lincoln was uncertain. But he would certainly try.

After breakfast on Good Friday morning Mr. Lincoln returned to his office in the south-east corner of the White House and flipped through the morning newspapers. He sat at a huge desk; nearby, over a mantel, hung an engraving of tough old Andrew Jackson, who, in 1835, was the first American President to be attacked by a would-be assassin. At 9 a.m., after signing some documents, Lincoln received his first visitor of the day, Speaker Colfax, who was hoping soon to become a member of the Cabinet.

1. Thomas Lincoln was nicknamed 'Tad' or 'Tadpole' by his father because as a baby he had an exceptionally large head.

The President viewed his promotion favourably; in time Colfax might well succeed Stanton as Secretary of War. The next callers were Congressmen Cornelius Cole of California, a Detroit lawyer, William Alanson Howard, and then former Senator John P. Hale of New Hampshire, newly appointed, 12,000 dollar a year Minister to Spain, whose daughter Bessie was being linked romantically with John Wilkes Booth. Utterly opposed to the liaison, Hale intended to take his daughter to Europe with him.

For another two hours the President received visitors in swift succession. Most had some personal favour to ask, such as the release of a friend or relative who was a prisoner of war, pardons, discharges, and passes to visit Richmond (Lincoln now ruled that passes were no longer necessary). Briefly, he interrupted this routine at 10.30 a.m. to send a White House messenger to Ford's Theatre to reserve the State Box for a presidential party which would include General Grant. Business manager James R. Ford received the request with surprise and delight. Good Friday was normally an atrocious box-office night; he had fully expected any theatregoers that night to attend the 'monster victory celebration' at Grover's, where the entertainment would include fireworks, the performance of *Aladdin*, special songs, and the reading of a new poem, 'The Flag of Sumter'.

At 11 a.m., Lincoln faced the major business of the day, a Cabinet meeting called to tackle the most pressing and controversial problem at hand, the reconstruction of the South. Congress had recently adjourned and he was determined to push far ahead with reconstruction plans before that body reassembled in December. It was therefore vital that the Cabinet should make speedy progress. Eager for the meeting to go as smoothly as possible, Lincoln now put on his most genial manner and led the round of applause for General Grant, who was sitting in his first session with a President and Cabinet. Others present were young Frederick Seward, Acting Secretary of State in place of his crippled father; Secretary of the Navy, Gideon Welles; Secretary of the Interior, John P. Usher; Secretary of the Treasury, Hugh McCulloch; Postmaster-General William Dennison from Ohio; Attorney-General, James Speed; and Colonel Horace Porter, one of Grant's aides. Vice-President Andrew Johnson had not been invited.

The members had already taken their places round the table when the Secretary of War arrived. Punctuality had never been among his virtues; this time he explained he had hoped to bring news of General Sherman and the surrender of General Joseph Johnston. But the news of a last major Union victory, expected at any moment, had not arrived. Stanton had better reason for being late. He had worked long after midnight, recopying his draft of proposals for peace in the South, and he had been working again on the draft that morning. The previous day Stanton had also held a meeting with Grant. Now he paid tribute to the General's splendid work, explaining to the Cabinet that Grant was to save the country vast expenditure by reducing the size of the Army and cancelling certain army contracts. He remarked that he would like to boost national morale by announcing the end of the draft. The proposal met with unanimous agreement.

Lincoln turned the discussion to the problem of re-establishing law and order and new state governments in the South. He said: 'I think it providential that this great rebellion is crushed just as Congress has adjourned and there are none of the disturbing elements of that body to hinder and embarrass us. If we are wise and discreet we shall reanimate the States and get their governments in successful operation, with order prevailing and the Union re-established before Congress comes together in December. . . . I hope there will be no persecution, no bloody work after the war is over. No one need expect me to take any part in hanging or killing those men, even the worst of them. Frighten them out of the country, open the gates, let down the bars, scare them off. Enough lives have been sacrificed.'

The President called for suggestions regarding the future of the South, and the basis for hours of debate was provided by

Frederick Seward. His bedridden father had given him innumerable proposals for the Cabinet to consider, such as the garrisoning or destruction of all Southern forts; taking over all Southern custom houses immediately and beginning to collect revenues; basing armed ships in all Southern ports and taking over all navy yards, ships and ordnance; the reassessing of Southern land by land agents and surveyors; appointing judges and reopening the courts; re-establishing full postal services. It was a huge canvas, but Lincoln was determined not to adjourn the meeting until the points had been covered and a skeleton picture of reconstruction plans had emerged. After much discussion, during which all members made suggestions, Stanton produced a fat sheaf of papers and began to read aloud his own detailed plan. Lincoln had invited his War Secretary to make this draft, but the proposals were by no means as conciliatory as he would have wished.

Navy Secretary Gideon Welles, a short, stocky man with a long white beard and kindly face, was the chief voice of the opposition to Stanton. In particular, he was critical of the plan to create a military territory, combining North Carolina and Virginia, with the district placed under the supervision of Stanton's own department. Welles declared that such violation of state lines would only aggravate the situation, and the majority of the Cabinet agreed. He also expressed the main concern of members when he said that the problem was to see that a state government was properly representative of the people of that state, while somehow it would have to be ensured that the leaders of the rebellion were not elected. Lincoln shared this view, but he tactfully suggested that copies of Stanton's draft proposals should be provided for all Cabinet members to study in detail.

During the meeting messengers frequently came in with notes for the President, but still the eagerly awaited news of Johnston's surrender failed to arrive. In remarking that he was sure favourable news would come soon, Lincoln deviated shortly to recount a recurring dream he had had. 'I seemed to be in some indescribable vessel and I was moving with great rapidity towards an indefinite shore. I had this dream preceding Sumter, Bull Run, Antietam, Gettysburg, Stone River, Vicksburg and Wilmington.' It was a dream, he said, which seemed to presage good news and great victories. 'I had this dream again last night and we shall, judging from the past, have great news very soon. I think it must be from Sherman.' Everyone shared his optimism, and possibly the congenial atmosphere of the meeting owed something to their mutual anticipation of a final victory.

The Cabinet meeting dragged on into the third hour, but it had progressed far more smoothly than Lincoln could have anticipated. True, Stanton pursued a tough line in his plans for the defeated South, but the differences among members did not appear insurmountable; indeed, there was a remarkable measure of agreement on broad issues. While many small details remained to be resolved, they all seemed to accept the hard economic fact that it was equally in the interest of the North to restore the financial well-being of the South.

At 2 p.m., when the four-hour Cabinet meeting was adjourned, one person lingered behind to raise a delicate, personal matter with the President. With some embarrassment, General Grant quietly mentioned to Lincoln that he faced some difficulty in joining him at the theatre that night. He and Mrs. Grant were most anxious to visit their children as soon as possible in Burlington, New Jersey; indeed, Mrs. Grant was planning to take the overnight train to Philadelphia.

In seeking to withdraw from the theatre party, Grant was acting for the second time in two days on the advice of Mr. Stanton. The war hero had simple tastes and no liking at all for public appearances or pomp and ceremony. His main purpose in visiting Washington had been to discuss with the War Minister how army personnel might be reduced and which army contracts might be cancelled. On the afternoon of April 13, however, Mrs. Lincoln invited him (no mention was made of Mrs. Grant) to join her and the President on an evening carriage drive round the city. Grant had not the slightest wish to go and he told Stanton so. At the War Secretary's suggestion he declined the invitation on the excuse of outstanding business. Instead, the Grants accepted an invitation to an informal evening at the Stantons' house. The persistent Mrs. Lincoln then came forward with her second invitation, for Grant to join them at the theatre the following evening, and this time she had the invitation sent in the President's name. Again Stanton advised the General to decline. The President, he pointed out, had been warned repeatedly against making such public appearances. In a meeting witnessed by telegraph operator David Homer Bates, Stanton urged him not to go and, moreover, to use his influence to persuade Lincoln to forget about the theatre trip.

Grant was unsure of himself as he now sought to excuse himself a second time. In his nervousness, he did not state his case firmly enough. Lincoln pointed out that, with the war ended, he would soon have ample time to see his children, but that he would not always have the opportunity of delighting the people so greatly by making a personal appearance. The victor of Appomattox was suffering a rare defeat, when providentially, and with perfect timing, he was provided with fresh ammunition. A note was delivered to him from Mrs. Grant, who reminded her husband that they had a train at six o'clock and that she hoped he would not cause them to be late. The General showed the note to the President and said he would regretfully have to leave Washington.

Lincoln, who yielded so readily to his own wife's wishes, accepted this decision. If Grant had excused himself earlier, he himself would have withdrawn from a theatre outing which did not appeal to him and which no longer had special appeal to the public. But now the visit had been advertised in the Press he would certainly attend rather than give the audience a double disappointment.

Around 2.20 p.m. the President left his office to lunch with

Mrs. Lincoln. This meal rarely constituted more than a biscuit, a glass of milk and fruit, and he soon returned, munching an apple. Now, at last, he tugged the bell-pull to ring for the man he had been avoiding for more than a month, Vice-President Johnson. The interview lasted twenty minutes, during which Lincoln almost certainly outlined the plans for reconstruction and the various views of Cabinet members.

Johnson had previously sought an interview without success. But the next visitor managed to see the President without formal application or permission. Mrs. Nancy Bushrod, a near-hysterical coloured woman, half starved, and exhausted from a five-mile walk, ducked under the arm of a soldier on duty at the White House porch and ran through a the corridor to the President's office where another guard halted her. 'Fo' Gawd's sake, please lemme see Mistah Lincoln,' she cried. And she made enough commotion to bring the President to the door. Smiling, he said: 'There is time for all who need me. Let the good woman come in.'

Mrs. Bushrod explained that she and her husband, Tom, had been plantation slaves near Richmond, that after the Emancipation Proclamation they had run away to seek freedom in the North. Tom had joined the Army, but his pay had since stopped coming to her. She was left with twin boys and a baby girl to support, and nowhere could she find work. Sobbing, the poor woman begged the President to help her. 'You are entitled to your soldier-husband's pay,' he replied. 'Come this time tomorrow and the papers will be signed and ready for you.' Then he escorted her to the door, bowed, and said softly: 'My good woman, perhaps you will see many a day when all the food in the house is a single loaf of bread. Even so, give every child a slice and send your children off to school.' Mrs. Bushrod never forgot Mr. Lincoln's courtesy, how he bowed to her 'lak I wuz a natchral bawn lady'. This was the President the people loved.

By 4 p.m. the President had finished work for the day and was preparing to leave his office when Assistant Secretary of War, Charles A. Dana, called with an enquiry from Stanton. Dana explained that the Provost Marshal of Portland had sent in a report that Jacob Thompson, the Confederate commissioner in Canada who had instigated raids and various acts of sabotage in the Great Lakes region, was due to pass through Portland that night. Stanton was eager to arrest the prominent rebel, but wished to have the President's opinion. 'No. I rather think not,' said Lincoln. 'When you have an elephant by the hind leg, and he's trying to run away, it is best to let him run.' That summed up his attitude towards all the Confederate leaders. He hoped they would flee the country. It was an attitude that infuriated Stanton. Thompson's activities had caused the North considerable difficulties, and, after years of suffering this thorn in his side, he could not contemplate allowing the old enemy to slip through his fingers. With typical duplicity the War Minister decided not to send any reply to the Provost Marshal and hoped that the law officer would use his own initiative and order the arrest. Stanton would then have achieved his aim, without leaving himself open to a charge of insubordination. With sound judgment, however, the Provost Marshal would anticipate the President's orders and let Thompson run.

Before joining his wife for their late afternoon carriage ride, Lincoln decided to call at the War Department to check for any news from Sherman. Bodyguard Crook accompanied him along Pennsylvania Avenue and at one point he had to clear a way for the President as they confronted two rowdy drunks. When they were safely past, Lincoln said, 'Crook, do you know, I believe there are men who want to take my life.' Then, after a pause, he added, 'And I have no doubt they will do it.'

The President was at pains to reassure Crook that he did not doubt his ability. 'I have perfect confidence in those who are around me—in every one of you men. I know no one could do it and escape alive. But if it is to be done, it is impossible to prevent it.'

There was no news of Sherman at the War Office. Lincoln

paused a few minutes to exchange a joke with cipher-operator Charles A. Tinker, then had a short conference with Stanton. The President asked whether the War Secretary could spare Major Thomas T. Eckert, chief of the War Department Telegraph Office, to accompany him to the theatre. Eckert was a massive officer, and Lincoln recalled that he had once seen him break five pokers, one after the other, over his arm, when he was testing the quality of a new delivery. 'I am thinking he would be the kind of man to go with me this evening.'

Stanton regretted that Eckert could not be spared. He had important work for him that night which could not be left over until tomorrow. In any case, he argued, with so many evil forces at work in the city, the President would be well advised to cancel his visit to the theatre. With rare persistence, Lincoln now went further, by approaching Eckert himself. But the telegraph superintendent, renowned for his loyalty to his immediate superior, also excused himself on the grounds of pressing work.

On their way back to the White House, Lincoln talked about the outing to Ford's and surprised Crook by saying that he was going because the visit had been advertised and he did not want to disappoint the people. 'Otherwise I would not go. I do not want to go.'

About 5 p.m., escorted by two cavalry outriders, the President set off from the White House on his afternoon carriage drive with his wife. He was in such good humour that Mrs. Lincoln remarked, 'You almost startle me by your great cheerfulness.'

'Mother,' he replied, 'I consider that this day the war has come to a close. We must both be cheerful in the future. Between the war and the loss of our darling Willie, we have both been very miserable.'

He talked of his hopes for the future; how, after completing his second term, he would like to take his family on holiday in Europe and then perhaps return to his law practice. At one point he said gaily, 'I never felt so happy in my life.'

Mrs. Lincoln paled. She lived in constant fear of omens, and such talk alarmed her. 'Don't you remember feeling just so before our little boy died?'

That Good Friday afternoon, as they talked sadly about the past and hopefully of the future, a stranger might have taken the Lincolns to be a reasonably contented and devoted couple. In truth, such relaxed moments together had been all too rare in their twenty-three years of married life. The President and his First Lady were complete opposites, in many ways quite unsuited to one another. Physically they presented such absurdly contrasting figures that Mrs. Lincoln would not allow them to be photographed together. He was tall, thin and gaunt; she was short, dumpy and round-faced. In temperament they were also diametrically opposed. He was calm, good humoured and patience personified; she was highly strung, moody, possessive and impatient. As Herndon put it, 'In her figure and physical proportions, in education, bearing, temperament, history—in everything she was the exact reverse of Lincoln.' According to Lincoln's law partner, she was even his reverse in that she was decidedly pro-slavery.

Born in Lexington, Kentucky, on December 13, 1818, Mary Todd was almost ten years younger than Lincoln and infinitely better educated. Hers was an influential, well-to-do family descended from generals on both sides, and in her youth she acquired all the social graces. She was witty, attractive, intensely ambitious. She told her school friends that she would one day become the First Lady of the land, and she continued to make that prophecy years later when she moved into Springfield society.

The details of Lincoln's stormy courtship of Mary Todd are much disputed. According to Herndon, they were to be married on the evening of New Year's Day, 1841. The guests were met, the feast was set, but the reluctant bridegroom failed to appear, leaving poor Mary stranded in veil and silken gown, with flowers in her hair. If we accept the version of his law partner, Lincoln did not love her and only went through with the marriage nearly two years later to save his honour. As for his bride, she never forgave him for deserting her on their original wedding day and married him solely to further her dreams of high social position. The accuracy of Herndon's account, apparently based on second-hand information, is questionable. But definitely it was Lincoln who, in his uncertainty, broke off their engagement. Later he wrote to his closest friend, Joshua Speed: 'I have no doubt that it is the peculiar misfortune of both you and me to dream dreams of Elysium far exceeding all that anything earthly can realise. . . . My old father used to have a saying that "If you make a bad bargain, hug it all the tighter." '

If Lincoln hoped for domestic bliss he most surely made a terrible bargain. It is recorded that once, in a moment of uncontrollable rage, his wife humiliated him in front of boarders at their Springfield home by dashing a cup of hot coffee in his face. Her persistent nagging in those days is supposed to have driven him to the point where he pushed her out of the house and cried: 'You make this house intolerable. Damn you, get out.' If he did make such a stand, it was probably his last. By the time they arrived at the White House, Mary had her husband firmly under control. He had learned the futility of questioning her wishes, the wisdom of humouring her in her many dark moods. On the eve of State functions he would invariably ask her which women he might speak to and so eliminate the risk of an embarrassing scene in public. He accepted her authority on all domestic matters. Once, when a man consulted him about cutting down a particularly fine tree in the grounds of his house, his immediate reaction was, 'What did Mrs. Lincoln say?'

'She consented to have it taken away,' said the woodman.

'Then, in God's name, cut it down to the roots,' he cried.

Lincoln himself left only one written comment on his marriage. In a business letter to a Mr. Samuel Marshall about a week after his wedding, he wrote, 'Nothing new here, except my marriage, which to me is a matter of profound wonder.'

With her husband's election, Mary Todd's gamble in marrying the prairie lawyer brought the fulfilment of her childhood dreams. But it failed to bring happiness. Extravagance and jealousy became her most notable vices, an ungovernable temper her saddest weakness. The President had only to make a passing reference to another woman to send his wife into an insane fit of jealousy, and, in her fearful rages, she terrified servants and antagonised tradesmen. In Springfield, when one tradesman complained to Lincoln about her rudeness, he replied, 'You ought to be able to stand for fifteen minutes what I have stood for fifteen years.' It was the same in Washington. Mrs. Lincoln was incapable of keeping White House servants for long; one girl who did remain in her service for several years was secretly paid an extra dollar a week by the President to suffer his wife's storms without complaint.

On her arrival in the capital, Mrs. Lincoln promptly began re-arranging the thirty-one-roomed White House. She insisted on being called 'Madame President', raged over food and clothing bills, dismissed servants, boycotted State functions when the mood took her to do so, complained constantly that Congress did not allow the President a large enough allowance for entertaining, nagged her husband into handing out minor appointments to her family connections. She was always ready to suggest a candidate when a government post became vacant and she would have decided a great many official appointments if her husband had allowed. Nor did she hesitate to express her opinions of leading figures of the day. General McClellan was a 'humbug', General Grant a 'butcher', Mr. Seward a 'dirty abolition sneak'. Once Lincoln replied to her criticisms: 'Well, Mother, supposing that we give you command of the Army. No doubt you would do much better than any general that has been tried.'

Her extravagance was alarming. She had an allowance of twenty thousand dollars a year to spend as she pleased, but it was never enough for Mrs. Lincoln. She used her position to run up huge bills; once she bought as many as three hundred pairs of gloves within four months, paid three thousand dollars for a set of earrings and a pin, five thousand dollars for a shawl. Yet, while she was to spend thousands of dollars on one day's shopping in New York, she continued to haggle with tradesmen over matters of pennies. As economy measures, she sacked long-serving members of the White House staff only to use their wages for more of her costly indulgences. Secretary John Hay called her 'the Hell-Cat'.

Doubtless, in her early days, Mrs. Lincoln was a considerable social asset to her rough-hewn husband. It can be argued that without her ambition and drive he might not have aspired to the highest office. Less kindly, it has been suggested that by making his domestic life a hell she forced Lincoln to seek escape in the world of business and politics, whereas by nature he was more inclined to lounge at home by the fireside with a good book. In fairness to Mrs. Lincoln, it should also be stressed that her husband, with his abstract moods and lack of social finesse, was not the easiest of men for such a cultured woman to live with. In his Springfield days he displayed complete indifference to his appearance, and his untidy habits would have been enough to drive any orderly woman to despair. He went about town sloppily dressed, answered the door with braces dangling at his side, liked to sprawl his long frame across the floor when reading, and at the dining table brought out an old penknife to stab the butter. These, and scores of other little irritating habits, brought the well-bred Mary Todd much distress and shame. As for her extravagance, this might have been avoided if her husband had had more time or inclination to pay attention to household budgeting. But as Herndon notes, Lincoln was weak in one respect: 'In dealing with the financial and commercial interests of a community or government he was equally as inadequate as he was ineffectual in managing the economy of his own household.'

Mrs. Lincoln's unfortunate disposition can also be partly explained by the unfriendly reception she received in official

Washington. City ladies at first looked down on the wife of the gangling, ill-bred Westerner, and it was largely in an effort to impress Washington society that she lavished so much money on clothes and glittering parties. This led to bitter attacks on her extravagance by the Press, who scrupulously reported her spectacular shopping sprees in New York. The First Lady was even more cruelly scorned because of her divided family connections. Those with Southern sympathies despised her for having deserted the South, while the Northern patriots mistrusted her and spread rumours that she was a Southern spy. While Mrs. Lincoln's eldest brother, Levi, and half-sister Margaret Kellogg had sided with the Union, she had one brother, three half-brothers and three brothers-in-law who had enlisted in the Confederate Army. It was reported at one time that she also had eleven second cousins in the Confederacy's Carolina Light Dragoons. One brother-in-law, Ben Helm, a West Pointer and son of a former Governor of Kentucky, was invited to the White House by the President and offered a major's commission in the U.S. Army. Helm left to think it over and then joined the Confederates. Most embarrassing of all, the First Lady had one half-brother, David Todd, who was violently hated in the North for his ill-treatment of Yankee prisoners in Richmond.

Three of Mrs. Lincoln's relatives died fighting for the South. But, above all, she suffered extreme mental anguish over the loss of two of her sons. Edward Baker Lincoln died shortly before his fourth birthday in 1850, the year that another son, William Wallace, was born. Then, in 1862, her beloved Willie died of typhoid. His death, more than any other event, seriously affected her mental condition. Two weeks before, wearing a daringly low-cut dress, she had entertained eight hundred guests at a White House ball. Now she began a period of nearly three years in mourning, during which she lived in almost complete seclusion, though in 1864 she began to make a more favourable impression with the public by her frequent visits to hospitals, bearing gifts of food and wine for the sick and wounded. She gave up completely her ostentatious social life. Yet Mrs. Lincoln still managed to overspend on buying mourning clothes, and in her private life she was as wildly emotional as ever and suffered violent headaches. She consulted mediums in her persistent efforts to communicate with her sons (spiritualism was not an unusual pursuit of Washington women during the war years); at night she had visions of Willie and Eddie and various lost relatives. So frequent were her wild hallucinations that one day the President took her arm, gently led her to a White House window, and pointed to the insane asylum. Then he said softly: 'Mother, do you see that large white building on the hill yonder? Try and control your grief, or it will drive you mad, and we may have to send you there.'[1]

The President was overjoyed when, on New Year's Day, 1865, his wife finally cast off her heavy mourning and resumed her social activities. True, she returned to her extravagant ways and demanded more of his valuable time for social functions. But the sympathetic Lincoln cared only that her mental condition was improving. Tragedy had brought them closer together than ever before, and that Good Friday, as they emerged from the darkness of the war years, he dearly hoped she would have a happier future.

The Lincolns' carriage drive took them as far as the Navy Yard, three miles away, where the President visited the monitor *Montauk*, and it was nearly 6 p.m. when they arrived back at the White House. As their carriage drew up outside, the President was delighted to see two old friends from his home state of Illinois. Though Mary advised him that supper would soon be ready, Lincoln insisted that Dick Oglesby, the new Governor of Illinois, and General Isham N. Haynie should join him in his office for a chat. They laughed about old times, and the President read them the latest satirical writings of his favourite columnist, Ohio editor David R. Locke, who wrote coarse dialect under the

1. Mrs. Lincoln was destined to be certified 'insane' in 1875.

pen of Petroleum V. Nasby. This piece, which was typical, read:

'I survived the defeet uv Michlellan (who wuz, trooly, the nashen's hope and pride likewise) becoz I felt assoored that the rane uv the Goriller Linkin wood be a short wun; that in a few months, at furthest, Ginral Lee wood capcher Washington, depose the ape, and set up there a constooshnal givernment, based upon the great and immutable trooth that a white man is better than a nigger.'

The satirist turned to the fall of Richmond and wrote: 'Linkin rides into Richmond! A Illinois rale-splitter, a buffoon, a ape, a goriller, a smutty joker, set hisself down in President Davis's cheer, and rites dispatchis. . . . This ends the chapter. . . . Linkin will serve his term out—the tax on whisky won't be repeeled—our leaders will die off uv chagrin. . . .'

Abraham Lincoln was never a teller of smutty stories as his enemies alleged. Artist Carpenter, who spent six months in the White House, could not recall one Lincoln story that could not have been happily told in a ladies' drawing-room. He was, however, the first great humorist to be elected to the White House. He was an unrivalled storyteller, once not unreasonably described as the 'American Aesop', and he could enjoy a joke against himself as much as any other man. For all his melancholy looks, Lincoln was famed for his sense of humour—a fact well illustrated by biographer Carl Sandburg, who recorded the following dialogue between two Quakeresses in a railway coach early in the civil war:

'I think Jefferson will succeed.'

'Why does thee think so?'

'Because Jefferson is a praying man.'

'And so is Abraham a praying man.'

'Yes, but the Lord will think Abraham is joking.'

Lincoln was called away from his Illinois friends with the news that his wife and sons were waiting for him to join them at a cold supper. At the table, Mrs. Lincoln told her husband that she had

invited two friends to join them at the theatre that night—Major
Henry Reed Rathbone and his dark, attractive fiancée, Clara
Harris. This young couple figured in an unusual romance. Miss
Harris was the daughter of New York Senator Ira T. Harris;
Rathbone, Assistant Adjutant General of Volunteers at twenty-
eight, a tall, slim, handsome officer with side whiskers and walrus
moustache, was the Senator's stepson. The President received the
news without comment and then left on one last visit to the War
Department in the hope of finding a wire from Sherman. There
was still no word from the General, and he found that Stanton and
Eckert, reputedly so busy that evening, had already left for home.

It was now around 7 p.m., and William Crook, an intensely
loyal and conscientious bodyguard, was becoming anxious. His
duty extended from 8 a.m. to 4 p.m. and yet he was still on
guard. The fact that his relief man was three hours overdue
caused him annoyance but no surprise. He was all too familiar
with the unreliability of Parker, a slack police officer of ill-repute.
When Parker finally arrived, Crook contained his anger and
merely outlined the evening programme in his most official
manner. Since the President's carriage would be full with four
passengers, he suggested that Parker should set out independently
for the theatre fifteen minutes ahead and stand by the main
entrance for the President's arrival. He asked his relief whether
he was armed and Parker patted the .38 Colt revolver in his hip
pocket.

As this alert young officer went off duty he said 'Good night'
to the President. Mr. Lincoln replied, 'Goodbye, Crook.' The
officer reflected that he could not recall the President ever having
said 'goodbye' before; always it had been 'good night'.

A few minutes later the President had a caller by appointment,
Speaker Colfax. During their brief interview, Lincoln threw out
an invitation for him to join their theatre party. Colfax declined
with thanks. Then came one last visitor, former Congressman
George Ashmun, who sought a favour for a friend. Lincoln could
hardly have refused to see the man who had presided over the

1860 party convention which had nominated him. But after a few minutes he cut their conversation short and arranged to see Ashmun again in the morning. He wrote on a card, 'April 14, 1865. Allow Mr. Ashmun and friend to come in at 9 a.m. to-morrow—A. Lincoln.' These were the last words ever written in the President's hand.

It was now just past 8 p.m. and Mrs. Lincoln, already dressed for the theatre, was becoming impatient. The performance at Ford's had begun. The President, as unconcerned as ever about his appearance, merely took up a silk hat and accompanied her to the waiting carriage. Mrs. Lincoln's preparations had taken rather more attention. She wore a low-necked white dress and was crowned with a pink-flowered bonnet. At 8.10 p.m. Mr. Lincoln walked out of the White House for the last time, into a chilly, gusty evening, on his way to a social engagement he had no wish to attend.

Meanwhile Stanton, who had apparently had so much urgent business at the War Office that night, paid a second call on old Mr. Seward, who was being nursed by two convalescent soldiers and watched at night by two of his children, daughter Fanny and Major Augustus Seward. Stanton would stay with the Secretary of State until about 9 p.m. and little more than an hour later he would be preparing for bed.

Although he had no interest in the theatre outing, Mr. Lincoln was in contented mood as he stepped out to his carriage. The terrible burden of the war years was becoming lighter at last, and he remarked to his companions, Ashmun, Colfax and secretary Noah Brooks, that the national debt would soon be greatly re-duced and that Grant planned to cut the cost of the army estab-lishment by at least half a million dollars a day. As he climbed into the carriage he was approached by his old staunch supporter, ex-Congressman Isaac N. Arnold of Chicago. After a brief, whispered exchange, the President told him: 'Excuse me now. I'm going to the theatre. Come and see me in the morning.'

The carriage rolled off in the direction of H Street, where the Lincolns called at the home of Senator Harris to collect Major Rathbone and his fiancée. Outside Ford's, coachman Francis Burns pulled up the horses and valet Charles Forbes jumped down to open the carriage door. The President's traditional escort of two cavalry outriders now went off duty until it was time for the return journey. Bodyguard Parker was left solely responsible for the President's safety.

The Lincolns were late. It was 8.25 p.m. and the first act of *Our American Cousin* was well under way. Parker led the way up to the presidential box, and as the Lincolns took their seats the near-capacity audience of 1,675 stood up and cheered. The performance momentarily stopped and Professor William Withers raised his baton for the orchestra to strike up 'Hail to the Chief'. Then the play was resumed.

The President, partly hidden from the audience by drapes, sat with his back to the door in a black walnut rocking-chair upholstered in red damask. Mrs. Lincoln sat on his right, towards the centre pillar of the double box. On the extreme right, Miss Harris occupied a seat with Major Rathbone, on a sofa, at her left. Bodyguard Parker, according to procedure, had already inspected the box that evening and had found nothing amiss. Now he took up his position outside the corridor leading to the State Box. Occasionally he left his seat to catch a glimpse of the play; then, some time shortly before nine o'clock, he tired of his duty. He left the theatre and outside he invited coachman Burns to join him for a drink at Taltavul's. Soon after they were joined by another member of the President's staff, the valet Forbes, who had left his seat at the back of the State box.

Meanwhile, President Lincoln was happily relaxed. Possibly, he was inspired by the sight of Major Rathbone and pretty Clara romantically holding hands in the darkness of the theatre. For now 'Old Abe' did an unusual thing. He reached out and fondly held Mrs. Lincoln's hand.

4

BRINGING DOWN THE COLOSSUS

LIKE THE MAJORITY of Washington citizens, John Wilkes Booth rose around seven o'clock on the misty Good Friday morning of April 14. He groomed himself meticulously, scenting his hair and fashionable moustache, donned a well-pressed suit and leather riding boots, and left his room (No. 228) at the National Hotel. Unlike the city's workers, who hastened over cobblestones to their shops and offices, he could enjoy a leisurely breakfast and then stroll around to the barber shop to complete his perfect grooming. As he passed by, casual acquaintances nodded and smiled, some possibly reflecting how much they would enjoy the seemingly carefree life of a nationally famous actor. Yet this Good Friday, which started so sedately, was to prove the stormiest, most eventful day of his life, the day when he would fulfil his boyhood dream of bringing down a 'Colossus of Rhodes'.

Around 9 a.m. Booth returned to his fourth-storey hotel room and shortly afterwards he had an unexpected visitor. It was his friend from schooldays, Michael O'Laughlin, and he had a hangover. The swarthy, long-haired Irishman had been drunk the night before and knew he would probably get drunk again today. He was passing by the hotel with three noisy revellers when, on the spur of the moment, he decided to call on his thespian friend. His three companions waited downstairs and when he rejoined them he explained he had been trying to collect a debt.

Two hours later Booth set out from the National Hotel with no definite programme for the day. As usual, his first stop was Ford's Theatre where, by a long-standing arrangement, he collected his mail each day. This morning he was in the manager's office when stage carpenter James J. Gifford was instructed by young Henry Clay Ford to have the partition removed between boxes 7 and 8 to accommodate the President's party. Thus, by chance, Booth was one of the first to learn of the quite unexpected visit which the President planned to make to Ford's that evening. Moreover, Henry Clay, who was running the theatre with James R. Ford while their brother John visited relatives in Richmond, proudly told the actor that the President would not be the only distinguished visitor that night. General Grant, the greatest hero of the day, would also be attending.

Outside, Booth sat on the granite step in front of the theatre and began to read his mail. A passer-by noticed he was laughing at the contents of one letter. Then the actor disappeared back inside the theatre, went up to box 7 and watched the casual rehearsal on stage. Almost certainly, he now made his precise plans while sitting at the intended scene of the crime. He had intimate knowledge of the theatre layout and he had always favoured Ford's as the place either to capture or kill the President. He was familiar with almost every line of the current play, *Our American Cousin*. No one was better equipped to calculate the timing of an attack there on Mr. Lincoln and General Grant.

Ford's Theatre, in downtown Washington on the east side of Tenth Street, stood about midway between the Capitol and the Executive Mansion, on a site occupied only six years before by the First Baptist Church. John T. Ford, an enterprising theatrical manager, purchased the old building in 1861 and converted it into a theatre, the Athenaeum, which was to be destroyed by fire the following year. The manager was undiscouraged; with financial support from wealthy citizens, he built a larger, more modern structure on the site of his first playhouse. It opened in

August, 1863, and the following October Mr. Lincoln visited the theatre for the first time. He was there again two weeks later to see John Wilkes Booth make his Ford's début in *The Marble Heart*.

Formally known as the Ford Opera House, the theatre had 1,700 seats, including 421 in the dress circle (first balcony), which sold at fifty cents each. Gas jets in bowls around the walls provided the lighting and for tonight's gala performance the interior would be properly rigged out with flags and banners. There were eight private boxes, but on such occasions the procedure was to unite boxes 7 and 8 to accommodate the President's party, and, as a mark of respect, to keep all other boxes unoccupied.

The presidential double-box hung above 'stage left', and, as he sat there, Booth must have noted that the distance from the ledge of the box to the stage below was no more than twelve feet. The 'gymnastic actor' had made greater leaps in *Macbeth*. Opposite the box, at 'stage right', was an enclosure for players who were shortly to make an entrance, and behind this enclosure was a door leading to the back alley. This impressed Booth as being the best escape route; he would drop to the stage and flee through the back door to a waiting horse. In choosing this route he was basically reverting to his original abduction plan but eliminating the greatest hazard. Now his escape would not be delayed by the difficult task of trussing up the President, lowering his heavy body to the stage and carrying him out to a carriage in the alley.

Making an entry into the President's box presented the biggest problem for the would-be assassin. Panelled pine doors led to boxes 7 and 8, and for this occasion only the door to box 7 would be used. There was a small hallway outside the boxes and behind it a narrow white door. The President's guard would normally sit with his back to this door and no one would be able to reach the box without passing him there.

Once past the sentry Booth knew he would have no difficulty in entering the box. Over four weeks before, ticket-seller Thomas Raybold had offered the presidential box to some dissatisfied customers who had arrived late and found their reserved seats taken. The door to the State box was locked that night and the usher in charge of the keys was at home ill. Raybold had impetuously smashed the lock and it had not been repaired since.

As Booth sat in the box, mentally rehearsing his greatest performance, the cast was engaged below in a most half-hearted rehearsal of Tom Taylor's celebrated eccentric comedy—*Our American Cousin*. It was an unnecessary formality. They were all too familiar with their parts; indeed, Miss Laura Keene, who was making her last appearance in the well-worn comedy, had played the role of Florence Trenchard over a thousand times. The players were now engaged in the second scene of the third act, where the scheming Englishwoman, Mrs. Mountchessington, who had been trying to match her daughter with a wealthy American, Asa Trenchard, discovers that the Yankee cousin is not rich at all. Mrs. Mountchessington complains loudly, 'I am aware, Mr. Trenchard, that you are not used to the manners of good society, and that alone will excuse the impertinence of which you have been guilty.' Then she arrogantly sweeps off stage, and Asa Trenchard, played by Mr. Harry Hawk, is left standing alone. 'Don't know the manners of good society, eh?' he soliloquizes. 'Well, I guess I know enough to turn you inside out, old gal— you sockdologizing old man-trap.'

This point of the play invariably drew one of the biggest laughs of the evening. Booth recognised it as the perfect moment for attacking the President. Only one actor would be on stage, and only Laura Keene would be in the wings, waiting for her entrance. Tonight he calculated this moment should be reached at around 10.15 p.m.

At noon, when Washington was comparatively peaceful, Booth was riding away from the theatre when he met James R. Ford, returning in a buggy with flags collected from the Treasury Department. Young Ford was in fine spirits. A few hours before he had been resigned to facing a near-empty house this evening while Grover's packed in the theatregoers at their gala performance. But the unexpected visit of Lincoln and Grant would change all that. In his eldest brother's absence, James was eager to make this evening a spectacular success. He chatted to Booth about his plans to have big American banners draped across the façade of the President's box. Flags would be hung at either flank of the box and two others would be draped on the balustrades. He also hoped to obtain the great blue regimental flag of the U.S. Treasury Guards to suspend at the centre pillar; his brother Harry had had the novel idea of hanging a picture of George Washington in the centre of the flag. Booth told James that he hoped to attend the performance, but he could not promise to be there. Then they parted. When Ford arrived back at the theatre he thoughtfully composed a special notice for the newspapers to advertise the forthcoming visit of Lincoln and Grant.

Booth walked on to Howard's Stable on Seventh Street where he arranged for his one-eyed roan to be taken to the stable behind Ford's Theatre and left there in the care of stagehand Ned Spangler. Booth knew he could trust Ned to look after the horse. The man had worked as a carpenter when Booth's father was building his new house at Belair in Maryland. He idolised John Wilkes, and though he had known the actor since childhood he still addressed him respectfully as 'Mr. Booth'.

Next Booth called at James W. Pumphrey's Stable on C Street in the rear of the National Hotel and arranged to hire a bay mare which, he was assured, had a fine turn of speed. He told the stableman to have her saddled for him to collect at four o'clock, then he headed back to the National Hotel to change his clothes. The actor dressed appropriately for the assassin's role, in a black hat and a black suit, with tight riding trousers, calf boots and new spurs. He took his wallet containing pictures of his girl friends, a folding pocket-knife, his unused diary, a pocket compass, a gold watch, a gimlet, a small brass derringer and a long sheathed knife which bore on its shining blade the inscription 'Liberty and independence. America—the land of the brave and the free. Sheffield, England'.

At 2.30 p.m. the actor briefly visited Mrs. Surratt's quiet little boarding house at 541 H Street. A few minutes later the widow left her house carrying a brown paper package, containing field-glasses, which Booth had asked her to deliver to tavern-keeper John Lloyd. Three days before, Mr. Weichmann had driven her ten miles south to Surrattsville where she hoped to collect a long-standing debt from Mr. John Nothey, who had bought land from her late husband. The poor woman had still to get the 479 dollars that was her due and now she was determined to settle the matter once and for all. Weichmann had agreed to drive her to Surratts-ville again for a final showdown with Nothey. Mrs. Surratt made no effort to hide Booth's package in her large hold-all. She simply told the inquisitive Weichmann that the parcel contained glass and she did not want to get it wet on the journey.

From the boarding house Booth walked to Herndon House on Ninth Street (only a block away from Ford's Theatre) where, several weeks before, Lewis Paine had registered on his instruc-tions. He went up to Paine's room and explained how he had changed his plans. At one time Booth had considered taking the giant ex-soldier with him to Ford's and giving him the task of eliminating Grant while he killed the President. Now he had decided against this. Possibly he considered that, as a well-known actor, he had more chance alone of reaching the State box with-out arousing suspicion; more probably, his colossal vanity per-suaded him that no one should share top billing with him in this supreme drama. He would kill Lincoln with his derringer and Grant with his knife.

Booth had another, equally dangerous mission for his strong man. Paine would be assigned the task of killing William H. Seward, Secretary of State, at sixty-three the oldest member of the Cabinet. It was only nine days since the white-haired states-man had narrowly cheated death when frightened horses had bolted with his carriage, taken a corner too sharply and smashed the front right wheel against the kerb. His right arm was broken, his jaw shattered, his mouth cruelly torn.

Though this grand old man of the Republican Party now lay

Above, the interior of Ford's Theatre on the night of April 14th, 1865; *below*, Ford's Theatre flanked by Ferguson's Restaurant, left, and Peter Taltavul's saloon, right

Above, the theatre box in which President Lincoln was shot. A portrait of George Washington is in the centre; *below*, the six-inch derringer which killed the President with a lead ball less than half an inch in diameter

helpless in bed, with a double iron brace round his neck and jaw, his murder presented a formidable challenge. Seward was in a front third-floor bedroom of The Old Clubhouse, his home in Lafayette Square, a residence in view of the White House and only three doors from the sentry-mounted district headquarters of General Christopher C. Augur. Moreover, there would be at least six persons—relatives, servants and male nurses—in the building at any given time.

Yet Paine accepted 'Cap's' orders without question, like the well-trained soldier he was. There remained only one obvious problem: Booth had tried many times in vain to acquaint the thick-skulled Paine with the geography of Washington, but the man only became more hopelessly confused. He could be trusted to kill but never to find his target and then escape without assistance. The role of guiding him to and from his target would be given to young Davy Herold, the former drug-store clerk, who was thrilled to be included in the momentous night's work.

Shortly after Booth's visit, Paine took an early dinner and checked out of the hotel. Meanwhile his leader went on to Kirkwood House to give a final briefing to George Atzerodt who had registered there the previous morning, taking Room 126, almost directly above that of Vice-President Andrew Johnson. The frightened German was out, so the actor left him a note which he pushed under his door. Then Booth did a strange thing: at the hotel desk he left a card presumably intended for the Vice-President. On it he had written: 'Don't wish to disturb you. Are you at home?—J. Wilkes Booth.' Soon after, Johnson's mail was collected by his private secretary, Colonel William A. Browning. But when Browning found Booth's card he immediately supposed it was intended for himself since he had been introduced to the actor some years ago. The Vice-President had never met John Wilkes.

It was now nearing four o'clock and, as arranged, Booth collected his excitable, deep-chested mare from Pumphrey's livery stable. He then rode over to Grover's Theatre, went upstairs to Deery's smoke-filled billiards saloon, and ordered a bottle of brandy and some water. The saloon keeper noted he was unusually remote. After watching a game of billiards for a while, the actor went down to the theatre manager's office. It was empty. Booth sat at Dwight Hess's desk, took out some writing paper and composed a letter which would explain his motive for murder and how he had abandoned his original plan for the President's capture. He addressed the envelope to 'Editor, *National Intelligencer*'.

The arrogant actor wanted to ensure that all the world knew that he, John Wilkes Booth, was responsible for the assassination of Abraham Lincoln, and that his name would be recorded in history for all time, just as he had dreamed in those days of his youth on the Maryland farm. This letter was his guarantee of immortality. Yet, maliciously, without consulting his fellow conspirators, he signed the confession: 'J. W. Booth—Paine—Atzerodt—Herold'. He sealed the letter and with it the fate of his followers, whether they collaborated with him that day or not.

On leaving Grover's, Booth just missed meeting David Herold who was across the road at Naylor's Stable, arranging to hire a mare. Stable foreman John Fletcher charged the lad five dollars and stressed that the horse must be returned by nine o'clock that evening at the very latest. He had had several horses stolen and was uneasy about dealing with such a boyish-looking customer.

Meanwhile the chief conspirator was walking his hired mare towards Ford's. Outside the theatre he showed off the spirited animal to propertyman James L. Maddox and demonstrated her fine turn of speed by racing her down the street. Then, as he rode slowly along Pennsylvania Avenue past Willard's, Washington's most famous hotel, he saw another person he knew. The man was actor John Matthews, who, like Sam Arnold, had declined to join the original plot to kidnap Lincoln. Despite his bitterness over that refusal, Booth now chatted pleasantly to him. He had one small favour to ask: would Matthews deliver a letter for him to the editor of the *National Intelligencer*? Booth explained that it could not be delivered today because of the nature of the news it contained and that tomorrow he expected to be out of town. Matthews readily agreed to deliver it Saturday morning.

At that moment their attention was drawn by the appearance of a long, bedraggled line of soldiers marching out of step down the street. With their unshaven faces bowed and their tattered grey uniforms thick with dust, these broken remnants of a once proud Confederate Army shuffled along the cobbled street while soldiers in blue guarded them on both sides.

'Who are those men?' Booth asked.

Matthews hesitated. 'They look like officers from Lee's army—probably being taken to the Old Capitol Prison.'

'Good God!' cried Booth. 'Matthews, I have no country left.'

He followed the marching column a short way until he was distracted by a carriage, escorted by two cavalry outriders, which had just drawn away from Willard's and was now heading towards the Capitol. Curious to see who was receiving such V.I.P. treatment, Booth galloped along the Avenue and saw that the passengers included General Grant and his wife. To his even greater surprise he learned from his enquiries that the General was leaving town by train that evening instead of attending the theatre as had been announced in the Press. Thus the ubiquitous actor had now gathered up-to-date information on all the day's happenings which were pertinent to his scheme. In each case he had gained the information in advance of the general public.

In this same hour, between 5 p.m. and 6 p.m., Booth was riding around Washington when he spotted yet another man he recognised—George Atzerodt, the conspirator he had missed earlier at Kirkwood House. He stopped to tell the frightened Prussian that their plot would now be made easier by Grant's absence from the theatre, and he stressed that Atzerodt should be sure to make his attack on the Vice-President as near to 10.15 p.m. as possible. It was vital that they should synchronise their separate attacks and so meet without delay on the far side of the Navy Yard Bridge.

But Atzerodt, befuddled with drink, didn't wish to know about Booth's terrifying plans; he wanted to back out of the conspiracy. The flabby Lutheran immigrant had been busy checking up on Mr. Johnson and from his enquiries in the Kirkwood House bar had learned of the Vice-President's considerable reputation for physical courage.

'You miserable coward,' snapped Booth. 'Anyway, it's too late to pull out now. We are all in this together.'

Atzerodt, who had never stood up to bullying in his life, nodded meekly in agreement. But it was an empty gesture. He was no man of action and knew that, whatever he might say to the contrary, he would never be able to steel himself to take the final step. Soon after leaving his leader, the man entrusted with the task of killing the Vice-President of the United States threw away his sheathed bowie knife in a deserted street and resumed his long saloon-crawl. In whisky bottles he would seek the courage he could never hope to find.

Booth now rode to the narrow alley behind Ford's Theatre, where he had his horse watered and fed. He asked Ned Spangler to stable the mare and then he invited the faithful Spangler, together with two other stagehands, James Maddox and Jacob Ritterspaugh, to join him for a drink at Taltavul's. It was now 6 p.m. When they set off for the nearby tavern, Ford's Theatre was left deserted except for a solitary ticket-seller at the front entrance.

Booth treated the stagehands to a bottle of whisky and then excused himself, explaining he had to attend to some business. That business took him back to the deserted theatre to prepare for the most dramatic performance of his life. He worked calmly and methodically. His chief concern was that, once he had entered the vestibule outside the State box, his evil work should not be interrupted by outsiders. For this purpose he took up a piece of pine board which had supported a music-stand and cut away about two inches of plaster from the wall of the vestibule. Thus he could jam one end of the board into the niche and brace the other end against the panel of the door which gave access to the corridor. Once he had entered the vestibule no one would be able to follow. Booth hid the pine board in a dark corner and efficiently collected up all the fragments of plaster. Then, with a gimlet, he bored a peep-hole into the door leading to the President's box and again cleaned up traces of his handiwork. Content that all was ready, he returned to the National Hotel for dinner and retired to his room. About this time James Maddox, acting as stage manager, returned to the theatre and inspected the President's box. He found everything in order.

Meanwhile, having set the stage, Booth now assembled his gear for the final act. He loaded a brass, single-shot derringer, about six inches in length, slid a sheathed knife into the waistband of his trousers, packed away a false beard, dark moustache, wig, make-up pencil, long scarf and two Colt revolvers. Then, at 7.45 p.m., he set out on his lively mare. His precise movements at this time are unknown, but he held a last meeting of his conspirators, probably on some side street.[1] In this final briefing he emphasised again that it was vital that they should all strike at 10.15 p.m.—Paine killing Secretary of State Seward at his home and Atzerodt shooting the Vice-President in his hotel room. Booth would take care of the President alone. Herold's task would be to guide Paine to Seward's house and escort him afterwards to the Navy Yard Bridge where, if all went well, the conspirators would meet and flee south together. If anything went wrong they should make their own way to Surrattsville and meet at the tavern where John Lloyd had guns and field-glasses awaiting them. Herold suggested that Paine could best enter Seward's house on the pretext that he carried a prescription

1. Where they met has been much disputed. It was arranged that they should meet in Paine's room at Herndon House about 8 p.m. But Paine had already booked out and there is no evidence that they gathered there.

from the Secretary of State's physician, Dr. Tullio Suzzaro Verdi. This was accepted. Then, possibly with the intent of killing any thoughts of last-minute withdrawal from the plot, Booth revealed that he had left a letter explaining the conspiracy and giving all their names. There could be no turning back.

John Wilkes Booth arrived at Ford's at 9.30 p.m., riding to the dark alley at the rear and calling for Spangler to hold his horse. But Spangler was on duty as a scene shifter, so stage-door attendant Joseph Burroughs, a young lad known to everyone as Johnny Peanut because he used to sell peanuts outside the theatre, agreed to hold the actor's mare until he returned. Booth now entered by the back door, nodded to actors as he passed by, and crossed the theatre under the stage. As he moved through the subterranean passage he could faintly hear the actors speaking the lines of the corn-packed comedy that he knew so well. There was still some time, he realised, before they reached the point where only one actor would be on stage and the audience's laughter would be at its loudest. To fill in time, Booth went across to the exit leading to Tenth Street and out to Peter Taltavul's adjoining saloon, where he ordered whisky instead of his usual brandy. In the same bar, coachman Burns and valet Forbes were drinking with a third member of the President's staff—bodyguard John F. Parker.

Outside Taltavul's, Booth talked to Lewis Carland, the theatre costumier, and James J. Gifford, the stage carpenter. There they were joined by Captain William Williams, an officer of the Washington Cavalry Police and an old fan of Booth's. He invited the actor for a drink, but Booth politely declined. 'I have promised to catch Miss Keene's performance,' he explained.

Ticket collector John Buckingham, a Navy Yard carpenter by day, nodded as this famous actor entered Ford's by the main door at about seven minutes after ten. He joked that Booth would hardly require a ticket and gave him a chew of his tobacco. Booth hurried on up to the dress circle, waited a few minutes, then slipped through the little white door leading to the President's box and barred the vestibule door behind him with the hidden pine board. In a few seconds now, Asa Trenchard, played by Harry Hawk, would be left alone on the stage.

Outraged at her discovery that Asa was not a millionaire after all, Mrs. Mountchessington haughtily proclaimed the line that was Booth's cue. Mrs. Mountchessington had ordered her daughter to go to her room and now she herself swept off the stage.

Booth crouched at the spy-hole and saw President Lincoln in his rocking-chair. Asa, alone on stage, began his laugh-line: 'Don't know the manners of good society, eh . . . ?' At that moment the assassin opened the door inwards, moved noiselessly over the carpet to within point-blank range of the President, and levelled his single-shot derringer at the back of Lincoln's head, just behind the left ear. Asa went on: 'Well, I guess I know enough to turn you inside out, old gal . . .' They were almost certainly the last words Mr. Lincoln ever heard. As the audience roared, Booth fired. The President moved only fractionally.

Few of the 1,675 theatregoers realised it was the sound of a gunshot; none immediately appreciated what had happened. Mrs. Lincoln and her companions were grinning one second, horror-stricken the next. At the sound of the explosion they turned to see the assassin, remarkably composed, standing amid a haze of blue smoke with the derringer still in his hand. With no dramatic cry or gesture, he softly spoke three words—'*Sic semper tyrannis*' (Thus always to tyrants),[1] the words of Brutus as he struck imperial Caesar down, the motto of Virginia, capital state of the Confederacy.

Major Rathbone instantly leaped to his feet and grabbed at the assassin. Simultaneously, Booth released the derringer, whipped

1. Some witnesses say Booth uttered these words in the box; some that he spoke them from the stage. It has even been reported that he said *Sic semper tyrannis* in both places. But Booth himself recorded that it was before he fired.

the Sheffield blade from his waistband and slashed the major's left arm to the bone. Now Booth reportedly cried, 'Revenge for the South,'[1] placed one hand on the balustrade and vaulted over the side to drop to the boards eleven or twelve feet below. It was a simple fall for the 'gymnastic actor', but he had not allowed for the possibility of catching the spur of his right foot in the Treasury Guards' flag drapped from the box. As he crashed heavily, landing in a kneeling position, his left leg took the full impact and snapped about two inches above the ankle.

The audience was bewildered, some believing that the strange interruption was part of the entertainment. Harry Hawk stood confused on stage as Booth stumbled past him towards the wings. The assassin, still flourishing his knife, brushed by Laura Keene, and then unexpectedly bumped into Withers. Twice he slashed wildly at the orchestra leader, cutting his coat and knocking him to the floor, and then he hobbled on to the back door. Now Mrs. Lincoln screamed hysterically, and a quick-witted army major in the first row of the orchestra shouted, 'Stop that man.' Major Joseph B. Stewart, a 6 ft. 6 in-tall lawyer, began to give chase. But the alarm had gone up too late. Booth was at the back door where 'Johnny Peanut', lying on a bench, was still holding his horse. He knocked the boy down with the butt end of his knife, swung into the saddle, and spurred his impatient mare down the alley, into the gas-lit streets, and out of Washington City.

No other conspirator played his part so efficiently.

At the appointed time of 10.15 p.m., the frightened Atzerodt was nowhere near the Vice-President's room. He spent most of Good Friday drinking at the Kirkwood hotel bar and pumping the barman for information about his intended victim—the position of Mr. Johnson's room, whether he was guarded or armed, the times he left the hotel. No one sent to spy on the Vice-President could have been more obvious in his behaviour,

1. Rathbone thought he shouted something like 'Freedom'.

and yet the Prussian, by his very nature, failed to arouse suspicion. He was such a ridiculous, sozzled figure that no one could take him seriously.

Around the saloons Atzerodt was well known as a comical character, a man pathetically eager to make friends, highly sensitive to criticism but incapable of replying to an insult. As soon as he sensed the faintest hostility among drinking companions he would doff his beaver hat and hasten out of the bar. Booth was too intelligent to have had any confidence in this conspirator. He despised Andrew Johnson, considering the statesman from Tennessee to be an arch-traitor and opportunist who had betrayed his birthright to serve the Union. Possibly he appointed Atzerodt as his executioner because he rated the Vice-President as the most insignificant of the war leaders, but certainly there was never a chance that the carriage-maker, terrified by the plan and too weak to resist Booth's authority, would ever carry out his role in the conspiracy. As John Wilkes entered Ford's Theatre, he was visiting the stables opposite Grover's Theatre, where he kept a rented horse. He invited Irishman John Fletcher to join him for a drink and then, confused with liquor, he rode aimlessly through the city. The alert Fletcher, growing more and more anxious about the horse he had hired out to Herold, decided to follow the Prussian on foot in the hope that he would lead him to his young friend. But he soon gave it up as a wild goose chase. Atzerodt stopped briefly at Kirkwood House, then rode slowly up the street. Fletcher could not be troubled to follow him further. He returned to his stables, while the German rode past Ford's and doubled back to the Kirkwood hotel, where he ventured no further than the bar.

In contrast, Lewis Paine, the desperado and Confederate deserter, carried out his part with horrifying determination. At precisely 10.15 p.m. he was knocking at the door of Mr. Seward's home in Lafayette Square, while Herold, who had guided him there, waited outside under orders to go to his assistance if necessary. William Bell, a young, white-coated Negro servant, answered the door. He looked up at a massive stranger who carried a package, 'medicine from Dr. Verdi', and who insisted that he had to deliver it to Seward in person. When Bell said that he had strict orders not to allow anyone upstairs, the stranger lost all control. 'Out of my way, nigger,' he growled, and forced his way into the house.

On the stairs the massive intruder was stopped by Frederick Seward, Assistant Secretary of State, and again Paine insisted that he had to deliver the prescription to the patient in person. In an attempt to humour the man, Seward asked him to wait there while he went to see whether his father was sleeping. He then disappeared into a third-floor room at the front of the hall on the left side and in a few seconds he returned to say that his father was indeed sleeping and could not possibly be disturbed. But it did not matter now; from this moment the dull-witted conspirator understood the position of the Cabinet Minister's bedroom.

Grumbling, Paine turned as though to go downstairs. He took one step down, then whipped out his Whitney Navy revolver, swung round and squeezed the trigger. There was a dull, metallic click. Still, the broken gun was scarcely a less dangerous weapon in his powerful hands. He smashed the butt against Seward's head, then senselessly hammered the unconscious man again and again. Meanwhile, William Bell fled down the stairs and into the street screaming 'Murder! Murder!' with such fearful intensity that young Herold rode off, leaving his friend to make his own escape.

Paine now ran berserk through the house. He threw away his blood-stained revolver, pulled out a knife, and hurled his huge frame against the bedroom door. In the semi-darkness of the room he savagely attacked three people, one of them a woman, Miss Fanny Seward. Slashing blindly with his knife, he reached the bed, then stabbed again and again at the body beneath him. With great courage and quick judgment, old William Seward rolled himself off his bed on the side near the wall, even though it meant falling on his broken arm. He was horribly slashed

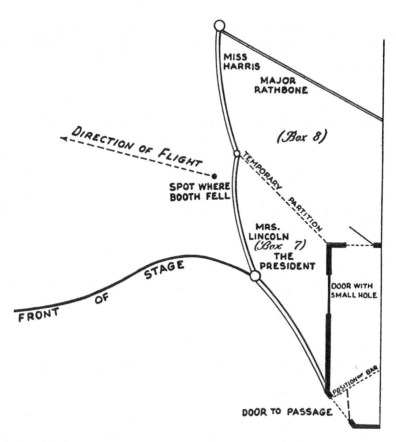

MISS HARRIS

MAJOR RATHBONE

(Box 8)

DIRECTION OF FLIGHT

TEMPORARY PARTITION

SPOT WHERE BOOTH FELL

MRS. LINCOLN *(Box 7)* THE PRESIDENT

FRONT OF STAGE

DOOR WITH SMALL HOLE

POSITION OF BAR

DOOR TO PASSAGE

around the face, but the iron brace around his neck and jaw saved him from a mortal blow.

Now, smashing a table and chairs in the nightmarish struggle, Paine shook himself free from the Secretary's attendants and rushed from the bedroom screaming 'I'm mad, I'm mad.' In the hall he met a State Department messenger, Mr. Emrick W. Hansell, and stabbed him in the chest. Then he fled out of the house and rode away with Bell, the faithful Negro servant, following him on foot and still screaming 'Murder!'

Behind him Paine left a miniature battlefield. Miss Fanny, who had been standing against the bedroom door when he smashed it inwards, now lay unconscious. Male nurse Sergeant George

Robinson, one of the two convalescent soldiers assigned to help the family, was bleeding from serious knife wounds. Major Augustus Seward, who had also been at his father's side, was badly bruised but not bleeding. His brother Frederick had two fractures of the skull and lay in a coma. Messenger Hansell was losing blood at a fearful rate. And Mr. Seward, the real target of the hired killer? Robinson could feel no pulse and took the old statesman for dead. But, miraculously, the great Republican was to recover and live on seven more years to the age of seventy-one. His deepest cut was a grotesque knife wound which ran down his right cheek from ear to lip, where the madman's knife had halted against the iron brace.

Without realising it, the hopelessly confused assailant now rode in his erratic flight to within half a mile of the Navy Yard Bridge, where he had been instructed to join his fellow conspirators. Then, seeing soldiers approaching, he panicked and abandoned his one-eyed horse. Lewis Paine spent the rest of the night of terror hiding in a patch of Washington woods.

Meanwhile Herold was fleeing in the right direction and was only a mile behind Booth. But he was not without a pursuer. Stableman Fletcher, for ever worrying about his horses, had spotted the young man by chance as he rode towards Pennsylvania Avenue. 'Get off that horse,' he shouted. 'You've had it long enough.' When Herold spurred the roan on faster, Fletcher saddled a horse and gave chase. He lost sight of the rider, but guessed which way he was heading and rode three miles towards the Navy Yard Bridge, the route to southern Maryland. Unknowingly, this persistent Irishman was leading the pursuit of conspirators soon to be sought by more than a million men.

At the north end of the Navy Yard Bridge, Sergeant Silas T. Cobb had little more than another hour on duty. With two sentries he was responsible for guarding the long wooden bridge and checking all persons entering or leaving the city. Normally this was dull routine since the bridge was officially closed to all travellers at 9 p.m. and he remained on guard until one o'clock in the morning. It was around 10.45 p.m. when he was approached by a rider dressed all in black. A sentry held the stranger's horse and Cobb asked the man to identify himself. 'Booth,' the rider replied.

Cobb's standing orders were to send back anyone without a special pass. But those were emergency orders; the war was virtually over and the sergeant was a reasonable man. He let the stranger pass. A few minutes later a second rider arrived at the north end of the bridge. He gave his name as Smith and his destination as White Plains. Cobb waved him on. That second rider was David Herold and now two conspirators had escaped from Washington across the east branch of the Potomac into Maryland.

After a further interval of a few minutes, yet another horseman pulled up at the sentry box. He learned that a young man on a roan horse had passed that way and asked whether he might follow the rider. Cobb told him he could cross the bridge, but added that he would not be allowed to cross back. John Fletcher thought for a moment, then decided to return to Washington. He would report the theft of his horse at police headquarters.

One conspirator panicked needlessly that night. When George Atzerodt heard of the attacks on Lincoln and Seward he took a horse car to the Navy Yard area and sought lodgings with a friend who kept a store there. The friend would not have him. The frightened Prussian was now in walking distance of the Navy Yard Bridge, but he would never join up with Booth and Herold. Confused with drink and fear, he wandered the streets without purpose or reason and, finally, in the early hours of the morning, booked in at a shabby hotel, Pennsylvania House. With a hangover and no money, Atzerodt left the hotel at 6 a.m. and tried to escape from Washington on foot. But he had nowhere to go, and no money for a horse. So he just walked openly through the streets. In the Georgetown farmland area, bordering Washington in the north-west, he sold his gun for ten dollars. Then he looked for somewhere to buy a drink.

5

PANIC IN WASHINGTON

'I'M GLAD it happened,' shouted one man on the street outside Ford's Theatre. Within seconds a lynch mob was dragging him towards a lamp-post and only the swift intervention of armed policemen saved his life. Outraged citizens, some wearing night attire, surged around the entrance and shouted 'Burn the theatre.' Men and women, from high-ranking government officials to lowly Negroes, wept openly at the news. Rumours spread that the entire Cabinet had been eliminated, that Grant had been killed on a train. Such was the first ripple of reaction which would mount into a tidal wave of hatred and grief engulfing an entire nation. With this first senseless killing of an American President, a country just emerging from its bloodiest war was plunged back into darkness. After ten days of victory celebrations came as many days of national mourning; just as joy turned to despair, so thoughts of peace turned to vengeance.

Washington was a city transformed overnight. Down came the colourful flags and banners; government and business offices, theatres, music-halls and saloons were closed; social functions postponed. The streets were strangely silent, except on Pennsylvania Avenue where hundreds of coloured people stood weeping outside the White House, the falling rain mingling with their tears. But there was hatred and fear as well as despair. At a mission church a preacher was dragged from his pulpit and arrested for making adverse comments about Mr. Lincoln in his

Sunday sermon. Some reckless fanatics who openly welcomed the news were sentenced to six months' hard labour. Newspapers blamed the Confederacy and screamed in their editorials for vengeance on the leaders of the rebellion. Secessionists, fearing for their lives, kept silent and joined in the mourning.

Some reacted hysterically to the news of the assassination. A young Swede took his own life because 'I want to join Lincoln', and Ella Turner, the prostitute who had loved Booth, tried to commit suicide with chloroform, only to be discovered and revived by doctors in time. One man who panicked that Good Friday night was actor John Matthews, who carried the most vital evidence of all in his coat pocket—the letter which he had promised Booth he would deliver next morning to the editor of the *National Intelligencer*. He rushed back to his hotel, read the letter, and then, terrified that it would incriminate him, burned it in the grate.

Edwin M. Stanton, who assumed the powers of a dictator for the next eight hours, reacted with disbelief. He was preparing for bed when a soldier brought news of the attacks on Lincoln and Seward. Now he went back to his bedroom and told his wife it was nonsense because he had left Mr. Seward little more than an hour before. There was one man who reacted with relief: Mr. Dwight Hess, manager of Grover's Theatre, where a gala performance had been staged that night. He hurried off a telegram to Leonard Grover in New York: 'President shot tonight in Ford's Theatre. Thank God it wasn't ours.'

When Lincoln was shot, matinée idol Edwin Booth was on stage playing Sir Edwin Mortimer at the Boston Theatre. Early next morning a Negro servant rushed into his bedroom with the news and the actor felt as though he had been 'struck on the forehead with a hammer'. Edwin, who had voted for Lincoln the year before, swore he would never act again. He never questioned the first report that his brother had done the foul deed; he recognised the melodramatic brand of the performance, knew instinctively that his brother was capable of such a senseless act. He wrote to his sister Asia: 'Think no more of him as your brother. He is dead to us now, as soon he must be to all the world, but imagine the boy you loved to be in that better part of his spirit, in another world.' In a log cabin in Illinois, Sarah Bush Lincoln, the President's seventy-six-year-old stepmother, received the news with shock but not surprise. 'I knowed they'd kill him,' she said. 'I been waiting for it.'

The police and military authorities reacted with an urgent flurry of activity which was fittingly prompt, and hopelessly misguided. General Christopher Augur, the District Commandant, immediately ordered out mounted patrols, but they searched aimlessly. There was no immediate effort to seal off all exits from the city, not even a prompt inspection of Booth's hotel room. Stanton was responsible for directing measures against the conspirators, but he created the impression of being a frightened man, convinced that this was just the beginning of a gigantic Confederate plot. His chief concern was the prevention of new terrorist outbreaks and so, between 10.15 p.m. and 11 p.m., no serious move was made to track down the President's assassin.

Reporter L. A. Gobright of Associated Press heard the news and, without checking for details, wired New York that the President had been shot, perhaps mortally wounded. He sent his message just in time. Shortly before 11 p.m., all commercial telegraph lines from Washington went dead. The authorities immediately presumed that a vast band of Confederate conspirators must have been at work to cut all the wires simultaneously. But the lines had not been cut; two wires in the main batteries had crossed, short-circuiting the whole service. It was not an exceptional mishap and soon after 12.30 a.m. the telegraph service was operating again. After sending his dramatic, twelve-word message, Gobright hurried over to Ford's Theatre and was on the murder spot quickly enough to take charge of Booth's derringer which had been found on the floor of the presidential box. The reporter handed the weapon over to Police Superintendent Richards and spent the rest of the night working

Three of the conspirators:
right, Michael O'Laughlin;
bottom left, Samuel Arnold;
bottom right, John Surratt

Left, Mrs. Mary Surratt, who was among those condemned to death; *below*, the execution of (left to right) Mrs. Surratt, Paine, Herold and Atzerodt

on stories about the confusion in the city. Yet Gobright, for all his swift efficiency, made no mention of Booth in his later cables that night. At the conspiracy trial some weeks later he testified: 'I was not perfectly satisfied that night that it was J. Wilkes Booth who had killed the President. . . . After I saw the official bulletin the next morning, I came to the conclusion that J. Wilkes Booth was the man.' Gobright was not alone in hesitating to name the alleged assassin in his first reports. Most newspapermen were unwilling to state a fact supported by innumerable eye-witnesses without the endorsement of an official source.

Like President Kennedy nearly a hundred years later, Abraham Lincoln virtually ended his life the moment an assassin's bullet ploughed into his brain. His great heart would beat for nine hours more, but he would never recover consciousness. Too weak to survive the journey back to the White House, Lincoln was carried by four soldiers and two doctors to the nearest house across the street from Ford's. In the three-storey home of William Petersen, a Swedish tailor, at 453 Tenth Street,[1] he was laid diagonally across a single bed[2] in a small room under the stairway. All of the Cabinet officers, except Seward, gathered there, and at least six doctors were present, with Surgeon-General Joseph Barnes in command. Mrs. Lincoln occupied the front parlour with her son Robert, Miss Harris and Laura Keene. Major Rathbone was there for a short while; then he fainted from loss of blood and was taken home.

Gideon Welles recorded in his diary: 'The quaint sufferer lay extended diagonally across the bed, which was not long enough

1. Now 516 Tenth Street.

2. Charles Warwick, the actor, later wrote that he was boarding in this room in March when Booth called on him. His visitor, feeling tired, filled a pipe and smoked himself off to sleep. 'Who would think, to look on that handsome face, so calm and peaceful in repose, that beneath it slumbered a volcano? Who could raise the curtain of the near future and peer upon the picture of the dying President on that very bed.'

for him. He had been stripped of his clothes. His large arms, which were occasionally exposed, were of a size which one would scarce have expected from his spare appearance. His slow, full respiration lifted the clothes with each breath he took. His features were calm and striking.' At times, the President sighed, but his breathing became more and more laboured. His case was hopeless. The lead ball, less than half an inch in diameter, had entered above the left ear, crossed the brain, and lodged itself behind the right eye.

Soon after 1 a.m. his condition was so critical that the ever-efficient Stanton had Attorney-General Speed draw up a formal note informing the Vice-President that the President had died and advising him to be ready to take over the highest office at once. Then the War Secretary made the unfortunate error of reading the message aloud while a fair copy was made. He did not realise that Mrs. Lincoln was nearby. When she heard the words, the First Lady presumed her husband to be already dead and was immediately launched on a fresh bout of hysterics. An hour later she began screaming again and then collapsed at the President's bedside. Stanton pointed at the unconscious Mrs. Lincoln and ordered, 'Take that woman away, and do not let her in here again.'

At 7 a.m., as rain fell outside, the President began moaning and breathing with extreme difficulty. Mrs. Lincoln was invited back in the room; at her side was her son Robert, grief-stricken, his tear-stained face buried in his hands. Twenty-two minutes later, Mr. Lincoln drew his last breath. Two silver dollars were placed over his eyes, and Stanton, standing at the foot of the bed, was reported to have muttered the words for posterity, 'Now he belongs to the ages.'[1] Then they began to pray until their meditations were broken by the screams of Mrs. Lincoln who threw herself on her husband's body. Half-carried, she was escorted from the room for the last time.

1. Sources vary on his exact words, but this was certainly the sentiment expressed.

The following day little Tad asked a visitor to the White House if his father was in heaven.

'I have no doubt of it,' the caller replied.

'Then I am glad he has gone,' said the boy, 'for he was never happy after he came here. This was not a good place for him.'

On Saturday morning, in his guarded rooms at Kirkwood House, Andrew Johnson was inducted into office as 17th President of the United States. But for the present he was only a figurehead. With Seward confined to his bed, Edwin McMasters Stanton had all the power in his hands. Throughout the long night he had directed all emergency operations from the back parlour of the Petersen house; he would be responsible for the pursuit of the conspirators for weeks ahead. Stanton took command with the same industry and firmness that had made him Lincoln's most valuable minister during the war. But at first his efforts were aimed largely at safeguarding the government and the city rather than apprehending the assassin as swiftly as possible. In this direction he was, as always, ruthlessly efficient. He assumed absolute authority, issued an endless stream of orders, summoned high officials, ordered arrests. At Stanton's command, Ford's Theatre was confiscated and 'every human being' in its service was arrested. All fire-engines stood at the alert, ready for mass outbreaks of arson. The homes of all high-ranking government officials were guarded. General Grant was recalled to defend the city against a last, desperate attack by the rebels. Stanton was not seeking one or two conspirators, but hundreds. He told General Augur that an army of Confederate terrorists was in the city and he wanted them sought out by some 650 municipal and military police, the U.S. Secret Service, the spies of the Bureau of Military Justice, and eight thousand soldiers encamped in the Washington area.

The first intelligent moves that Good Friday night were made by Major A. C. Richards, Superintendent of the Metropolitan Washington Police. As a member of the audience at Ford's Theatre, he had recognised Booth as the assassin. Immediately after the crime he had looked in vain for bodyguard John F. Parker and then had ordered the night detective squad to round up witnesses. Between 11 p.m. and midnight he interviewed seventeen persons who provided information which 'goes to show that the assassin is a man named John Wilkes Booth'. These witnesses included actor Harry Hawk, stagehand James Maddox and John Fletcher, the foreman at Naylor's livery stable. With higher Federal authority, General Augur also arranged for witnesses to be interviewed at the Petersen house, where Stanton set up a preliminary court of inquiry, took charge of the interrogations and unnerved many witnesses with his brusque and bullying manner. Major Richards, at police headquarters, and Stanton, in the Petersen parlour, separately found numerous witnesses who were willing to swear that John Wilkes Booth was the assassin. Indeed, this part of the investigation went so well that Corporal James Tanner, who made a shorthand note of testimony for Stanton, stated in a letter written two days later: 'In fifteen minutes I had testimony to hang Wilkes Booth higher than ever Haman hung.' And yet Stanton still delayed in ordering Booth's arrest. At 11.45 p.m., General Augur gave orders for all persons attempting to leave the city to be arrested and for troops encamped in the district to arrest all suspicious persons. Yet, one and a half hours after the crime of the century, the various orders still did not mention Booth by name. This omission can hardly have been due to uncertainty about the assassin's identity. In an official report, dated April 23, Colonel John A. Foster, investigator for the War Department, stated that Booth 'was recognised by at least a hundred men, some of whom were on the most intimate relations with him'.

The northern authorities were alerted first that night and by midnight three squadrons were patrolling roads to the north of Washington. Then the military forces at Alexandria, south-west of the capital, were alerted, and shortly after midnight eight hundred troops were ordered out at Fairfax Court House, directly to the west. The alert was also sounded beyond Fairfax, as far west as Winchester, and as far as Cumberland and Harper's Ferry in the north-west. At 3.0 a.m. General Morris, commander of the Baltimore district in the north-east, was ordered to patrol his area heavily. Troops were also out in great numbers in southeast Maryland. It was virtually impossible for Booth to escape in any of these directions. Only one feasible escape route remained—directly south through Port Tobacco, the route a Southern agent was most likely to choose, the shortest route to the Confederacy, the known underground route of spies and couriers, and the route on which Booth could most reasonably expect to find extreme secessionist sympathisers willing to help him. On the night of April 14-15, the War Department failed to send out wires alerting forces in that direction.

Equally extraordinary is the fact that one exit from Washington was completely ignored—the Navy Yard Bridge by which Booth had escaped. Since this bridge was officially closed at nine o'clock every evening, it was presumed that no one could have escaped that way. When Sergeant Cobb, the guard commander, went off duty a few minutes before one o'clock in the morning, he was still unaware of the dramatic events in the city—and so was the sergeant who relieved him. The significance of the Navy Yard Bridge was apparently still not realised even after stable foreman Fletcher had appeared among numerous witnesses at General Augur's headquarters. Richards had already heard Fletcher's story and he had immediately asked Augur for permission to mount his police and head south. His request was not granted that night. But the following day Richards would ride directly to Surrattsville, on Booth's precise trail.

At Augur's headquarters Fletcher again explained how he had followed Herold to the Navy Yard Bridge, but the commander was not interested in his story of a boyish-looking horse-thief. He wanted a man of Booth's description. More strangely, while Augur and Stanton presumed that a gigantic Confederate plot was in motion, they at first took for granted that the attacks on Seward and Lincoln were probably the work of one madman.

This was an absurd assumption; that it was not checked out sooner is a fair reflection of the pathetically slow workings of Washington's detective force that night. There was no lack of clues, only of quick, intelligent thinking.

Before midnight a large brown horse, blind in one eye, was picked up stray on the outskirts of the city. The saddle and bridle were taken to Augur's headquarters and Fletcher was now asked if he could identify them. Fletcher checked his stable records and reported back that he had stabled this horse and one man who had ridden it recently was a Mr. George Atzerodt. In fact, the horse had been used that night by Lewis Paine. But Augur could make nothing of these scraps of information and, in his haste to question others, he did not examine Fletcher long enough to learn that both Herold, the horse-thief, and the mysterious Atzerodt were friends of John Wilkes Booth. Augur missed another great opportunity when he refused a young captain's request to lead a mounted squad in pursuit of the conspirators. The officer was Captain D. H. L. Gleason who, through his official association with Louis Weichmann, had first reported the suspicions that a plot against the President was being hatched at the Surratt boarding house. Gleason knew that Booth and his friends sometimes met in Surrattsville, but he was not giving out this information for any would-be hero or reward-seeker to use.

Among the figures, great and small, who were involved in the complex investigations that night, one stands out as being reasonably efficient. This was detective John Lee of the U.S. Marshal's office who was sent shortly after midnight to take charge of security for Vice-President Andrew Johnson. Lee thoroughly examined Kirkwood House and from bartender Michael Henry he learned about the curious behaviour of a recent customer, one George Atzerodt, who had been asking so many questions about the Vice-President. The detective then broke down the locked door of Atzerodt's hotel room; inside, he found one Colt revolver below a pillow on the bed, a Canadian bankbook made out to J. Wilkes Booth and bearing a credit of 455 dollars, a detailed map of Virginia, a handkerchief embroidered 'Mary R. Booth', one marked 'F. M. Nelson' (the name of one of Herold's seven sisters), and a third handkerchief marked 'H'. Lee meticulously reported that he also found three boxes of cartridges, a piece of liquorice, a toothbrush, a brass spur, a pair of socks, two collars, a pair of gauntlets, and, beneath the bed sheets, a large bowie knife. At the same time Detective William Eaton was sent to Booth's room at the National Hotel. The only clue found among a pile of papers in the actor's trunk was a letter from Samuel Arnold urging the actor to forget about his complex plot. But this letter was simply signed 'Sam' and not until April 17 was the handwriting identified by an ambulance worker, one Robert G. Mowry, as probably belonging to his acquaintance, Samuel Arnold.

Towards one o'clock in the morning Stanton held a conference at the Petersen house for military, police and judicial chiefs. It was now certain, he announced, that the assassin had fired the shot that killed Lincoln through the door behind the presidential box. The bullet hole had been located. He went on to say that John Wilkes Booth was almost certainly the assassin, but he did not wish the assassination to be announced publicly yet. Perhaps fearing that the news would encourage fresh acts of violence by Confederates, he ordered that no reports of Lincoln's critical condition should be allowed to reach military districts of the South. By 1 a.m., Stanton had sufficient evidence to order the arrest not only of Booth, but also of Atzerodt and Herold. Only one of the four main conspirators had still to be identified, Seward's attacker, Lewis Paine. But it was not until 1.30 a.m., after members of the Cabinet had signed a formal notification of Lincoln's death, that Stanton at last decided to release the news of the attacks on the President and Mr. Seward. He sent a most succinct account of events to Major-General John Adams Dix, Commandant, New York, from whose headquarters official statements were traditionally sent out on general release to the Press. In the circumstances, it was an admirable account with one most notable exception. Remarkably, the assassin was still not mentioned by name in the message which did not leave Washington until 2.15 a.m.—four hours after the assassination.

Newspapers anxiously awaited an official source to which they could attribute Booth's name. When official statements refrained from naming the assassin they felt obliged to do the same—even though the Press of both Washington and New York knew that Booth was the hunted man. Some reporters included Booth's name in their stories only to have it removed because it seemed libellous. Some newspapers hinted that the authorities sought a famous actor, but this did not serve the purpose of broadcasting a general alarm for John Wilkes Booth. One big daily, the *New York Tribune*, was most daring of all; it stated boldly that 'Laura Keene and the leader of the orchestra declare that they recognised him as J. Wilkes Booth, the actor'. The *National Intelligencer* would have had the greatest scoop of the century if Matthews had delivered Booth's letter as promised. Instead, it came out with a tame story and named no names. Astonishingly, the *Washington Chronicle* said, 'Evidence taken amid such excitement would, perhaps, not justify us in naming the suspected man, nor could it aid in his apprehension.'

Nevertheless, after a feebly cranked start, the machinery of the law was now moving into top gear, and if the police were slow to pick up Booth's trail across the Navy Yard Bridge, they certainly lost little time in closing in on Mrs. Surratt's boarding house. General Augur had ordered cavalry patrols to make enquiries at every stable in the city. This profitable line of investigation quickly brought back the information that Booth and a man called John Surratt seemed to share ownership of horses and that they sometimes allowed their horses to be used by a David Herold and a George Atzerodt. Detectives began to wonder whether Booth might still be within the city boundaries, and the Surratt boarding house appeared to be the most likely hide-out. It was shortly after 2 a.m. that Superintendent Richards ordered a squad of eleven detectives to raid the place. Detective

John A. W. Clarvoe led the raid. He was let into the house by a frightened Louis Weichmann who had hastily slipped his trousers over the tail of his nightshirt. Weichmann had stayed indoors all evening after his journey to Surrattsville and was still unaware of the cause of so much excitement. Mrs. Surratt also claimed no knowledge of the affair and Clarvoe was impressed that both seemed genuinely horrified and surprised when he told them the news. After questioning all the boarders, and satisfying himself that John Surratt and Booth had not been seen there that evening, Clarvoe left without making any arrests.

It was 3 a.m.—too late to catch the early editions of the big circulation newspapers—when Stanton finally named Booth as the probable assassin in a further report to Major-General Dix. In this message, which left Washington five hours after the shooting of the President, he stated: 'Investigation strongly indicates J. Wilkes Booth as the assassin of the President. Whether it was the same or a different person that attempted to murder Mr. Seward remains in doubt. . . . Every exertion has been made to prevent the escape of the murderer. His horse has been found on the road near Washington.'[1] At last Stanton was beginning to doubt his theory that there was a widespread Confederate plot; perhaps, after all, this violent conspiracy against the government had been the work of only one or two fanatics. By 4.30 a.m. he was sufficiently sure of the facts to send a third Press release to General Dix which stated: 'It is now ascertained with reasonable certainty that two assassins were engaged in the horrible crime. Wilkes Booth being the one that shot the President, the other a companion of his whose name is not known, but whose description is so clear that he can hardly escape. It appears from a letter found in Booth's trunk that the murder was planned before the 4th of March, but fell through then because the accomplice backed out until "Richmond could be heard from". One of them has evidently made his way to Baltimore, the other has not yet been traced.' Stanton presumably took Arnold to be one assassin,

1. This, of course, was the horse abandoned by Lewis Paine.

and because Arnold's letter to Booth was headed 'Hookstown, Balto, Co', he guessed he had escaped in that direction. Baltimore police were ordered to find Arnold and arrest him.

All the evidence now suggested that Booth had escaped to southern Maryland. Stanton had learned of the actor's connection with the Surratt family and that he and his friends quite often rode to Surrattsville. All other routes from the city had been carefully guarded and no suspicious persons had been seen. Therefore, the great manhunt at last turned towards the Maryland shore. To assist the searchers, Stanton sensibly ordered a picture of Booth to be issued. An official went to Ford's Theatre and turned out what seemed a suitable photograph from the files. It was a picture of Edwin Booth.

Between 4 a.m. and 5 a.m., while regiments patrolled in all other directions, the first Federal troops were sent out on the road taken by Booth. A troop of cavalry, under the command of Lieutenant David D. Dana, younger brother of the Assistant Secretary of War, was directed to patrol the region of Piscataway, Maryland. But Dana did not stop to make enquiries at the Navy Yard Bridge as he led his group of twelve soldiers over to Maryland. He believed the assassin was still hiding within the city.

At 11.15 p.m. on Monday, April 17, four officers, led by Major H. W. Smith, were sent to 541 H Street to arrest Mrs. Surratt and search her boarding house. While the officers were waiting for the lady of the house to get dressed, the door-bell rang. Major Smith opened the front door to a tall, burly man, dressed like a labourer and carrying a pick-axe. The caller was Lewis Paine.

'What do you want?' asked the Major.

'I came to see Mrs. Surratt, but I think there must be some mistake. It's not important.'

'There's no mistake. Why do you want to see Mrs. Surratt?'

'She wanted me to dig a gutter in her back garden, but if she's busy . . .'

The officer assured the reluctant visitor that Mrs. Surratt was not too busy to see him and that he would call her. Paine was then invited into the house. Once he had the labourer inside, the efficient officer questioned him about his business and background. The man admitted that he was a Confederate deserter and produced a paper showing he had taken the oath of allegiance to the Union. The name on the crumpled document was Lewis Paine and it stated the deserter was to stay north of Philadelphia for the duration of the war. It was a common enough case, but the Major said that Paine would have to come along with him for routine questioning. That same day, O'Laughlin was arrested in Baltimore and Arnold was picked up at Fort Monroe. Three days later Atzerodt was arrested in his cousin's house in Maryland. These four conspirators, together with scene-shifter Ned Spangler, were clapped in irons and thrown into the holds of monitors anchored off the Navy Yard.

On April 20, a few hours before Atzerodt's arrest, Stanton announced rewards of 50,000 dollars for the capture of Booth, and 25,000 each for Herold and Atzerodt, with various lesser rewards for information leading to their capture. He also announced that anyone harbouring or aiding these men would be subject to trial before a military commission and liable to sentence of death. By referring to the wanted men as 'criminals and murderers' he had already condemned them without trial.

According to reports of the day, the search for John Wilkes Booth was the greatest manhunt of all time. Estimates of the number of soldiers engaged in the search have been as high as ten thousand. In reality, the actor was hunted by more than a million men; not only the police and Army were on his trail, but hundreds of civilians eager to avenge Lincoln's death or collect the reward offered for Booth, dead or alive. Certainly the manhunt was organised on a scale hitherto unknown, as over sixteen hundred soldiers combed the swamps of Maryland. But never can such a gigantic operation have been so incompetently directed. The searchers were so inefficient that Booth was able to hide out for six days in a tobacco patch close enough to the public road for him to hear the hoofbeats of passing soldiers. Strangest of all, no troops were sent south of the Potomac before April 23.

While the great manhunt went on its erratic way, wild rumours of Booth's capture or whereabouts regularly excited the capital. At one time, a house-to-house search was prompted by the story that Booth, disguised as a Negro woman on crutches, had entered a building near the Kirkwood House. The embarrassing delay in capturing Booth was largely due to the lack of co-operation among the main groups engaged in the pursuit. With the various rewards totalling over 100,000 dollars, the manhunt had become an inter-department contest. Police, detectives and soldiers were organising independent searches, and each group, eager for money or prestige, jealously guarded its clues. Superintendent Richards, for example, had the aid of Louis Weichmann, who could identify all the main conspirators, and he kept this key witness exclusively to himself. He took Weichmann to Maryland one day, to Baltimore the next, and then to Canada. Two years later, at the trial of John Surratt, he explained, 'It was our intention to hold him (Weichmann) as a witness for the reason that certain other parties were monopolising all the information, and we wanted to hold him as we thought we had not been treated altogether proper (sic).'

On Sunday morning, April 16, Lafayette Baker was summoned to Washington from New York and, according to this egotistical chief of detectives, he was told by Stanton, 'My entire dependence is upon you.' But General Augur gave Baker no useful co-operation; after he and his staff had worked night and day on strenuous ground work, the military chief had no intention of handing over all his clues to a latecomer to the chase. Indeed, when Augur received news on April 22 that Booth was crippled, he kept this valuable information to himself for at least a day and released it only to his own search parties. Baker had virtually to start his investigation from scratch. He sent detectives into lower Maryland, circulated wanted notices with photographs and descriptions of Booth and John Surratt, offered additional rewards of 30,000 dollars.

Baker made little progress in the first week, but on April 24, by some mysterious source, he learned that Booth and Herold had crossed into Virginia. At that time Major James R. O'Beirne, the Washington Provost Marshal, was already hot on the conspirators' trail across the Potomac. Then, to his astonishment, he was ordered to remain on the Maryland side of the river. Shortly afterwards, Baker sent for his most trusted subordinates, his own cousin Lieutenant L. B. Baker and Lieutenant-Colonel E. J. Conger. He put them in charge of a detachment of the Sixteenth New York Cavalry and ordered them to search around Port Royal on the Rappahannock. 'You're going after Booth,' he told his cousin. Then he added: 'Lieutenant, we've got a sure thing.' Two days later Conger reported back. The news he whispered into his chief's ear sent Baker leaping from his chair with a look of triumph. The detective hurried with Conger to Stanton's house, rushed into a room where the War Secretary was lying on a sofa, and proudly shouted his news—'We've got Booth.' Stanton put his hands over his eyes and rested in silence for a brief moment. Then Baker showed him Booth's effects—two pistols, a knife, a compass, a pipe, and a small red leather diary. The assassin had not been taken alive.

6

THE GREAT MANHUNT

WHEN JOHN WILKES BOOTH galloped furiously out of
Washington City, his broken leg gave him constant pain that
was sharpened by every jolt of his fast bay mare. Yet he felt
elation, too, at having struck a vital blow for the Confederate
cause. With one shot of his derringer he had silenced the rejoicing of twenty million Northerners, and, so he believed, had
enabled the proud South to lift her head high once more. By
killing the President he illogically thought that he had made
himself the undying hero of all secessionists; now that vain belief
spurred him on towards Virginia where he firmly expected to
find security and honour. Thousands of grateful Southerners
would surely be ready to aid his escape; with their help he might
move on to Mexico or Spain, countries which had no extradition
treaties with the United States, or even further eastwards since
so many well-born Europeans had supported the Confederacy.
Without injury, Booth could have expected to reach Port
Tobacco by 4 a.m. and then make the crossing to Virginia. In
fact, he made such slow progress that he was still some fifteen
miles from Port Tobacco at 4 p.m., and if his pursuers had begun
their search in the direction of Anacostia they would have
captured him within a few hours of the assassination.

Young Davy Herold had no difficulty in overhauling his
leader and by loyally riding on with the crippled assassin he
sacrificed his own excellent chance of escape. By midnight they
had ridden over ten miles to within sight of the crossroads at

Surrattsville. A light still burned in the tavern where they found John Lloyd alone, and drunk. Here they collected one Spencer carbine (Booth left another rifle behind so that he might travel faster), one cartridge box, field-glasses, and a bottle of whisky to ease the stabbing pain from Wilkes's leg. The pain was now so severe that Booth was convinced his leg was broken and in need of urgent medical attention. His anxiety compelled him to change his escape route which would have taken him eighteen miles directly south to Port Tobacco, across the Potomac to Virginia. Instead, he headed for the home of Dr. Samuel Mudd near Bryantown, about seventeen miles to the south-east, a deviation costing them at least an extra hour.

It was after 4 a.m. when they reached the isolated five-hundred acre farm of Dr. Mudd. The retired doctor was a former slave owner and a conservative supporter of the South, but Booth did not trust the man. He had met him the previous winter, when he had explored the area posing as a horse trader and a farm buyer, and he had actually spent a night under his roof. He had found the middle-aged doctor too rational and too practical a man to be attracted by his 'romantic' enterprises. Booth judged that Mudd might well betray him if he learned that he had shot Lincoln, so he took the precaution of using false whiskers and make-up to disguise himself as an old man. His aim was to be away quickly from the doctor's house and to reach Port Tobacco by 7.30 a.m., then crossing to a hero's welcome in Virginia.

The forty-year-old doctor was brought from his bed by the hammerings of Herold, who explained that his elderly companion had fallen from his horse as they rode to Washington. Booth, his face half covered by a huge muffler, was helped inside the farm-house; there, working by candlelight, the doctor made a ten-inch cut in the leather boot on the actor's left leg. He found a simple fracture of the tibia almost two inches above the ankle, applied a home-made splint, and suggested that the 'old man' would be well advised to rest a few hours. Booth, who was now complaining of a pain in his back and difficulty with his breathing, readily accepted. He felt incapable of travelling further that night. While Lincoln's assassin rested on a bed, Herold was invited to join the doctor for an early breakfast. He gave his name as Henston and Booth's as Mr. Tyser,[1] and later he aroused his host's suspicions by asking to borrow a razor for his friend. Mudd was surprised that the heavily bearded old man upstairs should have need of a cut-throat, but he provided the razor (Booth used it to shave off his real moustache) and then left to start another day's farming. Meanwhile the assassin slept soundly upstairs, and Herold dozed in a chair below.

It was noon before Booth awoke. He was then given a crude pair of crutches and left alone while Dr. Mudd rode with Herold over to his father's house to see if they could borrow a carriage for the injured man. When they were unsuccessful there, Herold rode on to Bryantown before returning to the farm and the doctor left him to visit a neighbour. It is uncertain whether Dr. Mudd had by this time recognised his patient as being his former visitor, John Wilkes Booth. But his suspicions were certainly aroused when he returned home that afternoon, for his wife then told him that she had seen the old man's beard slip out of place as he came downstairs. According to the doctor's sworn statement, made on April 22, he returned home that Saturday afternoon to find that the two strangers were preparing to leave. His patient insisted on paying a fee of twenty-five dollars and the two men left soon after four o'clock. He did not see them go and was surprised that the old man was intent on travelling so soon. Why did they make such a sudden departure? Most probably it was prompted by Herold's discovery that Federal soldiers were in Bryantown searching for Booth.

The fugitives, now forced to go into hiding, headed for the nearby Zekiah Swamps, a stretch of marshland divided by a stream that ran south into the Potomac. They took both horses, but only Herold mounted at first. Booth could not face the

1. In a later statement Dr Mudd was not certain whether the name was Tyser or Tyler.

jogging and hobbled behind on crutches, but when his crude sticks sunk deeper and deeper into the slimy mud he was compelled to face the discomforts of the saddle. Thus, while thousands of soldiers and police searched for him far and wide, Lincoln's assassin floundered in swampland, not thirty miles from Washington city. They were desperate men now, hunted like wild and dangerous animals, and their flight was still severely restricted by Booth's broken leg. The pain was as bad as ever; he urgently needed food and rest. Then they had a lucky break: in the marshland Herold found a backwoods Negro, one Oswald Swann, who was able to guide them to the home of Captain Samuel Cox, a plantation owner, whom, they had been told by John Surratt, had often put up Confederate couriers for the night. Swann was also able to bring them bread and ham.

About 9 p.m., Swann brought them to a large white house surrounded by outbuildings. Dogs barked and a thick-set Southern gentleman of forty-five came to the door in his nightshirt. To Booth's surprise, Cox displayed no marked enthusiasm for sheltering Lincoln's assassin; the unwelcome visitors had to hide in a nearby tobacco patch surrounded by a thicket and wait there on the understanding that Cox's foster brother, Mr. Thomas A. Jones, would eventually find them a boat for crossing the Potomac. Thus, for the first time in his life, Booth had to spend a night outdoors, rolled up in a blanket and lying on damp ground. By one senseless act he had played into the hands of Northern politicians who sought vengeance on the South, and never again would he receive the Southern hospitality which he had so firmly expected.

On Easter Sunday, Booth awoke with cramp and cold, his blanket heavy with dew, his leg still aching. He badly wanted a drink and, as he lay there, he might well have recalled a line from *Our American Cousin*—'I shall die if I don't have a drop of brandy, yes, brandy.' The pampered actor had no stomach for such extreme discomforts. But for catching his spur in that damned Yankee flag he would have been safely into Virginia by now;

instead, he was rotting in the open, about seven miles from Bryantown, with no guarantee of help or escape. He was becoming feverish. Another day and another night went by. On Monday, Jones brought a blanket, whisky, food and newspapers, and Booth searched in vain for his letter to the *National Intelligencer*. There was not even a mention of the motives he had explained; nor was there a report of an attack on Andrew Johnson, not even an obituary for the Secretary of State. Atzerodt, Paine, Matthews . . . it seemed that they had all failed him. He alone had succeeded on that fateful Good Friday night.

For five days and six nights the fugitives were destined to hide out near Cox's house. At one time Union soldiers came so near that they were prompted to destroy their horses lest they gave their position away. Herold was given the unsavoury task of leading them to a bog and shooting them. During the long wait Booth could read in the newspapers of the great manhunt, of the huge rewards offered for his capture, dead or alive. On Wednesday, Jones told him that he had met a detective in Port Tobacco who was offering one hundred thousand dollars for information leading to the assassin's arrest. From the description given to him, Booth recognised the officer as being Captain Williams—the policeman he had met outside Ford's only a few minutes before the assassination.

To pass the idle hours, Booth now began to make entries in his old, 1864 diary. He found a page blank except for the words '*Te amo*' and below he wrote: 'April 13, 14, Friday the Ides. Until today nothing was ever thought of sacrificing to our country's wrongs. For six months we had worked to capture. But our cause being almost lost, something decisive and great must be done. But its failure was owing to others, who did not strike for their country with a heart. I struck boldly and not as the papers say.' (The newspapers had described the assassination as a cowardly crime, in which the victim had been struck down from behind, without warning.)

'I walked with a firm step through a thousand of his friends, was stopped, but pushed on. A colonel was at his side. I shouted "*Sic semper*" before I fired. In jumping broke my leg. I passed all his pickets. Rode sixty miles that night, with the bone of my leg tearing at every jump.' (Even now, having committed the greatest crime of the century, the vain Booth was instinctively compelled to magnify details.)

Booth wrote on: 'I can never repent it, though we hated to kill. Our country owed all her troubles to him, and God simply made me the instrument of His punishment. The country is not what it was. This forced Union is not what I have loved. I care not what becomes of me. I have no desire to outlive my country. . . .'

On Thursday, April 20, Jones brought newspapers again. By now Booth could read of the arrest of Mrs. Surratt, Paine, Arnold and O'Laughlin, and of Lincoln's great funeral. He knew that he was the most hated man in the country, and, with every hour, he felt the danger of his position was increasing. They would have to move tonight. Jones was persuaded to bring an old mare for Booth to ride, and in darkness they reached a small boat hidden in weeds at the river's edge. But again their plans were thwarted. No sooner had they moved away from the shore than they sighted a gunboat and hastily turned back. The rest of the night was spent in hiding near Jones's own farmhouse. He could not risk taking the fugitives inside; his Negro servants would tear them to pieces if they discovered that one was the killer of 'Father Abraham'.

With daylight on Friday, April 21, Booth could see the gunboat through his field-glasses. He planned another attempt at a night crossing, but this time Jones refused to risk going with them. They faced another long day's wait and Booth recorded in his diary: 'After being hunted like a dog through swamps and woods, and last night being chased by gunboats till I was forced to return, wet, cold and starving, with every man's hand against me, I am here in despair. And why? For doing what Brutus was honoured for—what made William Tell a hero; and yet I, for striking down an even greater tyrant than they ever knew, am looked upon as a common cut-throat. My act was purer than either of theirs. One hoped to be great himself; the other had not only his country's but his own wrongs to avenge. I hoped for no gain; I knew no private wrong. I struck for my country, and her alone. A people ground beneath this tyranny prayed for this end, and yet now see the cold hands they extend to me! I cannot see any wrong, except in serving a degenerate people. The little, the very little, I left behind to clear my name, the Government will not allow to be printed. So ends all! For my country I have given up all that makes life sweet and holy—tonight misfortune upon my family, and am sure there is no pardon for me in the heavens, since man condemns me so. I have only heard of what has been done (except what I did myself), and it fills me with horror. God, try and forgive me and bless my mother. Tonight I will once more try the river, with the intention to cross; though I have a greater desire and almost a mind to return to Washington, and in a measure clear my name, which I feel I can do.

'I do not repent the blow I struck. I may before my God, but not to man. I think I have done well, though I am abandoned, with the curse of Cain upon me, when, if the world knew my heart, that one blow would have made me great, though I did desire no greatness. Tonight I try once more to escape these bloodhounds. Who, who, can read his fate? God's will be done. I have too great a soul to die like a criminal. Oh! may He spare me that, and let me die bravely. I bless the entire world. I have never hated nor wronged anyone. This last was not a wrong, unless God deems it so, and it is with Him to damn or bless me. And for this brave boy, Herold, here with me, who often prays (yes, before and since) with a true and sincere heart, was it a crime in him? If so, why can he pray the same? I do not wish to shed a drop of blood, but I must fight the course. 'Tis all that's left me.'

The gunboat had moved away by nightfall. Jones advised the conspirators to cross to Machadoc Creek and get in touch with a Mrs. Quesenberry who, in turn, would tell them how to find his brother-in-law, Thomas Hardin. Farmer Jones, who might have collected 100,000 dollars for betraying Booth, was paid eighteen dollars for his invaluable services; then the fugitives rowed out into the darkness of the Potomac, with only Booth's pocket compass to guide them. It was just one week since they had escaped from Washington.

Early Saturday morning they landed at a strange inlet which, after a scouting trip, Herold identified as Nanjemoy Creek in Maryland. They had drifted so far off course that they had simply crossed the great mouth of the Port Tobacco River and were now still further from their intended escape route. But Herold had once hunted ducks in the area and he knew a Colonel Hughes who lived nearby. He called alone at the Colonel's house and returned with food and whisky, and the advice that the outgoing tide after midnight should carry them to Machadoc Creek. This time they at last crossed the Potomac to Virginia. After eight days on the run, Booth was out of his native state of Maryland and on Confederate soil. Though they had landed north of Machadoc Creek, they were still in easy reach of Mrs. Quesenberry's house. This lady was much too frightened to help them, but through her daughter they learned of a Mr. Bryant who lived nearby and might be sympathetic to their cause. Bryant, a shabby, struggling farmer who lived in a run-down shack with a Negress house-keeper, was certainly sympathetic when the assassin, introduced as a wounded Confederate soldier seeking to avoid Federal forces, offered to pay for any help he could be given. Booth again wanted medical attention and he paid the farmer ten dollars to take them to the nearest doctor's house, some eight miles away.

After nightfall late on Sunday, April 23, they reached the home of a Dr. Richard H. Stewart. He provided food, but he could do no more for Booth's leg than advise complete rest for a couple of weeks. Then, at the doctor's suggestion, they spent the night at the cabin of William Lucas, a Negro freedman. To have had to ask for the aid of a 'nigger' would have been the final indignity for John Wilkes Booth, self-appointed protector of the slave-owning aristocracy. He did not request accommodation from Lucas; he demanded it—at knife point. The Negro and his wife were turned out of their shack and ordered to have a team of horses ready in the morning to take them to Port Conway.

Mid-morning on the Monday, Booth and Herold arrived at this small town and headed directly for the ferry wharf on the shore of the River Rappahannock. William Rollins, owner of the ferry, explained that the tide was too low for a crossing and, while they waited in Lucas's wagon, three more ferry passengers arrived—dressed in Confederate grey. Headstrong Davy Herold was delighted to see the soldiers. He ran to meet them and, abandoning all discretion, told them the true identity of his famous companion who had previously posed as Mr. John William Boyd, Confederate soldier. He proudly announced 'We are the assassinators of the President.' Fortunately for Booth, these young men—Lieutenant Mortimer B. Ruggles, Lieutenant A. R. Bainbridge and Captain William S. Jett—were hardened guerillas who had served with Mosby's Rangers, one of the most daring of Confederate Army groups, and who were not afraid to help such desperate fugitives. After they had crossed the river, Ruggles allowed Booth to ride his horse and Jett suggested that they visit a farmer who had a son in the Confederate Army and who would probably give them food and shelter.

Richard Garrett's farm, three miles south of Port Royal and tucked away off the road to Bowling Green, seemed an admirable hide-out. They could see from a distance anyone approaching by the road and there were thick woods at the back to facilitate any sudden flight. There were several outbuildings at the rear and a large old tobacco barn stood at the end of the track leading in from the road. The farmer, who had recently welcomed home his elder son Bill, was pleased to help the wounded soldier introduced to him as 'J. W. Boyd'. News of the assassination had still not reached the isolated Garrett farm. That Monday night, Booth slept on a bed, sharing a room with the two Garrett boys, Bill and Bob. Meanwhile Herold had ridden on to Bowling

Green with the soldiers so that he might buy new shoes in town. Ten days had now passed since the assassination of President Lincoln; the chief conspirator, crippled and without a horse, sought by thousands of troops, remained at large only through a remarkable succession of blunders by his pursuers.

The first official to be close on the trail of John Wilkes Booth was Major Richards of the Washington police who, at 8 a.m. on April 15, arrived with troops at John Lloyd's tavern at Surratts-ville. But Richards was soon sent off on the wrong track. Lloyd, who had once served as a policeman in the capital, held back the information that Booth and Herold had stopped there the previous night; moreover, he misguided the troops by directing them towards Piscataway instead of directly south. Meanwhile, Lieutenant David Dana and his search party had reached Piscata-way an hour before. On his own initiative, Dana sent news of the assassination to the cavalry at Chapel Point, near Port Tobacco. These soldiers were stationed almost directly on Booth's escape route. But they would not meet up with the conspirators; Dana removed that possibility when he took it upon himself to order the men to spread out and search along the shores of the Patuxent river. Then this misguided officer wired to Washington that he had reliable information that Seward's attacker was a notorious desperado named Boyle who had recently terrorised the district.

About midday, Dana arrived at Bryantown, four miles from Dr. Mudd's house where the assassin was sleeping. But he never suspected that he was hot on Booth's trail. He did not search the district immediately and most probably he only chose to stop at the town because it boasted the best hotel in the neighbour-hood. The following day Dana might have been spurred into action by information given to him by a Dr. George Mudd. This doctor explained that his cousin Samuel was suspicious of two strangers who had recently visited his farm; he had urged him to report the fact to the authorities. Dana made no effort to investigate the report that day.

Another group of searchers was equally slow to follow up Mudd's information. This was the cavalry squad, led by Lieutenant Alexander Lovett, and sent out by Provost Marshal O'Beirne on the morning of April 17. The detective chosen to direct the squad was Captain William Williams, who had spoken to Booth shortly before the assassination. Though the conspirators had a start of two and a half days, this policeman, mounted on a magnificent charger, led the cavalry over the Navy Yard Bridge with such haste that he knocked a sentry down with his horse. Unfortunately, Williams later revealed that his physical agility was not matched by quickness of mind. The squad went directly to Surrattsville, arrested tavern-keeper Lloyd, then rode on to Bryantown where they joined up with Dana's men. They learned about Dr. Mudd's story, and on Tuesday, when Booth was lying only about ten miles away on Cox's farm, the officers visited the doctor's house. Yet not until Friday, April 21, did they search the farmhouse. They were content to keep a secret watch on the house for four days in the optimistic belief that the conspirators might be tempted to come out of hiding in the swamps or that Dr. Mudd might slip out to take them food and supplies. When Lovett's men finally decided to make a search, they were given Booth's riding boot with the name 'J. Wilkes' inscribed on the inside. Immediately they arrested the unfortunate doctor.

At this time Provost Marshal O'Beirne was personally leading a search party farther south, along the shores of the Potomac. His expedition took him to Cox's farm where his men learned through a servant that food was being taken 'to persons down in the swamps'. But O'Beirne did not have enough men to follow up all the reports gathered by his detectives. Anyway, he was more interested in following the trail left by two farm labourers who had crossed the Potomac near the point where Booth was destined to cross a few days later.

On Sunday, April 23, Captain S. H. Beckwith, Grant's cipher operator, was sent out to join the search. Stanton ordered him to take soldiers to Port Tobacco and there he met O'Beirne. The

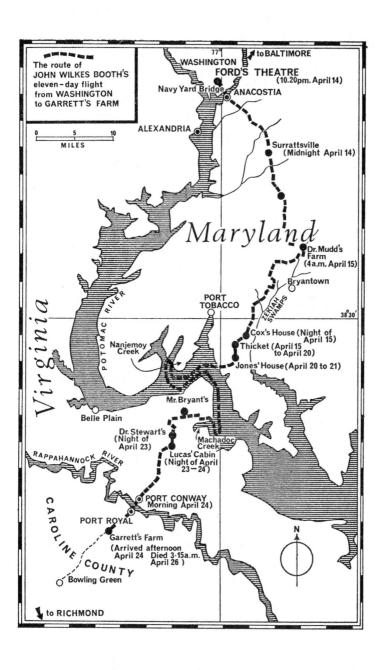

The route of
JOHN WILKES BOOTH'S
eleven-day flight
from WASHINGTON
to GARRETT'S FARM

0   5   10
MILES

77°   to BALTIMORE
WASHINGTON
FORD'S THEATRE
(10.20pm. April 14)
Navy Yard Bridge   ANACOSTIA

ALEXANDRIA

Surrattsville
(Midnight April 14)

Maryland

Dr. Mudd's
Farm
(4 a.m. April 15)

Bryantown

PORT
TOBACCO   ZEKIAH SWAMPS   38°30'

Cox's House (Night of
April 15)

POTOMAC RIVER   Thicket (April 15
to April 20)

Nanjemoy
Creek   Jones' House (April 20 to 21)

Virginia

Mr. Bryant's

Belle Plain

Dr. Stewart's
(Night of
April 23)   Machadoc
Creek

RAPPAHANNOCK RIVER   Lucas' Cabin
(Night of April
23—24)

CAROLINE   PORT CONWAY
Morning April 24)

PORT ROYAL   N

Garrett's Farm
(Arrived afternoon
April 24 Died 3·15a.m.
April 26)

COUNTY   Bowling Green

to RICHMOND

Major, who had stumbled by chance on the right track, was now eager to cross into Virginia in pursuit of the labourers he believed to be Booth and Herold. When Captain Beckwith heard his story, he promptly telegraphed a progress report to the War Department in Washington. To his great surprise, O'Beirne then received a wire from the capital ordering him to give up the pursuit and remain in Maryland. The frustrated Major followed up less fruitful clues around Bryantown and for the rest of his days claimed that he could have captured Booth but for official interference.

By a dubious coincidence, Colonel Lafayette Baker, Chief of the Detective Bureau, launched the main pursuit of Booth immediately after O'Beirne had been ordered to hold back. On Stanton's authority he applied to Major-General Hancock on April 24 for 'a small cavalry force of twenty-five men, well mounted, to be commanded by a reliable and discreet commanding officer'. Baker's twenty-five men, commanded by Lieutenant Doherty, came from the Sixteenth New York Cavalry. He put the troops under the orders of Lieutenant Luther B. Baker, his cousin, though one of his detectives, former Lieutenant-Colonel Everton J. Conger, was accorded command in respect of his senior rank. Remarkably, Lafayette Baker was able to give his cousin a most accurate briefing of where they could expect to find the conspirators. He marked a ten-mile area on the map. Within this area his men would find the President's assassin.

On the late evening of Monday, April 24, while Booth slept at the Garrett farm, the men of the Sixteenth New York Cavalry were landing at Belle Plain by boat from Washington. Without rest, they rode all night along the Virginia shore towards Port Conway. Despite the confidence of Lafayette Baker, their task seemed hopeless as they roused sleeping farmers and questioned them in vain. Locals were not especially co-operative, and a variety of wounded men who might be taken for the conspirators were moving about the countryside at the end of the war. The sleep-starved soldiers were becoming dispirited when, unexpectedly, they were given a really promising lead. Around noon, on Tuesday, April 25, they reached Port Conway and questioned ferry-owner William Rollins. He positively identified Booth and Herold from the pictures produced by the commanding officer and explained that the wanted men had crossed to Port Royal only the previous day with some Confederate soldiers. He understood they were going to Bowling Green. Rollins was persuaded to act as a guide, but he shrewdly arranged that he should appear to have been arrested so that he would not lose face with local Southern patriots. Conger's saddle-weary troops were driven hard, and they were so intent on following the Richmond road to Bowling Green that they passed the side turning to the Garrett farm without noticing it. Shortly before midnight they reached Bowling Green, surrounded the town's only hotel, and found one of the three ex-Confederate soldiers. Willie Jett was ordered out of his bed and quickly made to talk by Conger, who explained that anyone aiding the fugitives would face punishment of death. The frightened young Confederate promptly offered to lead the hunters back to the Garrett farm.

It was now eleven days since Booth had fled from Washington less than sixty miles away, and he was becoming desperately anxious to move further south. News of the assassination had reached the Garretts early that Tuesday and he had since heard that Federal soldiers were in the area. Booth had outstayed his welcome. That night he and Herold slept in the draughty, weather-beaten tobacco barn and they resolved to slip away at dawn. Conger's men arrived at 2 a.m.

The officers of this troop displayed efficiency and determination which was sadly lacking in leaders of other search parties. Six men were posted behind the tobacco barn to prevent anyone escaping into the woods; others formed a ring around the farmhouse. The soldiers were instructed to shoot only in absolute necessity. When Richard Garrett answered Baker's hammerings on the kitchen door he was roughly seized and ordered to reveal the whereabouts of Booth and Herold. Conger was standing no nonsense from this farmer who tried to explain at length that the fugitives had gone and that they had stayed at his house without his consent. 'I do not want a long story out of you,' snapped the Colonel. 'I just want to know where these men have gone.' Then, as the farmer started hedging again, Conger called out to one of his men, 'Bring in a lariat rope here, and I will put that man to the top of one of those locust trees.'

This was too much for young Bill Garrett, the farmer's son. He cried out: 'Don't hurt the old man. He's scared. I'll tell you where the men you want to find are—in the barn.'

Three sides of the tobacco barn were now covered by soldiers stationed about thirty feet away. Conger and Baker covered the front. The latter sent in the frightened Bill Garrett to bring out their firearms and persuade them to surrender, but he quickly returned after Booth had threatened to shoot him for betraying them. Now began a series of melodramatic exchanges between the hunter and the hunted: 'We'll give you just five minutes to surrender, then we'll set the barn on fire,' shouted Baker.

Booth replied: 'Captain, I know you to be a brave man, and I believe you to be honourable. I'm a cripple. I have got but one leg. If you withdraw your men in line one hundred yards from the door, I will come out and fight you.'

Baker answered that he had not come to fight, only to take him prisoner. Booth repeated his offer, this time asking the soldiers to withdraw only fifty yards. Again Baker refused. In what Conger later described as a 'singular theatrical voice', the actor called out, 'Well, my brave boys, prepare a stretcher for me.'

Booth had an audience one more time and he was playing his dramatic role to the bitter end. But Herold had no romantic dreams to comfort him. As Conger piled brush and hay against one corner of the barn, the young conspirator gave the carbine to his companion and surrendered himself to the soldiers. 'You damned coward,' said Booth. 'Will you leave me now? Go, go; I would not have you stay with me.'

Now the brush was crackling and the flames quickly enveloped a whole side of the barn. Such barns have wide spaces between the boards to allow air to circulate freely through the hanging tobacco. Booth was visible through the cracks and it was as though he were trapped in a giant wooden cage. As the soldiers closed in, Booth abandoned his carbine and took out his pistol. Then, at about 3.15 a.m., there came the explosion of a single gun shot. The assassin slumped to the floor.

What happened exactly at that time is much disputed, but the most reliable account would appear to be that given later by Conger at the conspiracy trial. The Colonel recalled: 'I put my eye up to the crack next to the one the fire was put through, and looked in, and I heard something drop on the floor, which I supposed to be Booth's crutch. He turned around towards me. When I first got a glimpse of him, he stood with his back partly to me, turning towards the front door. He came back within five feet of the corner of the barn. The only thing I noticed he had in his hands when he came was a carbine. He came back and looked along the cracks, one after another, rapidly. He could not see anything. He looked at the fire and from the expression on his face I'm satisfied he looked to see if he could put it out, and was satisfied that he couldn't do it; it was burning so much. He dropped his arm, relaxed his muscles, turned around and started for the door at the front of the barn. I ran around to the other side, and when about half round I heard the report of a pistol. I went right to the door, and went into the barn and found Lieutenant Baker looking at Booth, holding him or raising him up, I do not know which. I said to him, "He shot himself." Said he, "No, he did not, either." Said I, "Whereabouts is he shot—in the head or neck?" I raised him then, and looked on the right side of the neck, and saw a place where the blood was running out. I said, "Yes, sir; he shot himself." Lieutenant Baker replied very earnestly that he did not. I then said, "Let us carry him out of here; this will soon be burning." We took him up and carried him out on the grass, underneath the locust trees.'

Booth was still alive. After Conger had put water on his face, he mumbled, 'Tell Mother I die for my country.' Then they carried him to the porch of the farmhouse and laid him on an old feather bed. At the same time Herold was being tied to a tree only a few yards away. Booth was in great pain now. For more than two and a half hours he laboured in death, coughing blood, asking to be turned on his back, on his side, on his face, and several times begging for his captors to kill him. Towards the end he regained consciousness for only a few seconds and spoke two more words, 'Useless, useless.' He died just as the sun rose on Wednesday, April 26, the day that the last major Confederate force, under General Joe Johnston, surrendered.

Had the assassin died by his own hand? Or had a soldier disobeyed orders and fired? Conger and Baker were uncertain until a member of their troop came forward and reported: 'I did it, sir. I shot John Wilkes Booth.' The man was Sergeant Boston Corbett, who had been stationed at the rear of the barn. Why did he shoot? 'Providence, sir,' he replied. 'Providence directed me to do it. I heard the voice of God.'

7

THE CONSPIRACY TRIAL

WITH ELABORATE secrecy the body of John Wilkes Booth was buried at night beneath the stones of a cell in the Old Penitentiary Building in the grounds of the Washington Arsenal. Three floors above him, held in solitary confinement, and all but one hideously hooded and manacled, were the eight prisoners singled out to answer for his crime of the century—David Herold, Lewis Paine, George Atzerodt, Michael O'Laughlin, Samuel Arnold, Dr. Samuel Mudd, Edward Spangler and Mrs. Mary E. Surratt.

At first Booth's alleged accomplices were held on board two ironclad warships, the *Saugus* and the *Montauk*, moored near the Navy Yard. There, the seven male prisoners had their heads covered with heavy sacks which hung over the shoulders and were knotted about the neck and chest. They could not see; they could not wash their swollen faces; food had to be pushed through an air hole in front of each man's mouth. These stifling sacks were introduced on the direction of Edwin Stanton, 'for better security against conversation', and when the prisoners were moved to the Penitentiary security was even stricter. They were placed in separate cells with an empty cell between each prisoner to prevent communication through the walls. The seven men were manacled head and foot and their handcuffs were linked by a rigid iron bar. Guards, who watched them by night and day, were strictly forbidden to speak to any of them. When the trial of the conspirators was due to begin, their head-sacks were replaced by even more diabolical devices, tight-fitting hoods padded with inch-thick cotton. Dr. George Loring Porter, the Arsenal's medical officer, offered the opinion that these hoods, worn during the hot summer days, might produce mental derangement, and he believed that Stanton was persuaded to have them removed. Porter was mistaken. They may have been removed from the heads of other suspects held in the prison, but the accused conspirators continued to be hooded during the period of their trial, only having their heads uncovered while they were in the court room. By the nature of their alleged crimes, the prisoners were regarded as fiends beyond the pale of human pity. Only Mrs. Surratt was spared the ordeal of wearing a hood and rigid wrist irons; only she at first was allowed visitors—her daughter and two Catholic priests; only she commanded a measure of public sympathy.

Edwin Stanton personally conducted the investigation into the conspiracy. He worked with fanatical zeal, often throughout the night, in a determined bid to have the accused condemned and executed as swiftly as possible. To help prepare the prosecution's case, he called in Colonel H. R. Burnett, a young judge advocate who had established an excellent record for gaining the maximum penalty in trials in the West. Burnett scrupulously sought out positive proof that Booth was the assassin and he was not finally convinced until he had the evidence of the actor's left riding boot with the inscription 'J. Wilkes'. In seeking evidence against the surviving suspects, Burnett was less particular. Much of this evidence was the kind that could be gathered by the third-degree methods of Colonel Baker who, in the pursuit of conspirators, had instructed his officers 'to exhort confessions and procure testimony to establish the conspiracy . . . by promises, rewards, threats, deceit, force, or any other effectual means'. One key witness was especially eager to co-operate to save his own neck—Mrs. Surratt's old friend and boarder, Louis Weichmann, now under arrest in Carroll Prison.

Stanton aimed to demonstrate his efficiency by having the

sordid case closed within three weeks, before the late President found his resting place in Springfield. This was an impossible dream; in fact, he did well to have everything ready for the trial by the time of Lincoln's funeral on May 4. Three days earlier, President Johnson had instructed the Assistant Adjutant-General to select nine army officers to constitute the military commission. This was to provide a bitter legal controversy for years to come—whether the accused should have been tried before a military tribunal or before a civil court. The President had been assassinated at a time of civil war, when martial law operated in the District of Columbia. On the other hand, the civil courts were open at the time, and the accused were civilians. Stanton, however, had no intention of allowing the conspirators to undergo long-drawn-out trials by jury in the civil courts; he and others argued that the assassination of the Commander-in-Chief of the Army and Navy of the United States was a military crime. After long consideration Attorney-General Speed declared himself 'of the opinion that the conspirators not only may but ought to be tried by a military tribunal'. It was a decision that promised the accused far severer punishment than they might have received in a civil court.

The nine-man military commission of seven generals and two colonels not only had extremely dubious legal authority but also included several notably biased officers. Of course, it would have been impossible at such a time to have found nine soldiers of complete impartiality. On the other hand, one might have chosen members with less personal interest in the case than the presiding officer, Major-General David Hunter. This officer, who wore a dyed moustache and dark brown wig, was the escort who dislocated his collarbone while protecting President-elect Lincoln on his journey to Washington. The same General Hunter had recently stood at the head of the late President's coffin, when Lincoln lay in state on the catafalque in the East Room of the White House. He had also accompanied the late President back to Illinois, a sentimental journey of seventeen hundred miles by train, with mass demonstrations of sorrow all the way. This emotion-charged experience was scarcely designed to prepare him as an impartial judge of Lincoln's alleged murderers. The best known of the other members was General Lew Wallace, later to be famed as the author of *Ben Hur*. He was to prove an intolerant personality, firmly opposed to all the defendants, and after the trial he would be singled out by Stanton to preside over the military court which tried and condemned Captain Wirz, former commandant of the notorious Andersonville prison. Another member, Brigadier-General T. M. Morris of West Virginia, wrote about the trial many years later in a book full of inaccuracies and ill-judgments. His writings leave no doubt at all that he was a thoroughly biased and incompetent judge, who ignored historical fact and readily accepted unsubstantiated evidence. Even a quarter of a century after the trial he was stubbornly repeating details of the conspiracy which had long since been proved utterly false.

Guiding the nine army officers were swarthy Joseph Holt, the Judge Advocate General, and his assistants John A. Bingham and Colonel H. L. Burnett. Holt and Bingham would strive relentlessly, and without special concern for the truth, in seeking the death sentence for all the defendants. Their aim was to find the prisoners guilty in a mass trial on the general charge of conspiracy. In this way it would be sufficient to prove that the prisoners were involved in the abduction plot to link them with the assassination; in the same way a case might be made against Mrs. Surratt, Dr. Mudd, Arnold and O'Laughlin, even though they had alibis for the night of April 14. All eight prisoners were charged with 'maliciously, unlawfully, and traitorously, and in aid of the existing armed rebellion against the United States of America . . . combining, confederating, and conspiring together with one John H. Surratt, John Wilkes Booth, Jefferson Davis, George N. Sanders, Beverly Tucker, Jacob Thompson, William C. Cleary, Clement C. Clay, George Harper, George Young, and others unknown, to kill and murder . . . Abraham Lincoln

... Andrew Johnson ... William H. Seward ... and Ulysses S. Grant'. Other charges were specified individually.

While the defendants were prosecuted by highly experienced lawyers, they themselves had great difficulty in procuring legal aid. The trial began at ten o'clock on the morning of Tuesday, May 9, when the defendants were led into court and asked whether they wanted counsel. The commission then adjourned to the following morning to 'afford the accused opportunity to secure counsel'. Justice, however rough, had to be seen to be done; so they were finally represented, but only at the eleventh hour when there was inadequate time for the defence to prepare its case properly. Heading the defence team was the brilliant Reverdy Johnson, former U.S. Attorney-General, now Senator for Maryland, who would act for Mary Surratt. Other notable attorneys were General Thomas Ewing Jr., brother-in-law of General Sherman, and the experienced William E. Doster, former Washington Provost Marshal, and Walter S. Cox. Unfortunately, Johnson took a back seat in the proceedings. At the offset, General Harris objected to his presence and questioned his loyalty to the government. The distinguished lawyer was so badly treated by the commission that he acted only in an advisory capacity, leaving much of the work in the inexperienced hands of his juniors, Frederick Aiken and John W. Clampitt.

Cox expressed the enormous handicap under which defence counsel laboured when he spoke on behalf of O'Laughlin and Arnold. He told the commission: 'The accused and their counsel have laboured under disadvantages not incident to the civil courts, and unusual even in military courts. . . . For the most part they (the accused) were unable to procure counsel until the trial had commenced; and, when counsel were admitted, they came to the discharge of their duties in utter ignorance of the whole case which they were to combat. . . .' The defence lawyers had to appear in court, usually from 10 a.m. to 6 p.m., and then seek their own witnesses and new evidence by night. Even when the defence did discover the ill-repute of a prosecution witness (Von

Steinacker) they were unable to recall him for cross-examination. The man had conveniently disappeared. Said the Judge Advocate, 'I am perfectly willing he shall be called—if he can be found.' Equally remarkable, the court was arranged so that the witnesses had their backs or left sides to the defence counsel. Thus the perjurers did not have to face the accused as they poured out their avalanche of lies.

The scene of this farcical conspiracy trial was a gas-lit room about forty-five feet by thirty, adjoining the prisoners' cells on the third floor of the Penitentiary. Iron gratings barred the four windows; the walls were newly whitewashed and the floor covered with coconut matting. The nine officers of the commission, all staunch Republicans, sat at a long, green-topped table, with the Judge Advocate and his assistants at an adjoining table. In front of them, at the centre of the room, was the witness stand, and on the opposite wall of the room a table for reporters. The prisoners' dock stretched along the wall to the commissioners' right; defence counsel sat at tables in front of the dock.

As the result of loud protests by the Press, the first plan to hold the trial in camera was abandoned. Reporters and visitors with special passes were admitted to the sessions, and it became the fashionable 'thing' in Washington society to have visited the historic scene. Townsend of the *New York World* wrote: 'A perfect park of carriages stands by the door to the left and from these dismount major-generals' wives in rustling silks, daughters of congressmen attired like the lilies of the milliner, little girls who hope to be young ladies and have come up with "Pa" to look at the assassins; even brides are here, in the fresh blush of their nuptials . . . they chatter and smile and go up the three flights of stairs to the courtroom, about as large as an ordinary town-house parlour.'

It was not a pretty scene that the elegant young ladies witnessed. A macabre, unforgettable moment came with the opening of the iron door leading from the cells to the court room. The sound of rattling chains drew nearer. Then they emerged into the light of day—seven shuffling figures with padded hoods gruesomely covering their heads. There was something horribly unreal about this picture—a nightmare transformed to complete reality as the pathetic prisoners, once seated, had their hoods removed and their tired eyes suddenly and cruelly exposed to the brilliant sunlight. One last prisoner came unhooded but no less pathetic—the harmless-looking widow, Mary Eugenia Jenkins Surratt, whose chains clanked beneath her skirts as she shuffled towards the railed platform to take her place alongside the seven dishevelled men. Though she was veiled rather than hooded, the ordeal would be no less for her. The poor woman had the added infliction of internal disorders relating to the 'change of life', and was really too distressed to face the trial.

Mrs. Surratt, whose hands were free, and Dr. Mudd, who wore ordinary chain handcuffs, were the only prisoners who did not have their hands linked by thick, ten-inch-long iron bars. Paine and Atzerodt had their feet chained to iron weights (said to be 75 lb.) that were so heavy that two guards were required to lift one of them; the others wore steel anklets linked by chains. This procession of outcasts, chained like wild animals, sat along one wall on a railed platform. With a guard between each prisoner, they took their places in the order: Arnold, Mudd, Spangler, O'Laughlin, Atzerotd, Paine, Herold, Mrs. Surratt. Of these, only one sat upright and defiant during the trial—the disciplined gladiator, Lewis Paine. He saw himself as a loyal Confederate soldier who had bravely done his duty. The rest were broken remnants of very ordinary citizens who had been brought to this place by the fame-seeking actor they once proudly called a friend.

It was an altogether distasteful scene, for as these miserable figures sat dishevelled and frightened, on trial for their lives, the various army officers of the court, all smartly dressed in full uniform, lounged casually in their chairs, in a manner neither becoming their military nor judicial roles. But then this was only an elaborate sham of a civilised trial. During these proceedings twelve objections raised by the defence were to be overruled, while only three of fifty-four objections from the other side would be similarly treated. It proved a fair indication of the leanings of the court.

A major part of the trial was devoted to demonstrating that Jefferson Davis and other Confederate leaders were directly implicated in the assassination plot. Late in April, Stanton had publicly declared that the plot had originated in Canada and been approved in Richmond. On May 3, a Presidential proclamation had announced the connivance of Jefferson Davis, Jacob Thompson, Clement C. Clay and other Southerners. There was a price of 100,000 dollars on Davis's head. The court, operating in an atmosphere of post-war hysteria, now sincerely believed that the Confederate government was behind the conspiracy, and the prosecution took a Machiavellian approach in attempting to prove it. They began by dragging out gory details of wartime atrocities to show that kidnapping and assassination were not crimes foreign to the Southern leaders; they produced letters and documents of dubious origin, and a procession of perjurers; they sought to connect Confederate guerilla warfare with Lincoln's murder. The first witness for the prosecution was a professional spy and a convicted thief, Richard Montgomery, who claimed that in his contacts with Jacob Thompson, the Confederacy's Canadian agent, he had heard of proposals to assassinate Lincoln, Stanton, Grant and other Union leaders. Thompson had refrained from approving such a plot until he was advised by the leaders in Richmond. Another witness, Dr. James B. Merritt of Windsor, Canada, had also heard talk of a plot to assassinate the President. He was a man of equally bad reputation and his testimony was shown to be completely false. As a witness the prosecution even called a pedlar, Samuel Jones, who claimed he had heard Confederate soldiers in Richmond discussing a plan to kill Lincoln. This man was blind. Next came an even more unreliable witness who went under the name of Henry von Steinacker. He was a horse thief and convicted deserter, who had been dishonourably discharged from the U.S. Army and later court martialled by the Confederates.

No solid evidence was produced to connect Confederate leaders with the assassination. But Davis was inevitably presumed guilty, though later a re-examination of his case by the judiciary committee of the House of Representatives would expose the perjury of several witnesses. On this occasion the witnesses were thoroughly cross-examined and it was found that one of them, Sandford Conover, had run a veritable school for perjurers at the National Hotel (where Booth had boarded), inventing testimony and then rehearsing it with various witnesses. This remarkable rogue was later captured and sentenced to ten years' imprisonment.

Having fanned the atmosphere of hatred and bitterness by recalling irrelevant war atrocities, the prosecution presented its evidence against the eight accused. Besides the general charge of conspiracy, the prisoners faced specific charges. Spangler was accused of having assisted Booth to enter the presidential box and bar the outer door leading to the box, and of having aided his escape after the murder. Atzerodt was charged with lying-in-wait with intent to kill Vice-President Johnson, O'Laughlin with lying-in-wait to kill General Grant. Mrs. Surratt and Dr. Mudd were both accused of receiving, harbouring, concealing and aiding the conspirators, with knowledge of the assassination plot. General Ewing sought in vain to convince the court that the general charge of conspiracy was contrary to accepted legal practice, that it should be made clear whether the prisoners were charged with conspiracy, murder, attempted murder, lying-in-wait—or all four offences. Bingham replied that all these crimes were embraced 'under the common law of war'.

Among the weird assortment of witnesses paraded before the military commission, none presents quite such a pitiable figure as Louis Weichmann, the flabby, self-confessed coward, who provided damning testimony in the trials of the widow Surratt and the country doctor Samuel Mudd. Weichmann was not a wicked man; witnesses averred that he was of good character, honest, truthful and moral. Yet in his way he was to be despised even more than the professional perjurers. For Weichmann, out of fear and self-interest, betrayed the 'mother' who, in his own words, had treated him like her own son. It would be less than just to presume that he intended to condemn Mrs. Surratt. He told the commission: 'During the whole time I have known her, her character, as far as I could judge, was exemplary and lady-like in every particular, and her conduct, in a religious and moral sense, altogether exemplary.' Nor can one say with certainty that he lied on the witness stand. Sometimes, however, the innocent can be hurt more by truths than by lies, more by insinuation than by accusation.

Weichmann was the perfect witness for the prosecution. He was a man of respectable position, a clerk in the office of the Commissary-General of Prisoners. He had known John Surratt since his youth when they were both students of divinity at St. Charles College, Maryland. He was intimately acquainted with most of the conspirators, and, with hypocritical zeal for duty, he had reported to police headquarters soon after the assassination and talked for hours about Booth and his friends at the Surratt boarding house. Weichmann, who might easily have found himself on trial with the alleged conspirators, was ready to drag anyone down in his desperation. Two years later, at the trial of John Surratt, he admitted, 'I always look out for self-interest.' He also said then that a statement had been prepared for him before the conspiracy trial and he was threatened with prosecution as a conspirator if he did not sign.

Before the military commission, Weichmann steadily weakened Mrs. Surratt's position by his suggestive statements. He explained that the widow 'would sometimes leave the parlour on being asked by Booth to spare him a word. She would then go into the passage and talk with him.' He told how, on April 11, Booth gave him ten dollars so that he might hire a carriage to take Mrs. Surratt to Surrattsville. Though the actor was well known among his friends for such generosity, the jury interpreted this as an indication that she did not make the journey merely to conduct her own business. Weichmann hardly changed this impression when he remarked, 'I thought at the time that it was nothing more than an act of friendship.' Then, in an affidavit by Weichmann after the trial, he stated that when police came to her house after the assassination, Mrs. Surratt said: 'For God's sake, let them come in. I expected the house to be searched. . . .'

But it was not Weichmann's words that sent Mrs. Surratt to the gallows; it was the testimony of the besotted tavern-keeper and former Washington policeman, John Lloyd. This notorious drunkard had been brought into the conspiracy shortly before the abortive attempt to seize Lincoln in his carriage en route for the Soldiers' Home. John Surratt persuaded him to store two army carbines, ammunition, some rope and a monkey wrench at his tavern; he showed him a suitable hiding place and said he would call for the equipment in a few days. Yet Lloyd, far guiltier of aiding Booth than either Spangler or Mudd, was never prosecuted. His evidence was needed to condemn the middle-aged widow who, for some strange motive, the authorities were determined to have convicted.

Lloyd's damning evidence concerned the widow's two journeys to Surrattsville, the tiny settlement which had been named after its postmaster, the late Mr. Surratt. On April 11, Weichmann drove her there for the purpose of trying to collect a long-standing debt from landowner John Nothey. On the road, she chanced to meet Lloyd and, according to the tavern-keeper, she asked him about the 'shooting-irons'. He testified, 'She told me to get them out ready, that they would be wanted soon.' Weichmann did not support this evidence; nor did he challenge it. Though he had been sitting next to the widow at the time, he said he had not heard her soft-spoken words. If the experienced Reverdy Johnson had not withdrawn into the background, and left most of Mrs. Surratt's defence in the hands of juniors Aiken and Clampitt, this evidence might have been more strongly challenged.

On the morning of Good Friday, both Mrs. Surratt and Weichmann attended Roman Catholic church services, and in the afternoon they again set out for Surrattsville to seek Mr. Nothey. They called at the tavern since the widow was to deliver Booth's package (containing field-glasses) to Lloyd. About 5 p.m. Lloyd arrived home much the worse for drink from a visit to Marlboro. He testified, 'She told me to have those shooting-irons ready that night; there would be some parties who would call for them.' Mrs. Surratt claimed that she talked to him about nothing more sinister than fish and oysters which the tavern-keeper had brought back in his buggy. But Lloyd stuck, somewhat vaguely, to his story. 'I'm cofident that she named the shooting-irons on both occasions; not so positive about the first as I am about the last; I know she did on the last occasion.'

No civil court would have convicted her on this unsupported evidence of a drunkard. But the commission readily accepted Lloyd's flimsy testimony. Bingham attacked Mrs. Surratt as the woman whose house was the headquarters of the conspirators, who was regularly visited by Booth, who was visited by Paine when he sought refuge, who had a picture of Jefferson Davis in her house. Much was made of the fact that Mrs. Surratt told a detective that she had never seen Paine in her life before. But the man she was asked to identify was posing as a labourer, dressed in a shabby grey coat, black pantaloons and boots, with a ridiculous grey shirt sleeve wrapped around his head. Mrs. Surratt, who was shown to have defective eyesight, only knew the visitor as Mr. Wood, a Baptist preacher with clerical collar. Moreover, one boarder, Honora Fitzpatrick, also failed to recognise Paine at first—'but I did at General Augur's office when the skull cap was taken off his head'.

It was generally expected that Mrs. Surratt would be sentenced to imprisonment, never that she would be sentenced to death. She herself was assured by her legal counsel and her daughter that imprisonment would be her worst fate. When the widow learned that her hopes had been falsely raised, she collapsed and was semi-delirious until she died.

In his testimony relating to Mary Surratt, Weichmann not only helped to seal the widow's fate, but also seriously handicapped the defence of Dr. Samuel Mudd. Describing his acquaintance with the Surratt family, he recalled that about January 15 he was walking down Washington's Seventh Street with John Surratt when they met the doctor in company with Booth. Mudd introduced Booth to Surratt and they all went to the actor's hotel room to have cigars and wine. 'Dr. Mudd then went out into the passage and called Booth out, and had a private conversation with him. When they returned, Booth called Surratt, and all three went out together and had a private conversation, leaving me alone. I did not hear the conversation. . . . Afterward they were seated round the centre table, when Booth took out an envelope, and on the back of it made marks with a pencil. I should not consider it writing, but from the motion of the pencil it was more like roads or lines.'

Both Booth and Mudd explained to Weichmann that they had been discussing the possible purchase of the doctor's farm. During the trial Bingham chose a much more sinister interpretation of the meeting. He described it as a conspiracy conference. On the other hand, Mudd's counsel, General Thomas Ewing Jr., claimed to 'have proved, beyond all controversy, that Dr. Mudd was not in Washington from the 23rd of December to the 23rd of March'. There was no doubt, however, that Mudd and Booth had met before the assassination. On the doctor's own admission, he was introduced to the actor in November or December of 1864 by a neighbour, Mr. J. C. Thompson. Booth was then posing as a prospective land buyer.

Had the doctor recognised Booth on the morning of April 15 when the actor arrived in an old man's guise? This inevitably became the most disputed point at his trial. Dr. Mudd, it should be stressed, had done much to damage his own position by contradicting himself several times in his statements to investigating officers and giving the impression that he had something to hide. Two detectives who called at his house swore that he denied any strangers had stayed at his farm. A third officer, Lieutenant Lovett, said he 'did not at first seem inclined to give us any satisfaction'. Colonel H. H. Wells, the first witness for the prosecution, testified that during the week after the assassination he showed the doctor a photograph of Booth, and Mudd said he could not recognise him from the picture. This was scarcely any wonder. The photograph was of John Wilkes' brother, Edwin. No one revealed this extraordinary error at the trial and the photograph duly passed into the files.

The prosecution was not concerned in seeking the truth, only in securing a conviction. A vital point for the defence was that the doctor had seen his cousin, Dr. George Mudd, at church at 11.30 a.m. on Sunday, April 16, and that he had urged him to report to the authorities his suspicions about the strangers who had visited his farm. But when Ewing asked Cousin George whether Dr. Mudd had said anything to him about persons at his house, the Judge Advocate promptly objected—and the commission sustained the objection. Only through the long and persistent efforts of Ewing was this story finally introduced as evidence. This testimony, however, did nothing to explain Dr. Mudd's delay in reporting his suspicions which were allegedly aroused on Saturday afternoon when his wife told him she had seen the old man adjust his whiskers. Ewing remarked that this delay was responsible in no small part for the doctor's arrest, but he fairly argued that the doctor was more prompt in passing on his information than the detectives were in acting upon it. Why did he delay? Mrs. Mudd claimed that he had been eager to go to Bryantown at once but that she had begged him not to leave her alone in the house that Saturday evening. The locals at this time still lived in fear of raids by the bandit Boyle who had recently terrorised the district and was believed to be one of the hunted assassins.

General Ewing made nonsense of much of the prosecution's

case. Referring to Weichmann's unsupported testimony, he pointed out that the doctor was unlikely to discuss a murder plot with a man he had met only a few minutes before. Mudd's residence was off the escape route to Port Tobacco and Booth only went there because of his accidental injury. The doctor would scarcely have exposed his old father to suspicion by borrowing his carriage if he had known it was wanted for the President's assassin. It was absurd that he should deny to detectives that strangers had visited his house when the officers had been indirectly summoned by him. As for the riding boot which bore the inscription 'J. Wilkes', this was found several days later by Mrs. Mudd and then the doctor had voluntarily produced it for the detectives.

But there could be no escape for this respectable country practitioner and farmer, who was accused of having prior knowledge of the crime, of having harboured the fugitives and aided their escape. As George A. Townsend wrote in the *New York World*, 'The military commission works as if it were delegated not to try, but to convict, and Dr. Mudd, if he be innocent, is in only less danger than if he were guilty.' The doctor was sentenced to hard labour for life.

In the defence of Lewis Thornton Powell (alias Paine, Wood, Moseby, etc.), the eloquent William E. Doster made a bold attempt to support a plea of insanity on behalf of a savage killer who had crazily attacked the entire Seward household, who had run into the street screaming, 'I'm mad,' who had stupidly returned to the Surratt house, who had tried to commit suicide by crashing his head against an iron wall of the monitor *Saugus*, who had displayed complete indifference throughout his trial and expressed a wish to die. In his final argument, Doster movingly described the tragic background of Powell, the son of a Baptist minister, who had been sent to war at the age of sixteen. He had lost his two brothers in the conflict, had been wounded at Gettysburg, and had become so unbalanced through his battle experiences that he once brutally attacked a coloured maidservant in

Baltimore. 'We now know that slavery made him immoral, that war made him a murderer, and that necessity, revenge and delusion made him an assassin.'

There could be no plea other than insanity. In court, Powell was identified as Seward's assailant by the coloured boy William Bell (the accused laughed as the young servant pointed him out), by nurse Sergeant Robinson, and by Major Augustus Seward. Doster called a mental health expert who had examined Powell and found that the prisoner's past actions, inert mind, high pulse rate and chronic constipation provided reasonable ground for suspicion of insanity. But the prosecution could line up heavier artillery on this front, most notably Surgeon-General J. K. Barnes, who had attended the President in his final hours. Barnes found 'no evidence of insanity—none whatever'. Doster conceded defeat on this issue, but he went to remarkable limits in making a passionate plea for mercy. 'In spite of the odious crime with which he is charged, I have formed an estimate of him little short of admiration, for his honesty of purpose, freedom from deception and malice, and courageous resolution to abide by the principles to which he was reared.' Doster, who loved spouting quotations, even ventured to apply to him the words said of Brutus:

> *'This was the noblest Roman of them all.*
> *All the conspirators, save only he,*
> *Did that they did in envy of great Caesar;*
> *He only, in a general honest thought,*
> *And common good to all, made one of them.*
> *His life was gentle, and the elements*
> *So mixed in him, that nature might stand up*
> *And say to all the world, "This was a man!"'*

David E. Herold was defended as a simple-minded boy who had been led astray. Witnesses described him as 'trifling . . . temperate . . . easily persuaded . . . more like a boy than a man'.

Three witnesses separately used the word 'trifling' to describe him, and Dr. Samuel A. H. McKim, who had known the prisoner well for six years, stated, 'In mind, I consider him about eleven years of age.' But for a simpleton Herold showed remarkable good sense in the way he claimed he was out of Washington at the time of Lincoln's assassination. Herold's story—the best possible in the circumstances—was that he had left the city at 8 p.m. on Good Friday in the hope of selling a horse in Maryland. He had met Booth on his homeward journey and was persuaded to accompany him on a trip to Bryantown where they would join a hunting party. Later he had discovered what Booth had done and only stayed with him because his life was threatened. There was one major flaw in this story. Stableman John Fletcher had seen Herold in Washington much later that night. This identification, however, was made in poor light and from a distance; a sharp defence attorney might have argued that Fletcher recognised his horse rather than the rider. As for Sergeant Cobb, he was unable to identify Herold as the second rider he had stopped at the Navy Yard Bridge after 10.30 p.m. But no effort was made to break down the stableman's testimony. Frederick Stone, defending Herold, tackled his task with a notable lack of enthusiasm, indeed almost apologetically. Herold was one prisoner certain to be condemned to death from the start.

The conviction of George Atzerodt (alias Andrew Atwood), coachmaker of Port Tobacco, was also a foregone conclusion. There was overwhelming evidence to show his connection with the kidnap plot and to suggest that he lay in wait to kill the Vice-President. Weapons had been found in his hotel room together with personal effects belonging to Booth and Herold. Witnesses testified that he had asked numerous questions about Andrew Johnson. Moreover, this little man, paralysed with fear, had readily confessed that he had agreed to help kidnap the President; that he had had knowledge of the assassination plot several hours before it was perpetrated, though he had flatly refused to take any part in it. Witnesses were called for the defence to affirm that Atzerodt was a 'notorious coward' and once again defence counsel Doster gushed forth with his familiar rhetoric:

'Why, gentlemen, this hero, who, under the influence of cocktail courage, would capture Presidents and change the destinies of empires, is the same fleet-footed Quaker, famous in Port Tobacco for jumping out of windows in bar-room fights; an excellent leader—of panic, this son of arms who buries his knife in a gutter and revolves his revolvers into a greenback. Well might it have been said to Booth:

> "O Cassius, you are yoked with a lamb
> That carries anger as the flint bears fire;
> Who, much enforced, shows a hasty spark,
> And straight is cold again." '

Besides the general indictment of conspiracy, Michael O'Laughlin faced a most curious charge: that on the nights of April 13 and 14 he did 'lie in wait . . . with the intent, then and there, to kill and murder the said Ulysses S. Grant'. But even with three reputable witnesses the prosecution failed to make this one stick. On the evening of April 13 Grant was being entertained at the Stantons' home, and a large crowd was gathered outside to serenade the conquering hero. According to the testimony of the War Secretary's son and of a Major Kilburn Knox, a stranger came to the door at 10.30 p.m. and asked for the War Minister. They judged the man to be intoxicated and after a short while the stranger left. Sergeant John C. Hatter, who was on duty at the house, also recollected a stranger calling—'at about nine o'clock'—and asking if Grant was there. Young Stanton, Knox and Hatter all identified O'Laughlin as being the stranger. Stanton first identified the accused on board a monitor when he had 'an indistinct view of him' in semi-darkness. Knox was 'pretty certain' that the prisoner was the man. Yet the defence was able to produce half a dozen witnesses, including James

In addition to Mrs. Surratt these men were sentenced to death: *right*, Lewis Paine; *bottom left*, David Herold; *bottom right*, George Atzerodt

Edwin McMasters Stanton, subject of the allegations found by Mr. Ray Neff in a second-hand book

General Lafayette Baker. His death was shrouded with the suspicion of murder

Henderson, an ensign in the U.S. Navy, who could give a detailed account of O'Laughlin's movements on both April 13 and 14. The Irishman had not been near Stanton's house. Assistant Judge Advocate John Bingham argued stubbornly, 'No man who reads their testimony can determine satisfactorily all the places that were visited by O'Laughlin and his drunken associates that evening from seven to eleven.' But for once the prosecution's case was looking exceedingly weak. And defence counsel Walter S. Cox raised a most intriguing question when he remarked, 'Why the Government, with this information, did not charge the lying-in-wait to have been for Secretary Stanton, is a matter of astonishment.' The prosecution also failed to show that O'Laughlin could have been on Grant's train leaving Washington on April 14. Possibly a would-be assassin was on the train, for long afterwards it was revealed that Grant had received an anonymous letter in which the writer said he had been on the train to kill the General but had been unable to reach him since the door to his private car was locked. But that man could not have been Michael O'Laughlin.

Yet this liquor-loving Irishman did not escape the wrath of the commission. It was his misfortune to have been in Washington on the day of the assassination, enjoying a drinking spree. More unfortunately, he had attempted to communicate with Booth at the National Hotel on April 13 and April 14. O'Laughlin had withdrawn from the great kidnap plot after the failure of March 20, but that association was enough to condemn him. He was found not guilty of lying in wait for Grant, but guilty on the vague charge of conspiracy. He was sentenced 'to be imprisoned at hard labour for life, at such place as the President shall direct'.

The same sentence was passed on Samuel Arnold, who, like O'Laughlin, was clearly involved in the original abduction plot, but who had a cast-iron alibi for the time of the assassination. Arnold was out of Washington for several weeks before Lincoln's murder. In mid-March, at the oyster dinner for the conspirators, he had firmly opposed Booth's complex plan to seize the Presi-

dent in a theatre. But his part in the kidnap plan was proven by
his letter of March 27, in which he urged Booth to hold back
and 'go and see how it will be taken at R——d'. The prosecution
made much of this phrase during the trial since it was one piece
of evidence that suggested a possible Confederate plot. In reality,
it proved nothing. An even more absurd argument was pursued
after it was shown that Arnold had been a Confederate soldier.
Ewing protested that the accused was not on trial for his military
service and that he did not enter the Army to assassinate the
President. Bingham replied passionately, 'Yes, he entered into it
to assassinate the President, and everybody else that entered into
the rebellion entered it to assassinate everybody that represented
this Government. . . .' By this argument, all men who had served
in the Confederate forces were guilty of the assassination. The
New York World commented that it was 'like attributing the
measles to the creation of man'.

Of the eight defendants, the most insignificant was Edward
Spangler, the hard-drinking scene-shifter, whose chief interest in
life was shown to be crab-fishing. Theatre proprietor John T.
Ford described him as a good-natured fellow, kind, willing and
harmless, but with no self-respect since he slept in the theatre.
The unfavourable testimony was provided by stage carpenter
Jacob Ritterspaugh; he recalled that Spangler slapped him acorss
the face with the back of his hand as Booth fled on his horse, and
told him, 'Don't say which way he went.' There was no evidence
whatsoever to connect Spangler with the conspiracy and yet
Bingham declared, 'The testimony of Spangler's complicity is
conclusive and brief.' Bingham argued that it was impossible for
Booth to have escaped without an accomplice at the theatre, that
Spangler had provided the stable at the rear of Ford's for Booth's
horse and the bar for the outer door leading to the President's
box. It was remarkable that a case was brought against Spangler
at all, still more remarkable that he was found guilty of aiding
and abetting Booth in his escape and sentenced to six years' hard
labour.

There were many strange and irregular features of this conspiracy trial that made it a travesty of justice, but perhaps there was no testimony more remarkable than that given by Colonel Everton Conger on May 17. This witness for the prosecution, who received 15,000 dollars of the reward money, gave a most comprehensive account of the capture of Booth and Herold which demonstrated that he had an excellent eye for detail. Finally he itemised Booth's personal effects which were produced in court. One by one he went over the articles—a knife, a pair of pistols, belt, holster, file, pocket compass, spur, pipe, Spencer rifle, cartridges and bills of exchange. Yet, incredibly, one vital piece of evidence was missing. Booth's diary was never mentioned by Conger, nor by other witnesses, nor by prosecution or defence counsel. As far as the court was concerned, it might never have existed.

Several newspapers had previously reported that a diary was among the personal effects found on the assassin. At the trial this was apparently forgotten. In fact, no other piece of evidence was more important to the defence. Booth's writing stressed most clearly that, until the fateful day, the conspirators' aim had been to kidnap, not to kill, the President. It would have greatly aided some of the defendants, Mrs. Surratt especially. The diary, so conveniently overlooked, was not discussed again until 1867 when it was mentioned several times in Lafayette Baker's *History of the United States Secret Service*.

There was another, equally astonishing, omission at the trial. No attempt was made in court to trace Booth's movements between leaving Dr. Mudd's house and arriving at Port Conway nine days later. As a result, men who had helped the fugitives during the nine lost days were never prosecuted. To Thomas Jones, who had helped Booth cross the Potomac, it must have seemed an extraordinary act of mercy. He was in a far more vulnerable position than Mudd, Arnold, O'Laughlin, Spangler and Mrs. Surratt since he admittedly knew that Booth had killed the President.

Another mystery was provided by the testimony of one Captain Theodore McGowan, who explained that, on the night of the assassination, he had been sitting in the aisle near the door to the vestibule which led to the President's box at Ford's. Shortly before the shooting he had seen a man take a small pack of visiting cards from his pocket, select one and hand it to the President's messenger, who was sitting just below him. 'Whether the messenger took the card into the box, or, after looking at it, allowed him to go in, I did not know; but in a moment or two more I saw him go through the door of the lobby leading to the box and close the door.' Presumably this messenger was the President's footman, Charles Forbes.[1] But he was not called to testify and no further questions were asked about the curious, and possibly significant, incident.

On June 29, immediately after Bingham had delivered his massive summing-up for the prosecution, the commission met behind closed doors to consider the evidence. They deliberated for two days, then sentenced four prisoners to death and four to imprisonment and hard labour. Friends of Mrs. Surratt worked frantically behind the scenes in an effort to gain her an eleventh-hour reprieve. Yet, on execution day, July 7, the widow in black was the first to be led to the gallows.

It was a broiling and oppressive summer's day, but huge crowds sweltered in the sun around the Arsenal grounds, hoping for a glimpse of the final act of vengeance. Men climbed the masts of tall ships in the river to spy the gallow-tops; many stood at the prison gates to hear the first news of the assassins' execution; well-connected citizens had passes to witness the hangings. New gallows had been built in the courtyard; nearby were four freshly dug graves, with four wooden coffins piled up in front of them. Beneath the execution platform four guards were stationed to

1. Some sources identify this 'messenger' as bodyguard John Parker, who returned from Taltavul's saloon but then abandoned his chair outside the President's box and took a seat in the dress circle to watch the play.

knock away the props supporting the hinged boards which served as a trap.

Supported by two priests, and followed by an officer and four soldiers, Mary Surratt shuffled across the yard and took a seat at one end of the platform. Her head was shielded from the glaring sun by an umbrella—officialdom's one small gesture of mercy. After the widow came Atzerodt, dishevelled and terrified, with a handkerchief protecting his head. He, too, was escorted by four soldiers, each with bayonets fixed. Next came Herold, looking pathetically young and bewildered, and finally the great Lewis Paine, who marched with military bearing and dignity, broken only momentarily as he grabbed a straw hat from an officer's head and doffed it. On the scaffold he protested Mrs. Surratt's innocence one more time, then called out: 'Goodbye, gentlemen. May we all meet in the other world.' Brave and defiant to the last, this bull-necked giant was destined to suffer a slow, agonising death by strangulation.

Three clergymen spoke for the male prisoners and led prayers. The two Roman Catholic priests stood in silence as Mrs. Surratt kissed her crucifix. Then the prisoners were ordered to stand, and were bound and hooded one more time. Even at this stage the prison commandant and the executioner could not quite believe that the widow was really to be hanged. General Winfield Scott Hancock, the officer in charge of the execution, delayed as long as he dared. He had cavalrymen stationed at intervals between the White House and the Arsenal so that they might relay to him at maximum speed the news of a last-minute reprieve by the President. But no pardon came. The General, standing anxiously at the prison gate, finally gave the signal from across the yard, and, at the executioner's word, the timber props were knocked away to let the hinged boards crash down. Four bodies swung in the bright sunshine and all was silence.

Why did Mary Surratt hang? That would become one of the most controversial questions in American history. Apparently the nine-man commission had failed to get the necessary two-thirds majority to sentence the woman to the maximum penalty; then the dissentients were persuaded to sign her death sentence on the understanding that a petition for mercy would be attached and addressed to the President. Unfortunately, President Johnson was seriously ill at the end of June and could not be approached until July 5, when Judge Advocate Holt took the papers of the case to the White House. The President approved all the sentences and later said he never saw the petition for clemency for Mrs. Surratt. Holt, who had fought so energetically to have the accused condemned, maintained that he did. Various efforts were made to save Mrs. Surratt. A writ of habeas corpus was granted, but on July 7 the President signed a declaration that the writ had been suspended. The widow's daughter, Anna, tried to reach the President on the morning of Friday, July 7, but no one was allowed to see him until after the execution. Weeping and pleading, she threw herself on the White House stairs only to be turned away by Senator James Lane of Kansas and Preston King, Johnson's adviser and closest friend.

Some person or persons were apparently determined that Mary Surratt should not live. Certainly no defendant in the conspiracy trial was prosecuted more vigorously. Why? The popular and most obvious explanation is that the prosecution was hoping to ferret out her elusive son John, the one established conspirator still at large. It is argued that the sentence of death passed on the widow was a last desperate bid to persuade the young man to come out of hiding to protest his mother's innocence. But if this were so, why was the hanging not delayed? What hope could there be that Surratt might surrender once his mother was dead? Some experts conclude that there must have been another explanation, that someone wanted her silenced. And the finger of suspicion has been pointed firmly at the power behind the throne, the Secretary of War, Edwin McMasters Stanton.

8

WAS LINCOLN BETRAYED BY STANTON?

WHO STOOD to profit most by the murder of Lincoln and Seward? Not the pro-slavery leaders whom it was fashionable to blame for the conspiracy. As the 1865 Annual Summary of the *London Times* fairly noted: 'Passionate charges of complicity against some of the Confederate leaders in the first burst of grief and indignation were at once disproved by the argument that the South was deeply interested in preserving the life of a President who was certain to practise clemency and moderation.'

As a group, the Republican radicals undoubtedly had the most to gain by the removal of a President and a Secretary of State who advocated a conciliatory attitude towards the defeated South. Most radicals welcomed Lincoln's death and saw his successor as the man to exact a just peace. But there is not a shred of evidence to implicate them in the assassination; nor is there an impressive case to be made against the individual who immediately profited most from the murder—Vice-President Andrew Johnson.

In direct opposition to the man he succeeded, Johnson had persistently declared that 'treason is a crime and must be made odious' and had screamed that the Confederate leaders should hang. Yet, like so many American Presidents, he revealed unrealised qualities once he had been elevated to the highest office. In fact, he underwent what Grant described as 'a complete revolution of sentiment'. Johnson the avenger became Johnson the pardoner; incredibly, he now favoured the re-establishment of state governments on the lines of Lincoln's reconstruction programme. As a result, the disappointed radicals made desperate efforts to connect Johnson with the assassination; he was even accused from the floor of Congress of having instigated Lincoln's murder. The investigation committee, appointed by the House, went so far as Dry Tortugas, Florida, to seek information from Mudd, Arnold and Spangler, but even for the reward of a pardon the condemned conspirators would not speak out against anyone. The radicals also turned in vain to John Surratt for new evidence. After all these determined efforts, the case against Andrew Johnson virtually rests on two flimsy points—that Booth *may* have left him a note and that the President *may* have refused to pardon Mary Surratt.

In contrast, a massive weight of circumstantial evidence can be presented against one man who had much to gain by the death of Lincoln and Seward, who was intensely ambitious and ruthless, and who assumed the powers of a dictator immediately after the assassination. Edwin McMasters Stanton had both the motive and the means. By industry and intrigue he had climbed to a position of power second only to the Presidency itself. He dreamed of emerging from the war as the nation's idol and Lincoln's heir apparent. But, in April, 1865, his hopes were threatened by a reconstruction programme that would restore the electoral power of the South and conceivably put the Democrats back in office.

Could it be that the War Secretary responsible for the President's security was also responsible for his death? Did he secretly conspire against Lincoln, or at least encourage would-be assassins by making security arrangements as lax as possible? A century of investigation has proved nothing, but it has produced many charges against Stanton that cannot be readily dismissed. The case against Lincoln's trusted Secretary of War is based on the following suggestions:

1. *That prior to the assassination Stanton was fully aware that conspirators were meeting at the Surratt house to plot against the President, and that he took no action against them.*

This is one serious charge against Stanton that can be supported to some extent by hard facts. In March, or possibly earlier, Louis Weichmann reluctantly reported to government officers that he believed a plot against Lincoln was being hatched at the boarding house where he lodged. At least three officials, Gleason, Sharp and McDavitt, noted his report and the information was passed on to the War Department. Stanton was for ever expressing his fear for Lincoln's safety and during the war he had had hundreds of citizens arrested on the vaguest suspicions. The writ of habeas corpus had been suspended; the practice of acquiring evidence before making an arrest had long been abandoned. Yet the Surratt boarders named by Weichmann were not even hauled in for questioning. Detectives later testified that they had the house under surveillance for weeks, but they were unable to produce a report for even one day's watch on the house; nor could they outline the day-to-day movements of any of the boarders. It would be surprising if the efficient Stanton did not see this sensational information furnished by Weichmann. Such reports probably reached his office every day, but they did not all emanate from a government employee, and they did not all cast suspicion on a well-known Shakespearean actor. However, it must be admitted possible that this report was pigeon-holed and forgotten along the way.

But there are other facts to suggest that Stanton had prior knowledge of a plot against the President. At 4.44 a.m. on April 15, he stated in a Press bulletin to Major-General Dix in New York: 'It appears from a letter found in Booth's trunk that the murder was planned before the 4th of March, but fell through because the accomplice backed out until "Richmond could be heard from".' But where did Stanton find this reference to March 4, inauguration day? Not from Sam Arnold's letter to which he was referring. That letter was dated March 27 and made no mention of March 4. There is one clear way Stanton could have been prompted to date the plot prior to March 4—if General Augur had just told him about the information which had earlier reached his department through Weichmann and Captain Gleason; or if Stanton had had this information all the time.

More suspicion is aroused by the way Arnold and O'Laughlin were speedily arrested on April 16, although Arnold's letter was simply signed 'Sam' and his handwriting was not identified until the 17th. It adds weight to the suggestion that the War Department already had information about their acquaintance with Booth.

In defence of Stanton, it might be argued that he chanced to mention March 4 because many vague stories of plots against the President were circulating immediately before his inauguration. It is also possible that the Washington police were put on to Arnold and O'Laughlin by Weichmann or some other unknown informer after the assassination. But whether or not Stanton was informed of Weichmann's suspicions, the fact remains that he headed the department responsible for following up such reports, and that at a time when Washington was buzzing with many similar reports he should have taken much firmer action to safeguard the President, if only by releasing Eckert for the evening and advising bodyguard Parker to be especially alert.

2. *That Stanton went to extraordinary lengths to dissuade Grant from joining Lincoln's theatre party.*

The point of this charge is that the General's presence at Ford's would have made an assassin's task doubly difficult. Hundreds of eyes would have been constantly turning towards the presidential box for a glimpse of the conquering hero, so rarely seen in Washington. It is probable that the General would have had one or two military aides close at hand, barring entry to the box. Moreover, on such a special occasion, bodyguard Parker would almost certainly have taken care to remain at his post.

Much significance had been attached to Grant's lack of etiquette in accepting Lincoln's invitation and then withdrawing, even though his appearance at Ford's had been given advance publicity. Some writers have been unable to accept the General's explanation that he urgently wanted to join his children in Burlington, New Jersey. After all, his wife and sons, Fred and Jesse, had been with him at Christmas, and Mrs. Grant and seven-year-old Jesse had recently joined him at City Point. The time-table for the journey to Burlington has also aroused suspicion. The Grants, with Jesse, left Washington at 6 p.m., Good Friday, on the slowest of four trains running daily to Burlington. The journey took thirteen hours. They could easily have attended the theatre, enjoyed a night's rest and taken a train at seven-thirty the following morning to arrive fresh at their destination after only seven and a half hours' travel. On the other hand, the earlier train offered Grant an extra eight hours in Burlington. And who can tell how deeply a soldier on leave from the front may feel a compelling urge to escape from official life to the peaceful oasis of his own family circle and friends? Even when he received, at Philadelphia, Stanton's telegram informing him of the assassination and requesting his immediate return, Grant continued on to Burlington and saw his three other children before hurrying back to Washington.

Other factors suggest that Grant's absence from the theatre hardly deserves the suspicion that some theorists attach to it. One must consider especially the feelings of Mrs. Grant, who had been exceedingly hurt and embarrassed by Mrs. Lincoln's outrageous and insulting behaviour during the visit to the front. On April 13, Mrs. Lincoln had displayed further discourtesy by inviting General Grant to join her and the President on a carriage drive and not extending the invitation to the General's wife. Mrs. Grant, a simple and good-natured woman, can scarcely have relished the thought of being closeted in a theatre box with a volatile First Lady who was liable to explode into a fit of jealousy at any time and cause a fearful scene in public. It was a note from his wife, telling him not to be late for their train, that enabled the nervous General to convince Mr. Lincoln that he would rather not attend the theatre. So it is quite conceivable that Mrs. Grant influenced her husband in his decision not to visit Ford's, just as Mrs. Lincoln influenced her husband in attending.

Another relevant factor is Grant's well-known distaste for high social life. So strong in battle, he felt uneasy in official Washington and shied away from pomp and ceremony. Indeed, his withdrawal from the theatre party was not an unprecedented action on his part. In March, 1864, Grant entered the city of Washington for the first time in his life and received his commission as Lieutenant-General commanding all the Union armies. He was mobbed at Willard's Hotel and even at a White House reception where the other guests persuaded him to stand on a crimson-covered sofa so they might all see the unknown hero. During the visit it was advertised that Grant would accompany the President to Grover's where Edwin Booth was playing *Richard III*. A great crowd turned out to see the mysterious generalissimo; Mrs. Lincoln arranged a dinner in his honour. But Grant hastily left the Capitol to return to his troops.

It is certainly true that Stanton contributed no small part to the General's decision to withdraw from the trip to Ford's. On two separate occasions he advised Grant to avoid the visit. But this becomes less suspicious when one appreciates that the puritanical Stanton disapproved of theatres on religious grounds, and of visits to the theatre for security reasons. An avid reader of the Bible, the War Secretary regarded theatres as dens of iniquity; only once did he attend the theatre in Washington and that was merely to deliver a message to the President at Grover's and get an immediate reply. There was nothing unusual about his attitude. After the assassination, many voices would be raised, expressing dismay that the great President should have met his death in a 'house of sin'. Innumerable times Stanton had warned the President to avoid theatres and crowded public places, so it was perfectly natural that he should give the same advice to the

General on whose leadership the fate of the Union so greatly depended.

3. *That Stanton aided Booth by refusing to release the powerful Eckert when Lincoln wanted him as a bodyguard for the theatre visit, and that he falsely stated that Eckert was engaged in vital work that evening.*

This is a difficult charge to answer. Telegraph operator Bates did not publish his account of Stanton's refusal to give protection until 1907, after a gap of forty-two years. Was his memory of events reliable? Bates wrote that Booth might have been prevented from the deed if Eckert had attended—'in view of Eckert's previous knowledge of the plot to kidnap or kill the President'. Was he writing loosely so long after the events took place? Or is this another indication that Eckert and Stanton were well informed of plans to capture or murder Lincoln?

If we accept Bates's story—and since he was a 'Stanton man' there is no special reason to challenge his account—it automatically follows that Stanton, with or without intent, made Booth's task easier. Why should he refuse to release Eckert? Possibly he was unwilling to co-operate, to make any gesture that might encourage the President in his plans to visit a theatre. Possibly he had been riled that same afternoon by Lincoln's refusal to arrest the high-ranking Confederate, Jacob Thompson, and was merely in a difficult mood. There would be nothing unusual in Stanton's readiness to lie or to hinder the President when circumstances enabled him to do so without damaging his own position. Possibly he had lost interest in security measures after warning the President so many times in vain. Only recently, when Lincoln was at City Point, he had telegraphed the President, advising him against going to the front. The following day Lincoln had casually walked in the burning chaos of Richmond, where the risks could scarcely have been greater.

But all this is pure speculation. The facts are that Stanton made no mention of Lincoln's request for Eckert's company when he later recalled his last interview with the President; that, on the other side, he made no secret of the fact that he went home early that evening, dined and retired for the night. As for Eckert declining the President's invitation, this would not be so remarkable since he was the complete subordinate who would never do anything that might cut across his chief's known wishes. Eckert also made no pretence at working late that night. Was this the behaviour of a man who knew an attempt was to be made that night on the President's life?

4. *That Stanton, who directed the pursuit of the assassin, endeavoured to let Booth escape until the news of his injury made capture almost inevitable.*

Numerous incidents can be cited to support this charge. He did not alert guards at the Navy Yard Bridge, the most obvious escape route from Washington. He did not immediately raise a general alarm by issuing a statement to the Press. He delayed in naming Booth as the assassin, even though scores of witnesses had identified Lincoln's murderer. He recalled Major O'Beirne when he was leading the one search party on the right track. With this indirect assistance from Stanton, Booth might very well have escaped if he had not been handicapped by a broken leg.

There can be no doubt that the War Secretary bungled his direction of emergency measures. It is far from certain, however, that he deliberately aided the assassin's escape. Why then was he so slow to act? The most likely answer is that the War Secretary was a frightened man. He interpreted the attacks on Lincoln and Seward as a final desperate move by the South, and for almost five hours he worked on the assumption that a gigantic conspiracy had been set in motion. Defeated in the open conflict, the Confederates could now only hope to establish an underground movement and seek to disrupt the capital by terrorist activities. Thus he alerted the fire brigade as well as the police, recalled Grant to defend the city and posted guards at the homes of leading members of the government. Considering the numerous plots and intrigues uncovered in the war years, this initial reaction would not be an unreasonable one. In the first hours of organised chaos after the assassination, he was apparently thinking in terms of defence rather than attack, and it can be argued that the breakdown of the commercial telegraph system that evening, and the discovery of Arnold's letter, telling Booth to 'go and see how it will be taken at R——d', increased, if not confirmed, his fears of a widespread Confederate conspiracy.

If one accepts that Stanton treated the events of that night as acts of war and Booth as one attacker among an army of invaders, his subsequent actions are more easily understood. But having responded as though he faced a mass invasion, Stanton could be exposed to public ridicule if it was shown that, with all the forces at his command, he had been outfoxed by one man whose face was known to thousands. It was therefore in his interests to keep alive the belief that this was a Richmond-directed conspiracy and that his prompt action had averted a far graver crisis. The greater the conspiracy, the greater Stanton could be made to appear.

Towards 1 a.m. on April 15, Stanton told a conference of military, police and judicial chiefs that he did not want a public announcement of the assassination to be made yet. There is a simple explanation for this delay. Some government officials believed that he was expecting a swift arrest to be made and that he dreamed of being able to announce the crime and the arrest at the same time. None of these explanations, however, can excuse his inept handling of the search for John Wilkes Booth.

5. *That once he had learned that Booth was crippled and certain to be captured, Stanton secretly arranged that the assassin should not be taken alive and allowed to give evidence against his accomplices.*

Although official instructions from Washington were that Booth should be taken alive if possible, one officer instructed his men to shoot the assassin on sight. This man was Colonel William P. Wood, Superintendent of the Old Capitol Prison, who was in charge of three detectives at Dr. Mudd's house. After the doctor's arrest, these men lay in wait, hoping to trap Booth if he returned from the nearby swamps. It would seem strange that Wood, with heavy duties in Washington, was given the task of watching Mudd's house. But Stanton's accusers point out meaningfully that Wood was a devoted confidant of the War Secretary; he owed his prison appointment to him, and after Stanton's death he wrote, 'While I regretted the course adopted by the Secretary of War towards Mrs. Surratt, I would never hesitate to perform any act of kindness for him.' Shortly before his own death, Wood made another interesting statement. He made an affidavit that he had used deception when appearing as a witness for the defence in the famous McCormick *v.* Manny reaper case of 1855. (See page 235.) He had altered the design of an early model of the McCormick reaper which was introduced in evidence to help to demonstrate that there had been no infringement of patent. This was the case in which Stanton crowded out an obscure lawyer called Abraham Lincoln to act as counsel for the defence. Wood stressed that Stanton never knew anything about his trickery, but there was certainly a very strong bond between the two men.

Then there were the strange circumstances in which Major O'Beirne, so close on Booth's trail, was ordered to stay on the Maryland side of the Potomac. Immediately after news of O'Beirne's progress reached Washington, Lafayette Baker, Stanton's Secret Service chief, sent for trusted subordinates Lieutenant Baker and Colonel Conger and was able to direct them almost to within a few miles of Booth's position in Virginia. Why was Colonel Baker confident enough to tell his cousin, 'We have got a sure thing'? The most obvious answer is that he knew of O'Beirne's progress and appropriated the Major's discoveries for his own purposes. Baker's own explanation was that his detectives had been busy around Port Tobacco; on April 24, one of his men, Theodore Woodall, had found a coloured man who claimed he had seen two men answering the

Ray Neff, holding his copy of *Colburn's United Service Magazine*, in which General Baker's signature was identified

QUESTIONED DOCUMENT SERVICE
ADVISORY CONSULTATIONS
COMPARISON OF HANDWRITING · TYPEWRITING
Detection of Documentary Frauds and Alterations

STANLEY S. SMITH
Examiner of Questioned Documents
1808 STATE STREET, HARRISBURG, PENNA.
CEdar 3-1663

DOCUMENT EXAMINER 1939-1959
CRIME LABORATORY—Penna. State Police
Court Qualified Expert since 1934

Member
International Association for Identification
American Academy of Forensic Sciences

June 20, 1961

Pennsylvania State Police
1921-1959 Captain (Retired)

Member
International Association of Chiefs of Police
Pennsylvania Chiefs of Police Association

Mr. R. H. Fowler, Editor,
Civil War Times Magazine,
1002 Apple Drive,
Mechanicsburg, Penna.

RE: L. C. Baker Signature Report

Dear Mr. Fowler:

1. Responsive to your request I received the following items from
you June 19, 1961, for the purpose of making a professional examination to determine whetherthe the signature designated: Q-1 was in
fact written by Brigadier General Lafayette C. Baker (1826-1868),
Chief of the United States Secret Service:

QUESTIONED:

Q-1   Signature: "L. C. Baker" (previously developed from a latent
condition as reported by you) appearing on the left margin
of page 574 in the printed book: "Colburn's / United Service
Magazine /and / Naval and Military Journal / 1864, Part II /
London."

STANDARDS:

S-1   Lafayette C. Baker exemplars:

A - "L. C. Baker" signature appearing in photostat of a
Codicil to his Will dated June 31, 1868, bequeathing
his literary remains to Laura Ann Duvall.

B - "L. C. Baker" signature appearing in photostat of his
Will dated April 30, 1866.

2. OPINION: The S-1 writer, Lafayette C. Baker, wrote the questione
signature: "L. C. Baker", item Q-1, as found supported by identicalit
of form, habits, pressures and individual characteristics which inclu
the form of the "a" like "u", absence of pen lifts, placement of peri
etc.

Yours truly,   _Stanley S. Smith_
                STANLEY S. SMITH
                Captain, P.S.P. Retired
                Examiner of Questioned Docume

The statement by a handwriting expert stating that the signature found in
Colburn's Magazine was genuine

description of Booth and Herold enter a small boat near Swan's Point. But this is an improbable story. In one day Woodall was supposed to have arrived in lower Maryland, found the Negro witness, and taken him back to Washington instead of sending the information by telegraph. There was insufficient time for all this to have been achieved before Baker sent his cousin on the manhunt, and there is no record of a coloured man having had a share of the reward money. In fact, there is quite sufficient evidence for it to be accepted that the Negro informer never existed, that he was an invention of Baker's to cover up the fact that he had stolen Major O'Beirne's thunder.

Next there are the strange circumstances in which Booth was killed. Twenty-eight men surrounded the barn where he was trapped; the soldiers were ordered to hold their fire. Yet they failed to take the assassin alive. Boston Corbett, an eccentric sergeant, claimed that he had shot Booth, and yet no one witnessed his action. To have killed Booth with a single shot, he would have needed to leave his position and approach the barn, and in the light of the blazing building he should have been clearly visible. Later, when a congressional committee discussed the sharing out of rewards, the chairman described Corbett as an insane man who 'forsook his place, thrust a pistol through a crack and fired it without knowing where the ball was going'. He was awarded only 1,653·85 dollars, no more than each of the non-commissioned members of the cavalry squad. The description of Corbett as 'an insane man' proved extremely accurate. Three years later he was so disgusted at being accosted by two prostitutes that he castrated himself, and in 1887, one year after his appointment as doorkeeper of the Kansas State Legislature, he locked all the doors to the chamber of the House of Representatives, drew two revolvers, and blazed away at the Members.

In the light of his later behaviour, Corbett might appear a likely candidate for the role of Lincoln's mad avenger. He was charged by Colonel Conger with a breach of military discipline and sent to Washington for court martial. Yet no action was taken against him for his self-confessed disobedience. Stanton dismissed the complaint against him, saying, 'The rebel is dead—the patriot lives; he has saved us continued excitement, delay and expense—the patriot is released.'

Did Corbett kill Booth? Was perhaps the assassin murdered by Lieutenant Baker, who first reached the body? Or was he shot by Conger? Before a congressional investigation committee, Baker testified: 'I supposed, at the time, that Conger shot him, and I said, "What on earth did you shoot him for?" Said he, "I did not shoot him." Then the idea flashed on my mind that if he did, it had better not be known.' Conger received 15,000 dollars of the reward money, compared with Baker's 3,000, but the difference might be explained by seniority of rank. The other possibility, and the one much favoured, is that Booth took his own life. Corbett himself testified at the conspiracy trial, 'I knew also, from his desperate language, that he would not be taken alive.' The nature of the wound, with the bullet passing downwards at an angle of about twenty degrees, would suggest it was inflicted at a very close range; in further support of a suicide theory, the downward angle might be explained by the fact that Booth was crippled and standing awkwardly without his crutch.

The truth about the shooting at Garrett's farm might easily have been established by an immediate examination of Booth's and Corbett's pistols. There is no evidence that this was ever done. Further suspicion has been aroused by the elaborate security which surrounded the disposal of Booth's body. Stanton sent Colonel Baker to Alexandria to meet the steamer carrying the assassin back to Washington. The corpse was then kept under heavy guard on the ironclad warship *Montauk*. Booth had the initials JWB tattooed on his wrist, but the body was properly identified by a surgeon who had operated on him, by a dentist who had filled two of the actor's teeth only a week before the assassination, by Alexander Gardner, a famous society photographer, by Henry Clay Ford, and by Charles Dawson, Chief Clerk of the National Hotel. Dr. John Frederick May, who had removed a tumour from the left side of Booth's neck, remarked to Surgeon-General Barnes, 'There is no resemblance in that corpse to Booth, nor can I believe it to be that of him.' He noted that it was a 'haggard corpse . . . with its yellow and discoloured skin, its unkempt and matted hair, and its whole facial expression sunken and sharpened by the exposure and starvation it had undergone'. But he positively identified the scar on Booth's neck.

The corpse was sewn up in a grey army blanket and, at Stanton's command, was buried at night in strict secrecy. Colonel Baker and his cousin went to extraordinary lengths to cover up the true destination of the assassin's body. One evening the two men lowered the body, temporarily encased in a pine gun-box, into a skiff drawn alongside the monitor. They also took on board a huge metal ball and heavy chain. Curious onlookers could clearly see this activity and they raced along the bank as the skiff moved downstream for two miles. But as darkness fell the skiff was eventually lost from sight. The rowing-boat was then pulled into the great swamp near the lonely Geeseborough Point, where the detectives waited for hours until they were satisfied that they were unobserved. Near midnight, the Bakers rowed upstream as quietly as possible until they reached the walls of the Old Penitentiary Building, where Booth was to be buried. Only a handful of men were involved in the operation and all were sworn to secrecy. A shallow hole was dug in a ground-floor cell used for storing ammunition and guns, and, by the light of a single lantern, Booth was placed in an unmarked grave. The cell was locked and the key was given to Stanton.

As intended, it was at first presumed that Booth's body had been dropped in the river. This extreme secrecy also heightened stories that Booth was not really the man shot at the Garrett farm; in later years there would come reports that he had been seen in such widely scattered places as London, Mexico and Oklahoma. But Stanton's handling of the burial can be satisfactorily explained. He feared that the corpse might become the 'subject of glorification by disloyal persons'; also that the body might be seized by fanatical Confederates. These fears were not altogether unjustified. Colonel Baker recorded that he once found the seam of the funeral sack ripped open and a lady visitor to the *Montauk* on the point of cutting a lock of the actor's raven hair.[1]

Stanton's reaction to the news that the pursuers had 'got Booth' has also been interpreted as an indication that he wanted the assassin killed. In his *History of the United States Secret Service*, Colonel Baker wrote: 'When I entered the room he was lying upon a sofa. . . . I rushed into the room and said, "We have got Booth." Secretary Stanton was distinguished during the whole war for his coolness, but I had never seen such an exhibition of it in my life as at that time. He put his hands over his eyes, and lay for nearly a moment without saying a word. Then he got up and put on his coat very coolly.' Was this the reaction of a man who dreaded the news and feared that it meant Booth had been taken alive? Possibly. But it proves nothing. Indeed, there is some reason to doubt the reliability of Baker's account. He was obviously straining for dramatic effect in his book, and this passage in itself demonstrates how he sacrificed accuracy for the sake of colour. In remarking that Stanton was distinguished for his coolness, he was stating the reverse of the truth.

6. *That Booth left a note for Andrew Johnson in order to compromise him*; *that with Lincoln and Seward assassinated, and the Vice-President incriminated, the three men ranking above Stanton would be removed.*

The significance of this note remains a tantalising mystery. The card left at Kirkwood House on the afternoon of April 14 read: 'Don't wish to disturb you. Are you at home?—J. Wilkes Booth.'

1. Except for the presence of newsmen, seven of whom acted as pallbearers, Lee Harvey Oswald was also buried with extreme security. A huge force of Secret Service men and police stood on guard in an isolated section of Rose Hill Cemetery, Forth Worth. The plain, pine coffin was placed six feet down in a vault reinforced with steel bars. Then a policeman was left on duty nearby, as a precaution against threats of desecration.

Contrary to many reports, it was not definitely left for the Vice-President. In fact, it was found in the mail box of Johnson's secretary, Colonel Browning. But as Browning remarked at the conspiracy trial, 'It was a very common mistake in the office to put cards intended for me into the Vice-President's box, and his would find their way into mine; the boxes being together.' The Colonel thought that Booth might have called on him since they had met several times when the actor was working in Nashville, Tennessee. 'But when his name was connected with the assassination, I looked upon it differently.' Of course, such an intriguing question was not pursued further at the trial.

The popular explanation is that Booth, having no faith in Atzerodt as the man assigned to kill Johnson, decided with diabolical cunning to leave this visiting card as a means of causing the Vice-President acute embarrassment, if not making his position untenable. The card would automatically link the new President with the killer of the man he had succeeded. Indeed, according to an account by Lieutenant Ruggles a quarter of a century later, Booth told the Confederate soldiers who aided his escape that he left the note to compromise Johnson. It seems a feasible answer, but another, more far-fetched, solution has been offered: that the entire plot to kill Johnson was only a sham to allay suspicion that the attacks on Lincoln and Seward might have been prompted by Republican radicals. Here it can be argued that the cowardly Atzerodt was an absurd choice for the task of killing any man, let alone a Vice-President who carried a gun and was famed for his physical courage; Booth can never have seriously believed that the Prussian carriage-maker would succeed. Secondly, it can be argued that the attacked statesmen, Lincoln and Seward, were the two leading figures who supported conciliation in the reconstruction of the South. Though he made an astonishing turnabout when he became President, Johnson previously favoured harsh measures against the defeated South, and death to the Confederate leaders. So did Stanton.

Did someone wish it to appear that Johnson, Grant and Stanton were in danger that Good Friday night, and so suggest that there was a massive conspiracy by the South? Stanton certainly made every effort to throw the blame on the Confederate leaders. He encouraged the belief that his own life had been in danger, and at the conspiracy trial his son was one of three witnesses who provided incredible testimony to suggest that O'Laughlin was lurking around the Stanton house, presumably lying in wait for Grant. But this is entering into the realms of pure imagination. There are no facts whatsoever to link Stanton with the assassin's note, possibly left for the Vice-President.

7. *That Stanton suppressed the evidence of Booth's diary and removed pages which may have indicated who really master-minded the assassination.*

Booth's diary, indicating that kidnapping and not murder was the original intent of the conspirators, was the most astounding omission in the evidence presented at the conspiracy trial. For two years the diary was locked up in the War Office archives and might have remained there if Baker had not recalled its existence in his *History of the United States Secret Service*, published in 1867. At that time, Congress was busy investigating the possibility of impeaching President Johnson, and the diary immediately became the subject of bitter controversy. Fiery General Ben Butler seized on Booth's statement: 'I have almost a mind to return to Washington and . . . clear my name, which I feel I can do.' As a member of Congress, the General stirred up a hornet's nest with this revelation. 'How clear himself?' he asked. 'By disclosing his accomplices?' Soon after, the House of Representatives appointed a special commission to investigate whether persons 'holding high positions of power and authority' were behind the assassination. The President was the target, but Stanton stood directly in the line of fire.

Another bombshell was dropped when Baker stated under oath that the diary had been mutilated since it was taken from Booth's body. He claimed that eighteen pages had been cut out, pages dated prior to the time of Lincoln's death, and he recalled having seen a pencil sketch of a house on one page—now missing. On the other hand, Stanton testified that the diary was without these pages when he first saw it. Conger also thought the pages were missing originally, but he was uncertain. So it was Baker's word against Stanton's. When Baker was recalled, he further embarrassed the War Secretary by revealing that some of his detectives had made copies of the diary, but they had been ordered to hand them over to Stanton. He reaffirmed that no pages were missing when he first saw the diary.

Did Stanton remove the pages? It is entirely uncertain. One cannot attach great credence to the word of Baker, for at the time he was an embittered ex-officer, released from the U.S. Army in February, 1866, when he might have hoped for greater reward for his faithful service to Stanton. He was also disgruntled because Stanton had refused to release the diary when he sought to include the contents in his book. Baker claimed that the War Secretary had previously promised to let him use the diary. Moreover, it is altogether possible that Baker was eager to publicise his book with his sensational statements. It becomes more difficult to trust the word of Baker when one considers that he wrote in his book that the diary recorded how Booth had killed his horse and kept warm by sleeping between the legs of the dead animal. Baker later admitted he had never actually read the diary; he had merely heard this story told by colleagues. Booth's diary does not mention a dead horse, so presumably it was mentioned on one of the missing pages. But then those pages were dated before April 13-14 and it is improbable that Booth would have entered the account in the wrong part of the diary.

Perhaps the most feasible explanation of the missing pages was hinted at by Lieutenant L. B. Baker. He said he thought some pages were originally missing and revealed that he had found one page on his travels in Virginia. During his flight, Booth sent two notes to Dr. Stewart who, he hoped, would treat his injured leg. It is eminently possible that the assassin sent out Herold with other messages, and that he scribbled them on unused pages in the first quarter of his diary.

Why then was the diary suppressed at the trial? The most obvious explanation is that it contributed nothing towards the prosecution's case; rather it provided an impediment. It can, of course, be argued that Stanton did not wish attention to be drawn to Booth's statement about returning to Washington to clear his name. Great stress has been laid on these words—'I have a greater desire and almost a mind to return to Washington, and in a measure clear my name, which I feel I can do.' Standing alone, it may seem a most meaningful sentence. But is it so sinister when read in the full context? At the time Booth was bitterly complaining because he was being looked upon as 'a common cutthroat'. He wanted the world to know that his motives were noble, but the explanatory letter he had left for the *National Intelligencer* had never appeared. By 'clear my name', Booth might easily have meant returning to try to justify his action, to show that his motives were not selfish, and that he was not the coward that the newspapers had labelled him. But we cannot tell for certain.

8. *That Stanton went to extraordinary lengths to ensure the silence of the alleged conspirators lest they might reveal information of conspiracy in high places.*

There is some evidence to support this charge. Firstly, the prisoners were hooded 'for better security against conversation', though why such an extreme measure was necessary has never been made clear. The prisoners were not permitted to utter a word at the trial in their own defence, and the prosecution strenuously sought the death penalty in all eight cases. The frantic efforts to save Mrs. Surratt were thwarted in mysterious circumstances, and when four of the accused escaped the maximum penalty they were isolated again by their sudden transfer from the state penitentiary at Albany to the military prison at far-off Dry Tortugas, Florida.

On July 15, 1865, President Johnson signed an order directing that Arnold, Mudd, Spangler and O'Laughlin should be moved to Fort Jefferson, Dry Tortugas, but, according to Gideon Welles, it was Stanton who suggested the move. En route, Captain George Dutton sent an affidavit to Judge Holt stating that Mudd had now confessed that he knew Booth when he came to his house on April 15 and that he had been with Booth at the National Hotel as Weichmann had testified. According to the Captain, Dr. Mudd exclaimed on learning their destination: 'Oh, there is now no hope for me. Oh, I cannot live in such a place.' The four prisoners arrived at this island fort off Key West on July 24 and soon they were again subjected to extreme security measures. In mid-August, Stanton's detective chief, Colonel Baker, informed Thomas Eckert, then acting Assistant Secretary of War, that a New Orleans group was planning to free the imprisoned conspirators. Eckert passed on this information to the commanding officer at Dry Tortugas, instructing him to 'at once take measures to prevent the accomplishment of such purpose'. The four luckless men, previously treated like ordinary prisoners, were now kept to hard labour and isolated from other prisoners. Years later, after his release, Arnold complained that when a case of smallpox broke out on the island, the patient was placed near their small cell as though it were intended that they should contract the dreaded disease. There is no evidence, however, that Stanton adopted such strict security measures to protect himself. It could be that he was merely being as severe and as cautious as possible in dealing with the hated conspirators. Moreover, it would be quite in character for Baker, on his own accord, to seek to boost the prestige of his force by dramatically reporting a far-fetched escape plot.

9. *That Stanton allowed guilty men to go free in an effort to cover up his feeble efforts to capture the assassin.*

In a proclamation on April 20, Stanton declared that all persons harbouring, secreting or aiding the fugitives 'will be treated as accomplices in the murder of the President . . . and shall be subject to trial before a military commission, and the punishment of death'. Accordingly, such minor figures as Dr. Mudd, Mrs. Surratt and Spangler were vigorously prosecuted and harshly punished. Yet no action was taken against persons who aided Booth after his departure from Mudd's farm. This extraordinary leniency, so inconsistent with the authorities' attitude to other suspects, was certainly not due to lack of evidence. The Negro Oswald Swann described how he met Booth and Herold about two miles from Bryantown and took them to the plantation of Captain Samuel Cox. He alleged that the fugitives stayed there three or four hours, that Booth then came out, paid him twelve dollars, and made some unflattering remarks about Cox. On this evidence Cox was arrested and told by Colonel Wells that if he made a false statement he would be tied up by his thumbs. The prisoner then confessed that two men had visited his house, but he had not known who they were. An excellent case could have been presented against this landowner, a known Southern sympathiser, on whose land Booth had hidden out for six days. Instead, he was released after a few weeks.

Cox's half-brother, Thomas Jones, provided the assassin with food, drink, newspapers and a boat for crossing the Potomac. He could have been condemned on the evidence of his Negro servant, ex-slave Henry Woodland, who was soon made to talk by detectives. Woodland told how Jones had hidden a boat; how, over the previous year, he had arranged other secret crossings to Virginia. This farmer, far guiltier than some of the alleged conspirators, was also released after a few weeks.

Dr. Richard Stewart (who gave the fugitives a meal), Mr. Bryant (who guided them to the doctor's house), the Negro Lucas (who gave them his wagon) and the farmer Garrett (who provided them with food and shelter), were lesser figures who might have been prosecuted but who were ignored. More remarkable, no action was taken against the three young Confederate soldiers, Jett, Ruggles and Bainbridge, who knowingly helped the assassins to hide and warned them that Federal troops were close at hand. The soldiers were arrested and taken to Washington, where they admitted having aided Booth's escape. Not only were they released, but Jett was called as a witness for the prosecution at the conspiracy trial.

Two other persons might easily have been prosecuted, John Lloyd and Louis Weichmann. The former's conviction would have been a foregone conclusion. Lloyd had hidden guns and other equipment for the conspirators. He had aided Booth's escape by directing pursuers to Piscataway instead of to Bryantown. For two days after his arrest he had falsely denied knowing anything about the assassination. Weichmann was also in a vulnerable position. He had long been a close friend of the conspirators; he had been slow to report his suspicions to the authorities; he had driven Mrs. Surratt on her compromising visits to Surrattsville. There is an obvious reason why they were not prosecuted. Under pressure, both of them could be persuaded to testify against the widow Surratt, whom the authorities were so eager to have condemned. But why did the others go free?

One suggestion is that Stanton was not especially concerned with these minor figures since it was unlikely that Booth would reveal to them any information about his secret contacts with high-level officials in Washington. It is not a very plausible explanation. Would Stanton, such a ruthlessly efficient politician, have gambled on letting these men go free if there was the faintest possibility that they could connect him with the plot? A more probable answer suggests itself: that Stanton had no wish to draw attention to the way a crippled assassin had so easily eluded his pursuers for ten days after he fled from Dr. Mudd's house into the swamps. Stanton, who directed the greatest manhunt in American history, wanted to maintain the impression of a highly competent search for the assassins, and quite possibly this may explain why nine days of Booth's flight were completely ignored at the conspiracy trial.

10. *That Stanton had the recorded testimony of the conspiracy trial specially edited to cover up his incompetent direction of the manhunt.*

The official report of the trial, as recorded by Mr. Benn Pitman, does not correspond entirely with the transcriptions of the trial found in the archives at Washington. Pitman leaves out John Fletcher's statement that he went to General Augur's head-quarters early on Saturday morning; that he 'gave him the name of Herold, his description, and his age, as far as I could judge, and told him I had pursued him to the Navy Yard Bridge'; that he identified the saddle and bridle of a horse often ridden by Atzerodt. Yet Pitman stressed that his report contained 'the entire testimony adduced at the trial'.

This re-editing of Fletcher's testimony obscured the fact that the authorities were given an invaluable lead before 2 a.m. and that their efforts should have been directed towards the Navy Yard Bridge. Why should Pitman leave out a large slice of the stableman's evidence? There is no reason to suppose that he did. His account was published 'by authority of the Secretary of War' and 'prepared and issued under the superintendence of Colonel Burnett'. And 'in obedience to the directions of the Secretary of War', Burnett certified 'to its faithfulness and accuracy'.

11. *That Stanton, who directed the investigation into the conspiracy, purposefully avoided taking any action against bodyguard John F. Parker to cover up his own negligence.*

Few men in history can have been so totally unworthy of a position of trust as John F. Parker, the Metropolitan policeman who was responsible for President Lincoln's safety, and who abandoned him to satisfy his own thirst. Born on May 19, 1830, this Washington carpenter joined the Metropolitan Police in 1861 and quickly established himself as the most irresponsible patrolman on the force. That same year he appeared before a police board, charged with using profane language to a grocer and obscene language to a superior officer. He was found guilty and reprimanded. In March, 1863, he was again before the board, again charged with being offensive towards an officer. This time he was also accused of insulting a woman who sought police protection, sleeping on duty and being drunk and disorderly in a brothel where, it was said, he had been living with a prostitute for some weeks. Employees of the brothel testified on his behalf and he was acquitted. Two weeks later Parker was accused of sleeping in a street car while on duty; then came another charge of insolent behaviour. Both were dismissed with remarkable generosity by the police board. Taking the most charitable view of Parker's weaknesses, an examination of his record leaves not the slightest doubt that here was a thoroughly undesirable character with no sense of duty, loyalty or responsibility. This was the man selected as one of the four plain-clothes men to guard the President.

Parker's selection is not so incredible when one considers that there were only forty policemen on the entire force. Some of these were not attracted by White House duty and, by seniority, were able to avoid it. But the post appealed to Parker, a married man with three children, and young enough for military service. When he learned that he was being drafted, he had no difficulty in obtaining a letter from Mrs. Lincoln requesting that he be excused military service. Eleven days later John Parker showed the measure of his gratitude. On Good Friday he was guilty of three offences—arriving three hours late for his evening shift, deserting his post, and drinking on duty. It might be imagined that the news of the assassination sent Parker scurrying back to his post, to join the pursuit of the assassin or at least to watch over the grief-stricken First Lady. In fact, he was not seen again until after 6 a.m. the next morning when he reported at the police station with a prisoner. He had arrested a drunk and frightened prostitute named Lizzie Williams. The duty sergeant dismissed Lizzie and told her to get out of town.

Where had Parker been since ten o'clock the previous evening?

What could he report about the killing of the man he had guarded? No questions were asked, and no information was offered. Parker was sent home to rest and remained on the force three more years. In November, another complaint was made against him for conduct unbecoming an officer. In July, 1868, he was discharged from the service after being found asleep yet again on his beat. Ironically, there was some evidence in this case to support his claim that he had been feeling ill. All he suffered for his fatal negligence at Ford's Theatre was the wrath of Mrs. Lincoln who told him to his face that he was a murderer and conspirator.

Major A. C. Richards was ultimately responsible for the choice of men for White House duty, and Lincoln automatically assumed that only men with outstanding qualifications would be given this honour. Quite properly, on May 1, 1865, Richards preferred charges of neglect of duty against Parker. But there are no records of the hearing and the complaint was dismissed on June 2. Parker was never punished. He was not called as a witness at the conspiracy trial. And, incredibly, he was not immediately relieved of his White House duty.

Now it cannot be reasoned that Parker was involved in a conspiracy, for there could be no certainty in advance that he would be on duty the night that Booth chose to strike. But Stanton must bear the final responsibility for Parker's appointment since in time of war he was ultimately responsible for the safety of the Commander-in-Chief. Equally, Stanton can be held responsible for the failure to prosecute Parker as he deserved. The War Secretary was never noted for his forgiving nature. He was ruthless and harsh, and he never acted without a motive. Why then did Parker go unpunished? There is only one logical explanation: that once again Stanton was desperately anxious to cover up the appalling slackness of his security service, and the fact that the authorities had been careless enough to appoint a worthless officer to guard the most worthy life.

12. That Stanton made no special effort to capture John Harrison Surratt and preferred this conspirator to stay in hiding overseas.

Contrary to perjured testimony at his trial, John Harrison Surratt was not in Washington on the night of the assassination. On April 3, he left the capital to take dispatches to Confederate leaders in Canada. On April 14, a girl friend received from him two letters, postmarked Montreal, but in fact he was then in Elmira, a small town in New York State, where some five thousand Confederate prisoners were held. Witnesses placed him in Elmira as early as 7 a.m. on April 15 and there was no possible way he could have reached the town overnight from Washington.

After the assassination Surratt escaped with remarkable ease to Canada and then to Europe. On April 15, Assistant Secretary of War, Charles Dana, wired a description of Atzerodt to northern police chiefs, but not of Surratt. Thus the conspirator reached Canada without trouble, even though detectives were on special watch when he passed through the border station at St. Albans. Major Richards then took Weichmann and his fellow boarder, John T. Holahan, to help him track down Surratt, and they came so close to succeeding that Surratt later recalled he had seen Weichmann 'on the lookout for me'. But Richards was acting on his own initiative, and the War Department severely reprimanded him for sending these men on a 'wild chase' into Canada. In September, Surratt reached Liverpool. His arrival was quickly reported to the U.S. Consulate, and this valuable information was rushed back to Washington. Imagine then the Vice-Consul's astonishment when he was instructed that 'upon a consultation with the Secretary of War and the Judge Advocate General, it is thought advisable that no action be taken in regard to the arrest of the supposed John Surratt at present'.

Surratt now moved across Europe without difficulty and in April, 1866, under the name of John Watson, he enlisted as a zouave in the Pope's service. By a million to one chance there was another American in his company who had met him before in Maryland, and who now betrayed him in the hope of gaining

25,000 dollars reward.[1] But again the authorities delayed in taking action. Surratt escaped to Naples and moved on to Alexandria, Egypt, before he was finally brought back to be tried in 1867. The prosecution then went to extraordinary lengths to secure a conviction and the judge was absurdly biased. But the mood of the country had changed; the case had gone cold. In the face of diametrically opposed evidence, the jurymen, some of them Southern sympathisers, failed to agree on a verdict and eventually John Surratt was released.

The records clearly show that Stanton made no special effort to have Surratt captured after he had fled the country. Did he perhaps recall Lincoln's words at the last Cabinet meeting: 'When you have an elephant by the hind leg, and he's trying to run away, it's best to let him run.'? That was hardly Stanton's way. He must have had some other reason, but it remains obscure. Possibly he feared that Surratt, tried in a civil court, would make accusations against members of the government in an effort to save his own neck. Radicals certainly hoped that the last conspirator would help them to connect President Johnson with Lincoln's murder. But Surratt had no useful information in this respect. Another possibility is that Stanton feared that the Surratt trial would expose improprieties in the prosecution of the other conspirators and draw attention especially to his harsh treatment of the accused's mother. It is true that the Surratt trial did nothing to enhance the War Secretary's reputation, but nor does the casual pursuit of John Surratt add much weight to the theory that Stanton was involved in the assassination. If Stanton feared that Surratt could implicate him, it is improbable that he would have allowed him to run loose with the constant possibility of being captured. In such desperate circumstances he would surely have taken steps to have had him silenced completely.

So far the case against Edwin Stanton is based on sheer speculation. Many unanswered questions arouse suspicions that he was

1. In fact the reward for Surratt had been withdrawn by then.

connected with the assassination plot, but the only charge on which he could be found guilty on this evidence is one of incompetence or negligence in safeguarding the President from attacks and in pursuing the conspirators. There the case against him might have rested but for the remarkable research of an amateur detective who uncovered new evidence—ninety-two years after the crime was committed.

9

NEW EVIDENCE

IN THE HUNDRED years since the assassination of Lincoln, historical investigators have searched diligently for fresh evidence to throw light on the first murder of an American President. Many new facts have been uncovered to strengthen the possibility of a high-level conspiracy, and yet the most extraordinary discovery in this field was not made until ninety-two years after the crime. More incredibly, this discovery was virtually made by chance when a research chemist, Ray A. Neff of Gibbsboro (New Jersey), innocently paid fifty cents for a faded, second-hand book at Leary's bookshop in Philadelphia. The book—a bound volume of issues of *Colburn's United Service Magazine* for the latter half of 1864—set its owner on a fascinating new line of research which, through rare persistence and scientific effort, uncovered evidence which strongly suggested two startling possibilities: (1) that Edwin Stanton engineered the assassination as part of a vast, well-financed plot to seize control of the Federal Government; (2) that General Lafayette Baker, chief of Stanton's National Detective Police Force, was poisoned to ensure his silence about the plot.

The true value of this second-hand volume was not remotely suspected by Ray Neff until several months after he bought it. He was then thumbing through the book when he observed that a series of numbers and letters were written in pencil in the margins close to the binding. He showed them to Mr. Leonard Fousche, a professional cryptographer, who confirmed his suspicion that the jottings were a form of code. Aided by his wife and Fousche, Neff deciphered two messages. The first which appeared on pages 181, 183 and 185-211, was in what Neff describes as 'substitution cipher of a sliding variety'. Each letter in the message was replaced by another letter with frequent changes in the pattern to make solution more difficult. Each number marked the end of a word and Neff had to add his own punctuation. The message, dated 2.5.68, was translated as follows:

'I am constantly being followed. They are professionals. I cannot fool them. In new Rome there walked three men, a Judas, a Brutus and a spy. Each planned that he should be the king when Abraham should die. One trusted not the other but they went on for that day, waiting for that final moment when, with pistol in his hand, one of the sons of Brutus could sneak behind that cursed man and put a bullet in his brain and lay his clumsey [sic] corpse away. As the fallen man lay dying, Judas came and paid respects to one he hated, and when at last he saw him die, he said, "Now the ages have him and the nation now have I." But, alas, fate would have it Judas slowly fell from grace, and with him went Brutus down to their proper place. But lest one is left to wonder what happened to the spy, I can safely tell you this, it was I.'

It was 'signed'—Lafayette C. Baker.

The second message, running from pages 106 to 120, and continuing on pages 126, 127 and 245, could have been decoded by a child since it simply involved dots being placed under letters on the printed pages. This was translated:

'It was on the tenth of April, sixty-five, when I first knew that the plan was in action. Ecert had made all the contacts, the deed to be done on the fourteenth. I did not know the identity of the assassin, but I knew most all else when I approached E.S. about it. He at once acted surprised and disbelieving. Later he said: "You are a party to it too. Let us wait and see what comes of it and then we will know better how to act in the matter." I soon discovered what he meant that I was a party to it when the following day I was shown a document that I knew to be a forgery but a clever one, which made it appear that I had been in charge of a plot to kidnap the President, the Vice-President being the instigator. Then I became a party to that deed even though I did not care to.' (Alternatively, this part could be translated 'which made it appear that I had been in charge of a plot to kidnap the President [and] the Vice-President. Being the instigator then, I became a party to that deed even though I did not care to.' But this alternative involves introducing a conjunction and makes less sense).

The message went on:

'On the thirteenth he discovered that the President had ordered that the Legislature of Virginia be allowed to assemble to withdraw that state's troops from action against the U.S. He fermented immediately into an insane tyrade [sic]. Then for the first time I realised his mental disunity and his insane and fanatical hatred for the President. There are few in the War Department that respect the President or his strategy, but there are not many who would countermand an order that the President had given. However, during that insane moment, he sent a telegram to Gen. Weitzel countermanding the President's order of the twelfth. Then he laughed in a most spine chilling manner and said: "If he would to know who recinded [sic] his order we will let Lucifer tell him. Be off, Tom, and see to the arrangements. There can be no mistakes." This is the first that I knew that he was the one responsible for the assassination plot. Always before I thought that either he did not trust me, for he really trusted no one, or he was protecting someone until it was to his benefit to expose them. But now I know the truth and it frightens me no end. I fear that somehow I may become the sacrificial goat.

'There were at least eleven members of Congress involved in the plot, no less than twelve Army officers, three Naval officers and at least twenty four civilians, of which one was a governor of a loyal state. Five were bankers of great repute, three were nationally known newspapermen and eleven were industrialists of great repute and wealth. There were probably more that I know nothing of.

'The names of these known conspirators is presented without comment or notation in Vol one of this series. Eighty-five thousand dollars was contributed by the named persons to pay for the deed. Only eight persons knew the details of the plot and the identity of the others.

'I fear for my life. L.C.B.'

No findings of such a sensational character could have been better designed to arouse extreme scepticism, if not utter disbelief. On the face of it, these messages would seem worthless pencilled jottings which might have been added by any practical joker with a smattering of American history. And how convenient that the names of the members of the power group behind the conspiracy should be missing from the text. Inevitably, the immediate thought is that the messages are the invention of Mr. Neff himself, a devoted student of the civil war period. Let us allay this suspicion from the start. The first full account of his findings and subsequent investigations, as presented in the *Civil War Times* number of August, 1961, demonstrates that he approached his dramatic discovery with all the scepticism and science one would expect from a man of his profession.

Had this volume indeed once belonged to Lafayette C. Baker, former chief of Stanton's powerful National Detective Police Force? This was the first essential question to be resolved; until such ownership was established the messages were not worthy of consideration. Neff began a detailed study to see if the volume held more 'secrets' and found several discoloured places which he subjected to 'ultra-short wavelength ultra-violet radiations'. One of these patches in a margin emitted a purple glow but prolonged exposure to the lamp produced no results. He then spread a tannic acid solution over the spot and it revealed a signature—'L. C. Baker'. Neff, who was working at this time in the office of the medical examiner of the City of Philadelphia, had the signature examined by a city handwriting expert. It was declared genuine. In Neff's view, the signature had been made with an invisible ink having a ferro-cyanide base. He points out, 'Ink of this type was widely used by secret agents on both sides during the Civil War and would become visible after exposure to the sunlight for about half an hour.' He considers that the ink lost some of its properties over the years so that it would not respond to the ultra-violet lamp.

It was now established that the volume, in all probability, had sometime been in Baker's possession. Unable to learn more from the book itself, Neff began to delve deeper into the detective's last days, with special reference to the statement that he feared for his life in 1868. Baker had moved to Philadelphia after his dismissal in February, 1866, which followed President Johnson's discovery that the Detective Bureau had the White House under surveillance. Now, in the city where the detective chief had died on July 3, 1868, Neff began an exhaustive examination of the records in the City Hall. For six weeks he searched among the stacks and bundles of musty old records, and he was well rewarded. On file in the Register of Wills office he found Baker's will, dated April 30, 1866, which left specific amounts to his three brothers and three sisters and willed the residue of his estate to his wife, Jane Curry Baker. So far the only notable point he observed was that the death certificate, signed by Dr. William S. Rickards, gave meningitis as the cause of death—whereas newspaper accounts of Baker's death gave typhoid. But this discrepancy was not a new discovery and it seemed to have no special significance at the time. Neff also found that Luther Byron Baker, a cousin and fellow spy, had declined, on July 29, 1868, to serve as executor as named in the will. Instead, the duties of executor fell entirely on co-executor Joseph E. Stidfole who, on August 24, reported to the Register of Wills that he had been unable to find any personal property belonging to Baker.

Here was another oddity, but still Neff had found nothing to substantiate the coded allegations, or indeed that they were really made by Baker. With admirable persistence and patience he began checking on the legal records of the four witnesses to Baker's will of 1866. Only one of the four witnesses proved interesting—Mary Baker, wife of John F. Baker, a cousin of the deceased detective. She had lived next door (1737 Coates Street) to Lafayette at the time of his death and she had left a will signed June 11, 1867, three years before she was to die of tuberculosis. Her records gave Neff a most positive line of research, for among her papers at City Hall was an unprobated codicil to Baker's will which was dated three days before his death. This codicil provided for 'all books, diaries and personal papers not of a financial nature' to be given to 'my longtime friend Laura Duvall of Washington D.C.' Across the bottom of the codicil was written the notation: 'Rejected by Orphans Court, MBF January 6, 1879.'

This note of rejection told Neff that there should be a record of the hearing into the codicil somewhere in the City Hall archives. Now began the longest and most discouraging part of his searches; day after day he examined documents until he had almost given up hope. Then came his moment of triumph. He moved a pile of old books to one side and discovered the ledger which contained a handwritten transcript 'in the matter of the probate of a paper propounded as a Codicil to the Last Will and Testament of Lafayette C. Baker, deceased'. This transcript of a two-day hearing, held on October 14 and 15, 1872, could easily have proved dull and irrelevant. Instead, it provided the strongest support for: (1) the belief that the coded messages in the English military journal were written by Baker; (2) suspicions that Baker might have been murdered to silence him on some secret matter, possibly the conspiracy against Lincoln. It is an astonishing document.

The hearing begins with Miss Elizabeth Baker, daughter of Mary Baker, being asked by Mr. John R. Rogers (representing the legatee Laura Duvall) why the codicil had not been presented for probate years before. The witness explained that she had recently found the unrecorded codicil and six boxes of General Baker's books and papers among the personal effects of her mother, who had died in 1870. Where did her mother get the codicil? Miss Baker replied: 'I remember that when Uncle Lafe died, Mother went next door to their home and helped with arrangements. . . . Mother got two coloured men to bring some boxes from Uncle Lafe's house to our house. She put all the stuff in the attic. . . . I think there were about ten or twelve heavy wooden boxes. They were rather large boxes and appeared heavy. It took two men to carry them.'

Miss Baker went on to explain in her answers that her family had been poor when she was a child and that her father had worked in a livery stable. Mr. Rogers then asked her a seemingly simple question: 'What is the amount of your mother's estate?' Eight times he pursued this point. Each time Miss Baker hedged —she was not sure; she could not give an accurate answer; a final accounting had not been made; she could not recall what had been the appraisal. Rogers pressed on: 'Miss Baker, we are not interested in exact figures. We only want to know approximately. What was the general range of the appraisal?'

Back came a reply which must have staggered those present that morning in the Office of the Register of Wills of Philadelphia. The appraisal was about a quarter of a million dollars. And Miss Baker was unable to explain how her mother could have acquired such a gigantic sum.

It was already fairly obvious that Mary Baker had suppressed the codicil; indeed, her signature was on it as a witness. But this hearing had not been called by the heirs of Lafayette Baker to dispute the ownership of a few boxes of books and papers left to Laura Duvall. They believed Baker had left a secret fortune to which they were entitled under his will of 1866. Their lawyer sought to establish that the General was insane in the last months of his life, that his belief that someone was trying to kill him was indicative of mental unbalance and that Mary Baker had access to his property immediately after his death. A key witness on behalf of Miss Duvall was Dr. William M. L. Rickards, a respected citizen of Philadelphia and an ardent abolitionist. He testified that he had been General Baker's physician and personal friend since about 1850; he considered him to be a brilliant and a truthful man. Mr. Rogers asked him about Baker's mental condition just before he died. 'He was sane,' replied the doctor. 'He was suffering great pain and was receiving paragoric every four hours, but this had not disturbed his mental clarity.'

On behalf of the legatees under the 1866 will, Mr. Walter Marshall asked whether Baker had ever expressed fear for his life. 'Many times,' said the doctor. 'He had been shot at and attacked by someone with a knife on several occasions. . . . Two days before Christmas of 1867 I dressed a knife wound under his left arm. It required six stitches and took several months to heal . . . the cut was made through his surcoat, his coat, shirt and undershirt.' Dr. Rickards made nonsense of Marshall's suggestions that the wound might have been self-inflicted. 'I have seen many attempted suicides and I have never seen one that attempted it fully dressed with a heavy surcoat on.'

Richards went on to recall that he removed splinters from Baker's face, an injury caused by a bullet striking the door of the General's carriage on 'about December 28, 1867'. He then told how Baker came to his office on January 5, 1868, complaining that his nerves were bad because two attacks had been made on his life and because someone had been following him for a week or more. The doctor gave him some 'nerve medicine' and left his surgery soon after the General. 'As I left I saw a man who was skulking up an alley and carefully watching General Baker. . . . As I walked along the street I saw another man step from an alley further down the street. . . . They were definitely following the General.' Rickards admitted that he had no knowledge of detective work, but he stressed, 'It does not take a detective to know when some scoundrel is skulking around spying on honest people.'

At this point a certain Mr. John P. Smallwood intervened. He introduced himself as a national detective and an agent of the

United States War Department. The point he wished to make to the doctor was that detective work was a fine art—'if these men had been actually following the General, you would not have been able to observe that they were observing him'. An interesting man is this Mr. Smallwood. He is recorded as having appeared for the War Department as 'an interested party'. No one had suggested that professional detectives were shadowing the General, but he was eager to dismiss the possibility.

The Register put him in his proper place. 'Mr. Lockwood, you are not a witness but an interrogator. If you wish to testify then you should be sworn and take the witness chair. Otherwise, please ask questions or sit down.'

'The name is Smallwood, sir.'

'Then, Mr. Smallwood, either ask questions or sit down.'

Mr. Smallwood sat down.

Dr. Rickards continued to recall attacks on the General. After Baker left his surgery on the evening of January 5, he 'was set upon and beaten, and an attempt was made to drag him into a carriage'. A policeman came to his rescue and the doctor was called out to treat the General for his injuries. 'He had been beaten rather severely. . . . As a result of this incident a policeman was stationed outside the Baker home for some time. The officer accompanied General Baker wherever he went for some weeks.'

Baker's heirs apparently suspected that he had died of arsenic poisoning, for Marshall pressed the doctor strongly on this possibility. Rickards, however, insisted that Baker had 'died of meningitis following typhoid fever of long standing'. He explained that his patient 'contracted ptomaine on January 12, 1868', and that he was almost constantly ill until about the first of February. He then began to recover, but on February 14 he showed symptoms of typhoid fever. Rickards admitted it was not a typical case of typhoid fever. 'He would partially recover and then, for no apparent reason, relapse. I attribute that to his debilitated condition. . . . Although there is often much vomiting with high fever connected with typhoid, General

Baker did not run a high fever much of the time and he would often develop the vomiting when he felt his best. He, on one occasion, had been up and about all afternoon and said that he had a very good appetite. He ate his supper and soon thereafter began to vomit. He became extremely ill for several days.'

The following testimony shows that Rickards was unconvincing in his opinion of the cause of death. He stated:

'From a strict medical standpoint of view, it would be possible that he was poisoned. But I know he was not. I know that household and no one there would or could have poisoned him.'

Q. 'Did his symptoms fit the symptoms observed with any known poison?'

A. 'Yes.'

Q. 'Which poison?'

A. 'Arsenic.'

Q. 'In other words, the symptoms shown by General Baker show more similarity to arsenic poisoning than they do to typhoid fever?'

A. 'Yes.'

Q. 'It is then possible that General Baker died of arsenic poisoning?'

A. 'From a medical standpoint, yes. But I know that he was not poisoned.'

Q. 'How do you know this?'

A. 'No one had the opportunity.'

Dr. Rickards explained that he had investigated the possibility of poisoning by having the General's medicine analysed by a different chemist. It did not show any arsenic. He first considered the possibility of poisoning when Baker was having very severe headaches. 'I applied leeches behind his ears. The leeches stuck at first and then dropped off. When reapplied they would again drop off. I returned them to the apothecary and got others. These did the same. I watched these second leeches and observed that they soon died. . . . It could indicate some sort of poison. After consulting an associate I concluded that it was due to the toxins of typhoid.'

Marshall again questioned the doctor about Baker's mental condition. 'Is it not true that with insanity one of the most frequent complaints is that someone is trying to kill them? Isn't it also true that these persons usually claim to have papers and money hidden, papers which their enemies would like to have, papers which would cause the downfall of their enemies?' Rickards agreed. But Baker had never told him about secret papers. The General, he insisted, was 'perfectly sane'.

Dr. Rickards appears to have been a somewhat biased witness, a loyal friend determined to speak no evil of the deceased. He praised Baker as a man, steadfastly refused to believe he would take his own life. He stated: 'Much of the false things which had been written about him gave him worry. It made no difference whether it was good or bad; if it was untruthful it worried him. He was very apprehensive about what history would say about him. He wanted it to be good but he also wanted it to be accurate. He often told me of his concern about this.'

The next witness, Mrs. Bridgit McBane, was more accommodating. She was hired on June 5, 1868, as a nurse for the General, and she readily agreed that Baker was insane. 'I think he was daft. . . . He was always talking about how somebody was tryin' to do him in and as how he had papers to prove it, and as how he had a lot of money hidden and they was after it.' Mrs. McBane had never seen any money; in fact, she complained she was still owed for her last two weeks' work at the General's house. But she did testify that Mrs. Baker rarely slept at home because she was afraid of something, and she claimed that she had seen the General sign the codicil.

Miss Kathleen Hawks, who worked in the Baker home from February 1, 1868, to June 1, 1868, gave the opinion that her employer was ' as sane as you or I'. He had good reason to be frightened for during February someone had tried to shoot him. 'The General was standing by the window and someone shot at him. The bullet narrowly missed him and struck the wall near my head. I screamed and ran out of the room.' According to Miss Hawks, Baker said that old friends wanted to kill him because he had papers which would send them to prison. 'There was a Mr. Cobb who would visit him, and when Mr. Cobb left the General would be all upset. One time he said to me that Mr. Cobb would like to see him dead. Another time he said that Mr. Cobb wanted some papers which he had. . . . Once I heard Mr. Cobb say: "Our patience is running short, Baker. You haven't much time." '

Miss Hawks was the one witness who testified that she had seen Baker's hidden fortune. When she had asked for her back wages of 'about eight dollars', Baker had given her a key and sent her to get a tin box from the attic. 'He took a key from a string around his neck and unlocked it. The box was full of money . . . all new and shiny . . . fifty- and hundred-dollar bills . . . all wrapped with little bands of papers. . . . He gave me twenty dollars in new five-dollar bills.'

The witness who provided the most vital evidence in respect of Ray Neff's discovery was one William Carter, then 'a drummer for the American Household Supply Company'. He had worked under Baker during the war and had last seen him on June 30, 1868, a few days before the General's death. Carter said he found that Baker was 'in fair spirits and seemed mentally sharp', but 'he did say some things which made me wonder. When I came into the room he had a stack of books by his bed and he had one open and was making marks in it. I asked him what he was doing and he said, "I'm writing my memoirs." I asked him to make sure that I had heard him right and he said it over again. Then I said, "But, General, them books is already wrote." And he said, "Right, they are going to have to get up early to get ahead of old Lafe Baker." And then he laughed. I picked up one of the books and looked at it, and I saw that he was writing cipher in it. But it was a different cipher than I'd ever seen before. I learned to read and write cipher when I was in the National Detective

Police during the war, but I never seen anything like he was writing that day. I asked him what it was and he just laughed. . . .

'No, he didn't seem insane, but he didn't seem hisself. It could have been the medicine but he seemed sort of funny. He kept laughing and kind of cackling. All the time that I was there he kept writing in the book. Once I picked up one of the books and looked at a title in it. It was an English military journal and it had a story in it that I was interested in. When I said that I was interested in it he gave me the book to take it home with me.'

Q. 'And did this book have cipher in it?'

A. 'Yes.'

Q. 'Did you ever try to decipher it?'

A. 'I couldn't.'

Q. 'Would you consider yourself an expert cipher clerk?'

A. 'No, I ain't no expert by any bargain. I have a hard time deciphering simple codes anymore. But this one is different.'

Q. 'Do you still have the book?'

A. 'Yes. He also tried to give me about a dozen boxes of books and papers . . . but I couldn't accept them. I live in a gentleman's hotel and travel a lot, and I don't have any place to store no large amount of books.'

Mr. Marshall then asked the witness a few questions, the purpose of which is unexplained:

Q. 'You were in the National Detective Police?'

A. 'Yes.'

Q. 'What was your title?'

A. 'I was an operative.'

Q. 'How long?'

A. 'Two years.'

Q. 'Do you know Mr. Smallwood?'

A. 'Yes.'

Q. 'Were you associates during the late war?'

A. 'We were both National Detective Police but we wasn't associates.'

After a recess and further testimony by Miss Elizabeth Baker, this remarkable hearing concluded with another interesting exchange between the Register and the mysterious Mr. Smallwood.

Smallwood: 'On behalf of the United States War Department, I would like to submit a motion to the effect that certain papers, which are in the inventory of contents of the six boxes found with the effects of the late Mary Baker, be released to the War Department. These documents were pilfered from the War Department files many years ago and they are important to the Government. I am here prepared to take charge of them for the Government.'

Register: 'Can you identify them?'

Smallwood: 'Yes.'

Register: 'Very well, if you will pick them out of the boxes and turn them over to the clerk, I will have them read into the record and upon presentation of proof, I will have them turned over to you.'

Smallwood: 'It is the desire of the Government to have these documents kept secret.'

Register: 'First of all, Mr. Lockwood, this is the improper time to make a motion concerning this material, but since the petition has been filed, I will entertain it, but in my own manner. If this is not to your liking you may withdraw the petition.'

Smallwood: 'The name is Smallwood, sir. I wish to withdraw the petition.'

Register: 'Petition is withdrawn.'

There the hearing was closed. A decision on the codicil was not made until January, 1879, when the Orphans Court of Philadelphia rejected it because: (1) no living witnesses could be found to verify Baker's sanity when he signed it; (2) there was 'reasonable doubt' as to his mental stability; (3) the legatee, Laura Duvall, was dead, having been killed by a runaway team in 1876. In July, 1879, the legatees of Baker's 1866 will settled out of court with the heirs of Mary Baker for 80,000 dollars. The estate had become worth 458,299 dollars by that time.

It is not clear why Miss Duvall was not at the original hearing, but possibly her relationship to the late General Baker would have provided some embarrassment. Elizabeth Baker identified her as a woman who frequently visited the General in his long sickness, brought him flowers, and was 'very kind'. But she also recalled that Mrs. Jane Baker was 'very jealous . . . and she said many nasty and unfair things about Miss Duvall'. Baker mentions Laura Duvall in his *History of the United States Secret Service* as being a witness against a Treasury Department official, Spencer H. Clark, whom Baker charged with seducing government girls. Miss Duvall admitted intimacies with Clark. There would appear to have been a very close personal bond between her and the General, but she did not live to gain possession of his 'books, diaries and personal papers' as he had wished. What happened to the impounded personal effects of Lafayette Baker remains a mystery. Neff believes that some of his belongings may have been pilfered and that the rest may lie in one of the dozens of storerooms in the Philadelphia City Hall. He has searched without success.

The inventory lists ten volumes of Baker's journals for 1858-68, five volumes of bound correspondence and twenty-two volumes of photographs. Also mentioned are bound volumes of *Colburn's U.S. Magazine* for the years 1860 to 1865, with one notable exception. The volume for the first half of 1864 is not listed. This is the book in which the names of the alleged conspirators are supposedly named in code, and, in all probability, it is the volume Baker gave to Carter. The inventory, plus Baker's authenticated signature and Carter's testimony, provides convincing evidence that Neff's English military journal once belonged to the detective chief and that the General almost certainly wrote coded messages in at least two books. Neff believes that the second volume for 1864 was pilfered sometime after the hearing and so found its way into a second-hand book store. All efforts to find the missing volume have failed.

This hearing also provides a strong suggestion that Baker's death may have been due to arsenic poisoning. Dr. Rickards

testified that on July 1, 1868, his patient showed symptoms of
meningitis and died at 12.10 a.m. on July 3. Two hours after his
death, a magistrate signed an order to have the coffin sealed
because of the contagious nature of the disease. Then the house
was fumigated. But there is much evidence that Baker's life was
being threatened, and arsenic poisoning was easily misdiagnosed
because its symptoms resembled those of other ailments. The
presence of arsenic would explain the reaction of the leeches
applied to the patient. Neff looked for Baker's grave to have his
remains tested for traces of arsenic, but he found that the part of
the cemetery where the detective was buried had been taken over
as a public playground in 1922. The bodies had then been removed to another North Philadelphia graveyard, and records
indicating the precise location of the reburied corpses cannot be
found. Neff tells me: 'Baker's grave can be located only to the
extent that it is known to be in a plot twenty to forty feet. This
makes chemical analysis impractical.'

The evidence of the hearing leaves other puzzles. It strongly
suggests that Baker had a secret fortune, possibly a quarter of a
million dollars, when he died. How could he have acquired such
a sum far beyond his saving capacity from legitimate earnings?
And who was the mysterious Mr. Cobb whose visits upset Baker
during his illness? One suggestion is that he may have been
Joseph Cobb, husband of a pardon broker, whom Baker arrested
in 1866, much to the annoyance of President Johnson. Mrs. Cobb
had Baker indicted for false arrest and extortion, and the General
was found guilty of wrongful arrest and fined one dollar. This
affair precipitated his dismissal from the detective force.

Presuming that the coded messages were by the hand of Baker
—and on the evidence of this transcript it seems a reasonable
presumption—what light, if any, do the cryptic writings throw
on the assassination plot? The first message refers to three men
walking in Rome—a Judas, a Brutus and a spy. The spy, we are
told, is Baker himself, and the Judas is quite obviously Stanton
since, in the same passage, the author paraphrases the War

Secretary's famous remark on the President's death: 'Now he belongs to the ages.' It is equally clear that 'one of the sons of Brutus' refers to the assassin, John Wilkes Booth.

According to the second coded message, Baker first knew of 'the plan' on April 10, four days before the assassination. 'Ecert had made all the contacts, the deed to be done on the fourteenth.' It is reasonable to presume that 'Ecert' refers to Major Thomas T. Eckert, who was in charge of the military telegraph headquarters in the War Department, the same Eckert who had declined the President's request that he accompany him to the theatre that ill-fated night. It is simple to explain the different spelling of his name. The words were indicated by placing dots beneath letters on the printed pages of the bound magazines. On page 107, where reference is made to 'Ecert', the letter 'k' does not appear in the text at a convenient position; to have used this letter would have involved a large gap in the coded message. Further indication that Eckert was the man is provided by the later quotation, attributed to Stanton, 'Be off, Tom, and see to the arrangements.'

The message later states that 'on the thirteenth he (Stanton) discovered that the President had ordered the Legislature of Virginia be allowed to assemble to withdraw that state's troops from action against the U.S. He fermented immediately into an insane tyrade [sic] . . . during that insane moment he sent a telegram to Gen. Weitzel countermanding the President's order of the twelfth. Then he laughed in a most spine chilling manner and said: "If he would to know who recinded [sic] his order we will let Lucifer tell him."' Here the statements can be checked against historical records and it is seen that Baker, if he was the author, made an error of a week in recalling these events. It was on April 6, when the crushed Confederate Army of Northern Virginia was retreating towards Appomattox, that Lincoln sent the following telegram to Major-General Godfrey Weitzel, whose 25th Corps occupied Richmond:

'It has been intimated to me that the gentlemen who have acted as the legislature of Virginia, in support of the rebellion, may now desire to assemble at Richmond, and take measures to with-draw the Virginia troops and other support from resistance to the general government. If they attempt it, give them permission and protection, until, if at all, they attempt some action hostile to the United States, in which case you will notify them and give them reasonable time to leave; and at the end of which time, arrest any who may remain. Allow Judge Campbell to see this, but do not make it public.'

One can well imagine that Stanton 'fermented immediately into an insane tyrade' over the contents of this telegram. He saw this as open recognition of the Confederate legislature and a plain indication that Lincoln was set upon restoring to the South its former rights.

It would appear that Judge John A. Campbell, who had served as Assistant Secretary of War for the Confederacy, did not treat Lincoln's message with the secrecy he requested. The Official Records show that a telegram was sent from Stanton to Weitzel (dated 8 p.m., April 9) in which the War Minister reprimanded the General for allowing the Episcopal churches of fallen Richmond to hold services which did not include prayers for the President of the United States. The message went on: 'You are, moreover, directed to hold no further conferences with Mr. Campbell on any subject without specific authority, to be given by the President or this Department; but if he desires to make any communications to you it must be in writing, and transmitted by you to this Department for instructions.'

Stanton and the radicals were furious at what they interpreted as open recognition of the seceded Virginia Legislature. But Lincoln diplomatically sought to avoid a major clash within the Cabinet by sending another message to Weitzel. In this telegram, sent on April 12 at 6 p.m., the President challenged the assumption 'that I have called the insurgent legislature of Virginia together, as the rightful legislature of the State, to settle all differences with the United States. . . . I have done no such thing. I spoke of them not as a legislature but as "the gentlemen who

have acted as the legislature of Virginia in support of the Rebellion"
. . . as Judge Campbell misconstrues this . . . let my letter to you,
and the paper to Judge Campbell, both be withdrawn or countermanded, and he be notified of it. Do not allow them to assemble,
but if any have come, allow them safe return to their homes'. In
effect, Lincoln had countermanded his own orders of April 6.

If, as the coded message states, Stanton discovered Lincoln's
original order on the 13th and countermanded it, there is no
record of such a message being sent. Anyway, it could not have
been done on the 13th since Lincoln had already sent his second
telegram, and that day Baker was no longer in Washington. He
left that day for New York and was there when the President
was killed. Most probably, the author of the ciphers had his dates
muddled and referred to Stanton's message of April 9 when he
stated that the War Secretary countermanded the President's
orders. The suggestion behind these facts is that Lincoln sent his
second message to Weitzel too late to appease Stanton and the
radicals. Two days later he was murdered.

Finally, one must consider the most sensational allegation of
all to appear in 'Baker's coded messages'—the concluding statement that 'there were at least eleven members of Congress involved in the plot, no less than twelve Army officers, three Naval
officers and at least twenty-four civilians, of which one was a
governor of a loyal state. Five were bankers of great repute, three
were nationally known newspapermen and eleven were industrialists of great repute and wealth . . . eighty-five thousand dollars
was contributed by the named persons to pay for the deed'.

Without any names named, these allegations are virtually
worthless, and even if a list of names was discovered it is difficult
to see what it could prove. The revelation of a mass conspiracy
scarcely adds weight to the allegations; rather it prompts several
questions which cannot be readily answered. Would Stanton
really run the risk of letting so many people (at least fifty) have
knowledge of a secret plot to overthrow the Government?
Would so many associates be needed to raise the capital for such

an enterprise? And is it conceivable that all these people would have taken the secret with them to the grave? It hardly seems credible. On the other hand, there is the fact that Booth told Chester that there were 'from fifty to one hundred persons engaged in the conspiracy', and that, after his arrest, Herold made a statement that Booth had told him that thirty-five men in Washington were involved in the plot. Moreover, the idea of a huge assassination fund is not so absurd in the light of history. On December 1, 1864, a Southern lawyer, George Washington Gayle, placed the following advertisement in the *Selma Dispatch*, an Alabama newspaper:

'One million dollars wanted to have peace by the 1st of March. If the citizens of the Southern Confederacy will furnish me with the cash, or good securities for the sum of one million dollars, I will cause the lives of Abraham Lincoln, Wm. H. Seward, and Andrew Johnson to be taken by the 1st of March next. This will give us peace, and satisfy the world that cruel tyrants can not live in a "land of liberty". If this is not accomplished, nothing will be claimed beyond the sum of fifty thousand dollars in advance, which is supposed to be necessary to reach and slaughter the three villains. I will give myself one thousand dollars towards this patriotic purpose. Every one wishing to contribute will address Box X, Cahawba, Alabama.'

The *Selma Dispatch*, with a circulation of eight hundred, published this ad several times. Gayle was eventually taken to Washington where he spent some time in prison. But he was never brought to trial and he said that he placed the ad 'in sport for the sake of playing a joke on the community'. Was General Baker, in the last days of his life, also playing a grim joke against Edwin Stanton? As in 1867, when the House Judiciary Committee investigating Lincoln's death considered suggestions that Booth's diary had been mutilated, all the evidence boils down simply to a question of Baker's word against Stanton's. Without proof on either side, one can only consider which man's word is more acceptable.

10

STANTON AND BAKER

GENERAL GEORGE B. MCCLELLAN, the Democrats' 1864
Presidential candidate, once gave his opinion of Edwin
McMasters Stanton in a letter to his wife. He wrote, 'I think
that (I do not wish to be irreverent) had he lived in the time of
the Saviour, Judas Iscariot would have remained a respected
member of the fraternity of the Apostles, and that the magnificent treachery and rascality of E. M. Stanton would have
caused Judas to have raised his name in holy horror.' Admittedly,
McClellan, the most controversial of Lincoln's war generals, had
been driven to almost hysterical condemnation of 'those hounds
in Washington', and had become prone to almost irrational
thinking. Yet he was by no means alone in this extreme view of
Stanton. Old Gideon Welles, Secretary of the Navy, was one of
many who distrusted him intensely. A shrewd judge of character,
he wrote in his diary that the Secretary of War 'has cunning and
skill . . . dissembles his feelings . . . is a hypocrite'.

Depending on the person's viewpoint, Stanton has been
variously described as loyal, industrious, highly strung, sensitive,
stubborn, cowardly and treacherous. Examples can be drawn to
show him to be all these things and more. But above all we are
concerned here with his treachery, his ruthlessness and his double-
dealing. Was he, in short, a man capable of an act of supreme
perfidy, of being the Judas in the killing of Abraham Lincoln?

Stanton certainly looked the part of a Judas. He was a gnomelike figure, burly, short-legged, with a black, bushy beard and long, black, perfumed whiskers streaked with grey; thick-lensed, gold-rimmed spectacles covering his darting eyes accentuated the picture of a sinister figure. In temperament, too, he fitted the role of a villain. He was a peppery little man, grim, aggressive and impatient, completely contrasting the patient, easy-going President he served. With his vehement glare and sneering tone, he had the ability to make even veteran generals cower in his presence. Yet the bullying, sharp-tongued Stanton was a physical coward and the few men who stood up to him found that he could be quickly subdued.

It is undeniable that Stanton was an efficient administrator who brought order out of chaos when he took over the War Department in 1862. He worked remarkably long hours, never took a holiday or seriously engaged in social activities. He lived for his work, worshipped power, and waged such a relentless war against treason and corruption that over a quarter of a million people were arrested under his authority during the civil conflict. Adroitly, he established himself as the second most powerful man in the land. He took charge of the military telegraph and the control of government censorship which he exercised drastically and to the despair of war correspondents. Eventually he had full control of the propaganda machine, and, apart from himself, only the President had access to official dispatches. Stanton also took over jurisdiction over political prisoners, and with that wide power the tyranny of his office steadily increased. More than thirteen thousand persons were arrested by the War Department as political offenders, many without recorded charges. His ruthlessness, domineering manner and disregard of human rights made him the most hated member of Lincoln's administration.

But Stanton had not always been a stern disciplinarian, apparently without any feeling for anyone except himself. Of humble origin, he worked his way through college and fell deeply in love with a clergyman's daughter. They married and lived in Steubenville, Ohio, where Stanton began as a young lawyer. But then he suffered two heart-breaking personal tragedies. Firstly, he brooded so much over the death in 1841 of their baby daughter Lucy that he had the remains exhumed a year later and kept the child's ashes in his room. Then, after seven years of marriage, the wife he adored died in childbirth. For a while Stanton surrendered himself to wild emotions. He insisted that his wife should be dressed in her coffin just as she had been on their wedding day; long afterwards he was a broken man who wept by night and day. Twelve years later he took another wife, a handsome woman called Ellen. But by now his one great love was power, and for the rest of his days he was noted for his hatred, never for affection.

Edwin Stanton was certainly a man capable of betraying a colleague in his own pursuit of power. Throughout his political career, intrigue played a major part in his progress. In December, 1860, President Buchanan made him his Attorney-General, but while Stanton flattered the Democratic leader *ad nauseam* he also curried favour with Republicans in Congress in anticipation of a new party administration. When Lincoln failed to send for him in forming his first administration, the disappointed office-seeker reacted by bitterly abusing the new President whom he called 'the original gorilla'. And in the same way he turned against Grant years later when another President omitted him from his Cabinet.

Stanton succeeded War Secretary Simon Cameron in ironic and highly suspicious circumstances. As his attorney, Stanton advised Cameron to include in his annual report a statement that 'it is as clearly the right of this Government to arm slaves when it may become necessary as it is to use gunpowder or guns taken from the enemy'. In this, Stanton was both serving the Radical Republicans and increasing the measure of disagreement between the President and his Secretary of War. The gulf between Lincoln and Cameron was now widened beyond repair. Cameron was appointed to replace Cassius Marcellus Clay as Minister to Russia, and Seward proposed Stanton as his successor. Apparently, Lincoln was not aware that the new War Minister favoured arming the slaves even more strongly than the man he was replacing.

Stanton displayed similar cunning in his dealings with General McClellan, whose rising popularity he bitterly resented. The War Secretary once proclaimed that McClellan hoped to take Richmond shortly. But he did so at a time when no such expectation was expressed in the General's telegrams; indeed, McClellan then feared a major defeat. This statement by Stanton might be interpreted as reasonable wartime propaganda, an effort to boost the Union's morale. More probably, it might be taken as a stab in McClellan's back. When Richmond was not captured, the General's public image was badly tarnished and newspapers condemned him. It was a typical Stanton manœuvre against a man who threatened to be a strong rival in the future struggle for power. He was for ever undermining McClellan's position by political interference in army affairs and by spreading the seeds of doubt concerning the General's loyalty. But while he conducted a personal campaign against McClellan, he communicated with him in the friendliest of terms, professing himself to be a true friend. McClellan was not deceived for an instant. He judged the War Secretary to be 'the vilest man . . . the most unmitigated scoundrel . . . the most depraved hypocrite and villain'. Similarly, Stanton's later efforts to weaken the political standing of Sherman prompted that general to accuse him of 'deadly malignity'.

As a boy, Stanton had the curious hobby of training snakes. Many of his contemporaries would judge that he had learned to behave like his pets. Certainly his intrigue was no less after Lincoln's death. On April 16, two days after the assassination, radical leaders met at the War Department where he outlined his plan for placing Virginia and North Carolina as one military territory under the supervision of his own department. This was the plan so coldly received at Lincoln's last Cabinet meeting. While Stanton flirted with the left wing of the Republican Party, he remained at loggerheads with President Johnson over his moderate reconstruction policies and had spies placed in the

White House. It has never been explained why Johnson, who was well aware of Stanton's duplicity, allowed him to remain in his Cabinet. When he finally felt compelled to get rid of his double-dealing Secretary of War, he could only do so with the maximum difficulty. By then the Tenure-of-Office Bill, enacted over the President's veto, had stripped the President of his constitutional right to dismiss appointed officials without the Senate's consent.

When Johnson sought to replace him with Grant, Stanton refused to resign, and the radical Congress had their excuse for the President's impeachment. The sordid impeachment proceedings began on March 5, 1868, and ended on May 16, with the radicals failing by one vote to gain the two-thirds majority in the Senate necessary for conviction. It was virtually the end of Stanton's dreams of power, and as his political standing declined so did his health. His last ambition was to be appointed to the Supreme Court of the United States, but he was a dying man when the appointment came in 1869.

Since Stanton either commanded extreme loyalty or more often aroused intense personal dislike, it is difficult to find a dispassionate assessment of him as a man. But the opinion of General Grant is worthy of note. The General, a tobacco-addict, was dying of cancer of the throat when he wrote about Stanton in his *Personal Memoirs*, and he had no special axe to grind. According to Grant, the War Secretary 'was a man who never questioned his own authority, and who always did in war time what he wanted to do. He was an able constitutional lawyer and jurist; but the Constitution was not an impediment to him while the war lasted. In this latter particular I entirely agree with the view he evidently held. The Constitution was not framed with a view to any such rebellion as that of 1861-5.'

Lincoln and Stanton 'were the very opposite of each other in almost every particular, except that each possessed great ability. . . . He [Stanton] cared nothing for the feeling of others. In fact, it seemed to be pleasanter to him to disappoint than to gratify.

He felt no hesitation in assuming the functions of the executive, or in acting without advising with him. It was generally supposed that these two officials formed the complement of each other. The Secretary was required to prevent the President's being imposed upon. The President was required in the more responsible place of seeing that injustice was not done to others. . . . It is not a correct view, however, in my estimation. Mr. Lincoln did not require a guardian to aid him in the fulfilment of a public trust. Mr. Lincoln was not timid, and he was willing to trust his generals in making and executing their plans. The Secretary was very timid, and it was impossible for him to avoid interfering with the armies covering the capital when it was sought to defend it by an offensive movement against the army guarding the Confederate capital. He could see our weakness, but he could not see the enemy was in danger. The enemy would not have been in danger if Mr. Stanton had been in the field.'

Grant, however, was not in the best position to evaluate the wartime partnership of Lincoln and Stanton, and it is necessary to go back much further to consider their attitude towards one another. Their first meeting came in 1855 and it scarcely augured a happy relationship. At that time Lincoln was an up and coming lawyer engaged by John H. Manny to defend him in an action brought by Cyrus H. McCormick, inventor of a reaping machine, for infringement of patent. It was the most important of Lincoln's patent cases—McCormick was suing for 400,000 dollars—and he looked forward to a great legal tussle with the brilliant Reverdy Johnson, representing the plaintiff. A second lawyer, George Harding, was to make the technical arguments for the defence, but when Lincoln arrived in Cincinnati for the trial he found a third lawyer had been engaged for the defence—Edwin M. Stanton. Only two lawyers were required to speak at the trial and, contrary to professional etiquette, Lincoln, the original counsel, was crowded out of his own case by the more experienced Stanton.

It was a bitter disappointment for the Springfield lawyer, who had prepared his arguments so carefully. Herndon quotes a local lawyer, W. M. Dickson, as recalling that 'Lincoln felt that Stanton had not only been very discourteous to him, but he had purposely ignored him in the case. . . . Stanton, in his brusque and abrupt way, it is said, described him as a "long, lank creature from Illinois, wearing a dirty linen duster for a coat, on the back of which the perspiration had splotched wide stains that resembled a map of the continent".' Back in Springfield, Lincoln told Herndon that he had been 'roughly treated by that man Stanton' and that he had overheard Stanton saying in an adjoining room, 'Where did that long-armed creature come from, and what can he expect to do in this case?'

Possibly the memory of their first meeting prompted Stanton to believe that he might again assert his will over the uncouth, backwoods lawyer, even though Lincoln was now President. Certainly Stanton had his way in most matters, and on at least one occasion he was known to send for the President rather than call at the White House himself. But there are also plenty of examples of Lincoln imposing his authority over Stanton. The President patiently suffered Stanton's domineering manner, but suggestions that he was cowed by his War Minister are erroneous. It sometimes amused the President to give the impression that he dared not defy Stanton's wishes, and sometimes it served as a tactful expedient when he was hard pressed by some favour-seeker. But on several occasions, when Stanton bluntly refused to execute a presidential order, Lincoln stood firm and saw that it was carried out.

For the sake of the Union it was vital that they should work in reasonable harmony and the President accepted a situation requiring a great deal of humility on his part. Lincoln's superb sense of humour made their uneasy partnership more bearable. He did not hesitate to make jokes about his War Secretary. When a Boston man asked him if he ever swore, Lincoln replied: 'Oh, I don't have to. You know I have Stanton in my Cabinet.' Once, when a trader sought a pass through army lines, Lincoln signed a permit and told him, 'You will have to take it over to Stanton for countersigning.' The trader returned later to complain that Stanton had torn up the permit and stamped on the pieces. Said Lincoln, 'You go back and tell Stanton that I will tear up a dozen of his papers before Saturday night.'

Charles A. Dana, Assistant Secretary of War, was perhaps not so far from the truth as some historians would suggest when he wrote: 'Lincoln was a supreme politician. He understood politics because he understood human nature.' Indeed, he worked so well with Stanton that Secretaries Nicolay and Hay observed, 'There grew up between them an intimacy in which the mind and heart of each were given without reserve to the great work in which they bore such conspicuous parts.' Certainly, Lincoln had a high regard for Stanton's ability and considered him to be indispensable at a time of war. 'Stanton,' he once remarked, 'is the rock upon which are beating the waves of this conflict. I do not see how he survives—why he is not crushed and torn to pieces. Without him I should be destroyed.' After the 1864 election there were persistent rumours that Lincoln would replace his Secretary of War. But, as it was noted by Grant's aide, Colonel Porter, the President declared: 'I doubt very much whether you could select as efficient a Secretary of War as the present incumbent. He is not only a man of untiring energy and devotion to duty, but even his worst enemies never for a moment doubt his personal integrity and the purity of his motives.' When Lincoln returned from Richmond on April 9, 1865, Stanton offered his written resignation, knowing full well that it would never be accepted at such a moment of triumph. Lincoln tore up the paper and told him: 'You cannot go. Reconstruction is more difficult and dangerous than construction or destruction. You have been our main reliance. You must help us through the final act. The bag is filled. It must be tied and tied securely. Some knots slip. Yours do not. You understand the situation better than anyone else, and it is my wish and the country's that you remain.'

Edwin Stanton remains a great enigma. Once, at the end of a

busy day at the office, he was found with his head slumped over his desk, inexplicably sobbing. He was sly, deceitful, domineering, ruthless, stubborn, power-seeking and ill-tempered. On the other hand, he was efficient, industrious, intensely religious (in his precious little spare time he worked on a book *The Poetry of the Bible*) and was loyal to the Union cause. And no one could accuse Stanton of using his high position for material gain. A man of simple tastes, dedicated to his work, he displayed no desire to make a personal fortune. As much cannot be said of his wartime subordinate, Lafayette C. Baker, the man now cast in the role of his accuser. Baker had all Stanton's vices, but not all of his virtues. Born on October 13, 1826, the son of a Michigan farmer, he migrated to California and became a leading member of the Vigilante Committee which ruthlessly and effectively tamed the lawless of San Francisco. This experience was to prove a first-class apprenticeship for the role he would take in the civil war years.

After the fall of Fort Sumter, this shrewd opportunist applied to General-in-Chief Winfield Scott as a secret agent and was sent on a mission behind Confederate lines. Baker went on foot to Richmond—along the underground route that Booth later planned to follow—and was eventually captured. According to his story—and Baker never failed to recount events to his own advantage—he had three interviews with Jefferson Davis and then escaped back to Washington with valuable information about the opposing armies. On Scott's recommendation, he was employed as a detective by the State Department, and when the Detective Bureau was taken over by the War Department, Stanton singled out Baker as the most suitable officer for work on the exposure of conspiracies and the capture of Confederate spies. Peter H. Watson, then Assistant Secretary of War, described Baker's appointment as a case of 'set a rogue to catch a rogue'.

Though he was often accused of dishonesty and duplicity, Baker appears to have been a master detective who made a valuable contribution to the war effort. From being an obscure agent he jumped, in May, 1863, to the rank of Colonel of the 1st D.C. Cavalry, a security regiment under direct control of the War Department. He used this position of immense power to build up a force of secret agents and informers estimated as great as two thousand strong. His so-called detectives, many of them men of dubious character and background, would seize suspects without a shred of evidence, handcuff them, and escort them to their chief's office in the basement of the Treasury, where they might be held for weeks, even months, without warrant, and grilled as long and as severely as Baker pleased. He became known as the czar of the underworld; his power and his ruthlessness made him one of the most feared and hated men in the land.

Gideon Welles judged that Baker was 'wholly unreliable, regardless of character and the rights of persons, incapable of discrimination, and zealous to do something sensational'. But while his bureau was notorious for its corruption and harshness, no one could accuse the secret service chief of lacking energy, and if his methods were often underhand they still achieved much in combating crime and vice within the capital. His men seized contraband supplies of drugs, raided brothels and gaming houses, arrested stewards and nurses who were robbing soldiers in hospitals, exposed immoral relationships between government employees. But innocent and guilty often suffered alike as his force relentlessly waged war against traitors, war profiteers, forgers, bounty-jumpers and prostitutes.

According to Lincoln's Register of the Treasury, Lucius E. Chittenden, a Stanton admirer: 'Corruption spread like a contagious disease, wherever the operations of these detectives extended. . . . Honest manufacturers and dealers, who paid their taxes, were pursued without mercy for the most technical breaches of the law, and were quickly driven out of business. The dishonest rapidly accumulated wealth, which they could well afford to share with their protectors.' Chittenden also records in his *Recollections of President Lincoln* that he once caught Baker in the act of committing a forgery—'perfectly unabashed, without a blush, the fellow smiled as he looked me in the face and said, "That game didn't work, did it?"'

By the end of the war Baker had the rank of brigadier-general, but now the value of his services inevitably diminished. Prying was his profession and in peacetime conditions he could no longer operate as a law unto himself. He finally lost his position in the War Department in February, 1866, after incurring the hostility of President Johnson by planting one of his agents in front of the White House. Apparently, the detective chief's last official aim was to seek evidence connecting the President himself with a ring of 'pardon brokers' who were doing brisk business in Washington.

The man who had established a reign of terror in the city during the war now suddenly found himself powerless, without work or good prospects. He had served Stanton faithfully, but, at the age of forty, he had been discharged through his extreme efforts to spy on the President, presumably in Stanton's interests. Unemployed, he busied himself, with the help of a professional writer, on his history of the secret service. That work, published in 1867, recalled many of the post-assassination blunders which Stanton would most certainly have preferred to remain forgotten. More embarrassing to Stanton, it aroused new interest in Booth's suppressed diary which, Baker claimed, had been mutilated since it had left his possession. But it was Baker who emerged as the tarnished figure from the investigation conducted by the judiciary committee of the House of Representatives. Some members of the committee felt that 'it is doubtful whether he has in any one thing told the truth, even by accident'. The House report on the hearing virtually labelled the ex-detective a liar.

It is difficult to accept on trust any of the dramatic revelations made by Lafayette Baker, the sinister, egotistical general who thrived on sensationalism, who was for ever publicising himself as the master detective. His book, for example, contains an obscure 'letter' praising 'Gen. L. C. Baker, chief Detective of the War Department during the late rebellion'. The letter continues:

'And now about certain facts Baker may state with respect to men in high official relation with the Government or otherwise! The half he will not tell. I know of many things he will not state which I would. I have no mercy on men who will corrupt and contaminate all with whom they come in official contact, and men who, in time of peace, after treason has been put down, again secretly plot the overthrow of a Government at once the best and noblest that the sun of the Eternal ever shone upon. I hope to see truth come, let it cut where it may, as I believe the country to be still in danger; and unless some master hand will seize the knife and lay open the festering wound, the disease of the Republic will never heal! I am, very respectfully ———.' And this so-called letter is unsigned.

Was this mysterious letter another invention by Baker intended to be a veiled threat to frighten Stanton? Were the coded messages discovered by Neff part of the same pattern, sensational suggestions, devoid of concrete evidence, designed to throw suspicion on the Secretary of War? Quite possibly. From history Baker emerges as a scoundrel perfectly capable of leaving behind false statements merely to cause mischief and boost his own name. Certainly he cannot be regarded as a reliable or impartial witness of events and any writings attributed to him must be considered in the light of his unsavoury character and personal feelings towards Stanton. In *The Age of Hate*, George Fort Milton wrote that Baker 'glorified in his title of General but was really one of the worst rapscallions in an age in which rascality paid high dividends'. No person, not even such a tyrant as Edwin Stanton, should be condemned on the word of such a man alone. Moreover, one must consider Baker's mental state in his last year. The first coded message attributed to him suggests a somewhat juvenile mind striving to achieve unnecessary rhyme such as 'spy' and 'I', 'day' and 'away', 'die' and 'I', 'Grace' and 'place'. Such writings give the impression of an old man doodling to pass the time rather than of an intelligent man seeking to pass on vital information. Nor is it highly significant that Baker died one year after the publication of his book and his appearance before the judiciary committee, events which must have given Stanton considerable alarm. Hundreds of men had sufficient cause to wish Baker dead.

The case against Stanton, supported by a vast but flimsy web of circumstantial evidence, must therefore remain unproven; without concrete evidence to support the charge, there is more than reasonable doubt that he either engineered or consciously encouraged the murder of the President. In defence of Stanton, there are several facts which his accusers cannot easily explain away. His desire for a harsh reconstruction programme for the South would hardly put him in sympathy with such a Southern fanatic as John Wilkes Booth. The suggested motives for murder —to assure Stanton of a position of power after the war and to end plans for a soft peace—are by no means convincing. Then there was his constantly expressed concern for the President's safety. Only eleven days before the assassination, when Lincoln informed him that he was about to visit war-shattered Richmond, Stanton telegraphed: 'Allow me respectfully to ask you to consider whether you ought to expose the nation to the consequences of any disaster to yourself in the pursuit of a treacherous and dangerous enemy like the rebel army. Commanding generals are in the line of their duty in running such risks. But is the political head of a nation in the same condition?' The following day, as part of the victory celebrations, Stanton had men stationed in every window of the War Department's eleven buildings and at the appointed moment they all struck matches as part of the grand illuminations in Washington. At that time the Secretary of War seemed joyful at the fall of Richmond. Could he have really been plotting Lincoln's downfall as he rejoiced at the closing of a terrible chapter in American history? Did he abandon within the next ten days his concern for the President's life? Or could it be that, with the war virtually over, he merely lowered his guard and relaxed his thoughts about possible conspiracies against the government?

The answers will probably never be known. But on the evidence at hand, Stanton can only be found guilty of gross negligence in not providing Lincoln with adequate protection, of displaying extreme self-interest in the way he exploited the crime of the century to his own advantage, and of covering up details of the crime and the ensuing investigation when they adversely reflected on his handllng of the situation. Perhaps the last word on Stanton might be given to his great-grandson, Ernest Lee Jahncke Jr., who wrote to the *New York Times* a few years ago: 'In these times it often seems easy to confuse unpopularity with treachery. It also seems that the character assassination involved in the smear for sensational impact is sometimes more acceptable than a reasoned view of history.'

Meanwhile, one century after the crime, the search for new evidence goes on. Though it is admitted that Stanton's guilt remains unproven, researchers like Ray Neff conclude that there was a conspiracy by persons high in the United States Government either to cause or allow the assassination, and that a large fund was established to finance the deed. More evidence may well come to light; in particular, there is scope for more thorough investigation into Booth's Canadian connections, his financial dealings in Montreal, and the part possibly played by Confederate agents there.

In the same way it is more than probable that investigators will be re-examining the circumstances behind President Kennedy's assassination a hundred years from now. The greater the crime, the more intriguing a mystery becomes, and since both John Wilkes Booth and Lee Harvey Oswald did not live to answer for their senseless deeds, some mysteries surrounding the killing of both Presidents will remain for ever.

POSTSCRIPT

STRANGELY, TRAGEDY OVERTOOK many of the characters who figured in the story of the most dramatic crime in American history. Major Rathbone, who accompanied the Lincolns to the theatre, married Clara Harris as planned, but in a moment of madness he murdered her and then tried to commit suicide. He ended his days in a lunatic asylum. Mrs. Lincoln and Boston Corbett, the sergeant who claimed he had shot Booth, were also certified insane.

Mrs. Lincoln continued to be plagued with self-made financial worries after her husband's death, even though Congress eventually voted her 22,000 dollars (she had asked for 100,000). She ran up new debts, finally had to give up her home and live in a boarding house. She had her poverty publicised in the hope of receiving gifts from sympathisers, sold part of her vast collection of clothes and jewellery, and became despised rather than pitied. Ten years after the assassination she was certified as a lunatic. She was committed to a private asylum but released one year later, and then she lived alone for a while in France. After being haunted for years by frightful nightmares, Mrs. Lincoln died in 1882 in the Springfield house in which she had married Abraham forty years before. She was buried with her husband and three of their four sons, Edward, William and Thomas (Tad), at Oak Ridge Cemetery, Springfield.

Lovable Tad lived only six years after his father, dying in 1871 of typhoid fever. Stanton lived only four years after the assassination; Andrew Johnson, ten years. General Grant served two undistinguished terms as President of the United States and then went into a disastrous business venture. On Christmas Eve, 1883, he slipped on an icy pavement and needed crutches for long afterwards and never completely recovered from the accident. The following year he revealed clear symptoms of cancer of the throat. Grant suffered considerable pain, swallowed with extreme difficulty, dropped in weight from 180 lb. to 125 lb. Courageously he laboured over his memoirs to save his family from poverty and completed the work in July, 1885, a few days before his death. It earned nearly half a million dollars for his widow.

Preston King, collector of customs in New York City, and James Henry Lane, Senator for Kansas, were the men who turned Annie Surratt away from the White House. Four months after Mrs. Surratt's execution, King tied a bag of shot round his body and slipped off a Hoboken ferry boat to drown himself. Eight months later Lane also became mentally deranged and shot himself.

On the day of Lincoln's death, 50,000 citizens gathered around Wall Street, New York, armed with revolvers, knives and sticks, ready to avenge his death. They lynched one man on a portable gallows and were about to smash the offices of Southern sympathisers when a man climbed on a platform and calmed the half-crazed mob with his oratory and reason. That man, General Garfield, was destined (in 1881) to become the second American President to be assassinated. He took eleven weeks to die from a bullet wound close to his spine and, like Lincoln, he was attended in vain by Surgeon-General Barnes.

In August, 1867, yellow fever broke out at the moated Dry Tortugas prison, killing, among others, Michael O'Laughlin and the prison doctor. Dr. Mudd volunteered to help fight the disease, saved many lives, and, on the recommendation of prison officers, was granted a free pardon by President Johnson early in

1869. Arnold and Spangler were also freed, but the latter was now suffering from tuberculosis and the kindly Dr. Mudd took him to his farm to spend his last days in peace. In fact, Spangler lived until 1879 and Mudd died three years afterwards. Arnold died in a Baltimore hospital in 1906, but not before he had recorded that Mudd had told him in prison that he had never had any connection with Booth's conspiracy. John Lloyd later claimed that he was forced to testify against Mrs. Surratt under the threat of death, and Louis Weichmann claimed that Stanton had promised him a job in reward for his co-operation as a witness. Weichmann took up a position in a Philadelphia customs house and was later sacked. He died in 1902, having signed on his death-bed a statement that he had told the truth at the trial of the conspirators.

Some figures in the story enjoyed good fortune. John Surratt, who remarkably escaped the gallows, settled down successfully to a business career as an auditor for the Baltimore Steam Packet Company. He revealed nothing new about the assassination plot. In 1870 he delivered a lecture on the subject at Rockville, Maryland, but it disappointed the audience and plans for an extensive lecture tour were abandoned. In 1898 he gave a newspaper interview which revealed new facts about his European travels. Otherwise, Surratt maintained a discreet silence about his part in the conspiracy and lived until 1916.

Thomas Eckert rose to the rank of General, became boss of several commercial telegraph companies, and served as presiding judge of the Texas Court of Appeal. He died in 1910. Miraculously, all the persons savagely attacked by Paine recovered from their injuries. William Seward, whose many notable achievements included the purchase of Alaska from Russia for 7,200,000 dollars, lived on until 1872 when he died of natural causes at the age of seventy-one. But his delicate wife lived only two months after the nightmare of April 14, and Miss Fanny Seward, whom Paine knocked unconscious, lived only one and a half years more. She was twenty-one. Ward Hill Lamon lived another twenty-eight years, for ever regretting that he had not been in Washington that night to safeguard the President. Robert Todd Lincoln outlived all the main characters in the story. The only son of Lincoln to reach maturity, he died in 1926, at the age of eighty-three, and was buried in Arlington National Cemetery.

Jefferson Davis, fleeing with his family and servants, was captured when dressed in a woman's coat and shawl. He was arrested at dawn on May 10, 1865, just as the conspiracy trial was opening. But Davis himself never faced trial. Charged with treason, the Confederate leader was put in chains in Fort Monroe and held prisoner for two years. He was then released on bail and on Christmas Day, 1868, the charge against him was dropped. Davis went into retirement, visiting Europe five times in the next two decades, and died in 1889, outliving Lincoln by nearly a quarter of a century. The rebel President was given the greatest funeral the South has ever seen and buried in his old capital of Richmond.

Bessie Hale, the senator's daughter who loved Booth, went with her father to Spain, later married a Mr. William Eaton Chandler and enjoyed a quiet married life in West Point, New York. She was untouched by scandal, though if Booth had struck on inauguration day when he had the opportunity, she would have been ruined as the woman who secured him a seat at the ceremony.

The surviving Booths lived in the shadow of shame for the rest of their lives. John Wilkes' brothers Junius and Joseph, and his brother-in-law, John Sleeper Clarke, were arrested shortly after the assassination. Clarke hated his wife ever after for being a Booth, and Asia's friends also turned against her. She died of heart disease in England at fifty-two, leaving behind a book which had a lock and key and contained all she could remember of John Wilkes. Contrary to his declaration, Edwin Booth did return to the stage—making his come-back as Hamlet at the Winter Gardens, New York, in 1866—and he found himself even more famous than before. People who had previously shown no interest in the theatre now flocked to see the assassin's brilliant brother. But not until 1871 would Edwin venture to play the assassin Brutus again, and then Laura Keene hailed his performance as 'a masterpiece'. Edwin reimbursed farmer Garrett for the loss of his tobacco barn and he was reluctant ever again to speak of his notorious brother. But in 1881 he recalled in a letter to a friend that he remembered John Wilkes as 'a rattle-pated fellow, filled with Quixotic notions . . . we regarded him as a good-hearted, harmless, though wild-brained boy, and used to laugh at his patriotic froth whenever secession was discussed. That he was insane on that one point no one who knew him well can doubt.' Oddly, Edwin Booth was appearing on a Chicago stage in 1879 when a madman shot at him and missed. He lived until 1893.

John T. Ford, held in prison for forty days, had his theatre confiscated after the assassination, but he later threatened legal proceedings and the government agreed to rent the building for 1,500 dollars a month until June 1, 1866, with the privilege of purchasing it for one hundred thousand dollars. Ford's was re-modelled into an office and storage building for Confederate records. In 1893, at the very time that Edwin Booth's funeral was being held in New York, three floors of the old theatre collapsed, killing twenty-two government workers and injuring sixty-eight. Ford's is now the home of the Lincoln Museum, where exhibits include Booth's left boot, derringer, diary, Spencer carbine and compass; the original door to Box 7 and the pine board used to secure the vestibule door. Across the street, the Petersen House where Lincoln died is also preserved as a national memorial.

John Wilkes's body did not remain in its secret hiding place. At his mother's request, Edwin wrote to Stanton seeking custody of the body. Stanton made no reply, and, in 1867, a similar request was ignored by Grant, then Secretary of War, even though the General had once offered to do Edwin any service after his rescue of Robert Lincoln at the railway station. But, on

October 1, 1867, when the Arsenal Prison was torn down, the corpse was removed from the penitentiary to the nearby Arsenal Warehouse. Finally, in February, 1869, John Wilkes's body was sent home where it was identified by the Booth family and then buried on the family plot in Greenmount Cemetery, Baltimore. There the assassin remained, though he was 'seen' in various parts of the world and numerous bogus Booths proclaimed themselves.

Nor was President Lincoln allowed to rest entirely in peace. In 1876 a gang of counterfeiters plotted to steal his body; again the aim was to 'kidnap' Lincoln to exchange him for prisoners, or rather one prisoner, master engraver Ben Boyd. 'Big Jim' Kinealy, head of the gang, conceived the macabre plan which had one outstanding virtue—body-snatching was not defined as a crime in the statute books of Illinois. The gang broke open the padlocked, iron door of Lincoln's tomb, entered, and lifted the wooden coffin half out of the sarcophagus. But the gang was double-crossed by a newly recruited member, Lewis G. Swegles, a former thief now working for the Secret Service. At his signal eight armed detectives jumped out of hiding. The body-snatchers escaped in the darkness but were arrested in Chicago a few days later. They were sentenced to one year's imprisonment.

Afterwards greater care was taken to safeguard the President's remains, and in 1901 his coffin was embedded in steel and solid concrete six feet beneath the floor of the tomb. At that time the coffin was opened and it was noted that Abraham Lincoln had changed remarkably little in appearance in the thirty-six years since his death.

BIBLIOGRAPHY

Adams, James Truslow, *America's Tragedy* (New York, 1934).

Arnold, Samuel, *The Lincoln Plot (Baltimore American*, 1902).

Badeau, Adam, *Grant in Peace* (Philadelphia, 1885).

Baker, L. C., *History of the United States Secret Service* (Philadelphia, 1867).

Baker, R. S., 'The Capture, Death and Burial of John Wilkes Booth' (*McClure's Magazine*, May, 1897).

Bates, David Homer, *Lincoln in the Telegraph Office* (New York, 1907).

Bishop, Jim, *The Day Lincoln Was Shot* (New York, 1955).

Chittenden, L. E., *Recollections of President Lincoln* (New York, 1891)

Civil War Times, Gettysburg, Pa.

Clarke, Asia Booth, *The Unlocked Booth, a Memoir of John Wilkes Booth* (New York, 1938).

Crook, William H., *Memories of the White House Through Five Administrations* (Boston, 1911).

De Witt, David Miller, *The Judicial Murder of Mary E. Surratt* (Baltimore, 1895).

De Witt, David Miller, *The Impeachment and Trial of Andrew Johnson* (New York, 1903).

De Witt, David Miller, *The Assassination of Abraham Lincoln and Its Expiation* (New York, 1909).

Dictionary of American Biography.

Donovan, Robert J., *The Assassins* (London, 1956).

Eisenschiml, Otto, *Why Was Lincoln Murdered?* (Boston, 1937).

Ferguson, W. J., *I Saw Booth Shoot Lincoln* (Boston, 1930).

Frank Leslie's Illustrated Weekly, 1861-5.

Gleason, D. H. L., 'Conspiracy Against Lincoln' (*Magazine of History*, Vol. 13, Feb., 1911).

Gobright, L. A., *Recollections of Men and Things in Washington During Half a Century* (Philadelphia, 1869).

Grant, U. S., *Personal Memoirs* (New York, 1885).

Harper's Weekly, 1861-5.

Herndon, William H., and Weik, Jesse W., *Herndon's Lincoln* (1889); with an introduction and notes by Paul M. Angle (New York, 1930).

Kimmel, Stanley, *The Mad Booths of Maryland* (New York, 1940).

Lamon, Ward Hill, *Recollections of Abraham Lincoln, 1847-1865* (1896).

Laughlin, Clara E., *The Death of Lincoln* (New York, 1909).

Leech, Margaret, *Reveille in Washington* (London, 1942).

Lorant, Stefan, *The Life of Abraham Lincoln* (New York, 1955).

McClellan, George B., *McClellan's Own Story* (New York, 1887).

McClure, Stanley W., *The Lincoln Museum and The House Where Lincoln Died* (Washington, 1949).

Milton, George Fort, *The Age of Hate* (New York, 1930).

Morris, Richard B., *Great Presidential Decisions, State Papers That Changed the Course of History* (New York, 1960).

Nicolay, John George, and Hay, John, *Abraham Lincoln: A History* (10 vols., New York, 1890).

Oldroyd, Osborn H., *Assassination of Abraham Lincoln: Flight, Pursuit, Capture, and Punishment of the Conspirators* (Washington, 1901).

Pitman, Benn, *The Assassination of President Lincoln and the Trial of the Conspirators* (Cincinnati and New York, 1865). Facsimile edition with an introduction by Philip Van Doren Stern (New York, 1954).

Poore, Benjamin Perley, *The Conspiracy Trial for the Murder of the President* (Boston, 1865).

Pratt, Fletcher, *Stanton* (New York, 1953).

Ruggles, Eleanor, *Prince of Players* (New York, 1953).

Ruggles, M. B., Bainbridge, A. R., and Doherty, E. P., 'Pursuit and Death of John Wilkes Booth' (*Century Magazine*, January, 1890).

Sandburg, Carl, *Abraham Lincoln, the Prairie Years and the War Years* (New York, 1954).

Starr, John W., *Lincoln's Last Day* (New York, 1922).

Stern, Philip Van Doren, *The Man Who Killed Lincoln* (New York, 1955).

Thomas, Benjamin P., *Abraham Lincoln, A Biography* (New York, 1952).

Trial of John H. Surratt (2 vols., Washington, 1867).

United States Senate, *Report of the Committee of the Judiciary on the Assassination of President Lincoln* (Washington, 1866).

Warren Commission *Report on the Assassination of President Kennedy* (Washington, 1964).

Welles, Gideon, *Diary* (3 vols., Boston, 1911).

Woodward, W. E., *Meet General Grant* (New York, 1928).

NEWSPAPERS

Baltimore Sun

London Daily Mail

London Times

National Intelligencer

National Republican

New York Commercial Advocate

New York Times

New York Tribune

New York World

Richmond Examiner

St. Louis Republican

Selma Dispatch

Washington Chronicle

INDEX